London Review OF BOOKS

VOLUME 5 NUMBER 24 22 DECEMBER 1983 TO 18 JANUARY 1984 70 P

London Reviews

A selection from the London Review of Books 1983–1985

edited by Nicholas Spice, with an introductory essay
by Karl Miller

Chatto & Windus · London

Published in 1985 by
Chatto & Windus Ltd
40 William IV Street, London WC2N 4DF

British Library Cataloguing in Publication Data
London reviews.
1. Books——Reviews
I. Spice, Nicholas II. London review of books
028.1 Z1035.A1

ISBN 0-7011-2988-3

Typeset at The Spartan Press Ltd, Lymington, Hants.
Printed by Redwood Burn Ltd
Trowbridge, Wiltshire

Contents

Section 4

Preface

Since 1982, when the last anthology of pieces from the *London Review of Books* was published, we have printed more than eight hundred articles, stories and poems in the paper. The present volume includes 28 of these. Making this selection was very difficult and, in the nature of things, many excellent pieces have had to be left out. As it is part of the purpose of this anthology to introduce the *London Review of Books* to new readers, I have chosen pieces which represent the paper in all its moods.

The book begins with an essay on the history and aims of the *London Review of Books*, written in the autumn of 1984 by Karl Miller, who has been the paper's editor since it was founded in October 1979. The pieces which follow are divided into four miscellaneous groups. This seemed the best way to introduce a certain pace into the progress of the book. There is no hidden design in the arrangement.

NICHOLAS SPICE
London, 1985

Introduction to the London Review of Books

There are many young people now who may well feel that they will never work, and there are many a generation older who are being driven into retirement. Atrocities, coercions, cuts, strikes have almost ceased to be news, and yet they are almost the only news we make. The country is filled with anxiety and ill-feeling, and with the sense of a dishonoured public life. There is a war on in Northern Ireland, and the Government is letting it run. There is a war on in the coalfields, and the Government is letting that run too. We have become the theatre for a battle of wills, of barbarous egotisms, between Margaret Thatcher and Arthur Scargill, with working people at each other's throats, miner against miner. Having dispatched its entire Armada to expel the garrison of Argentinian conscripts which had been thrust into the Falklands, the Government is maintaining an exorbitant and improvident British presence there, while cutting the costs of the universities, and making their teachers feel that they belong to Mrs Thatcher's 'enemy within', her domestic counterpart of the Falklands invader.

In the 1840s, Carlyle wrote that 'insurrection' was 'a most sad necessity; and governors who wait for that to instruct them, are surely getting into the fatalest courses . . . for violence does even justice unjustly.' He may be thought to have discredited the apocalypse evoked in *Past and Present* with his prescription of hero-worship and of an Oliver Cromwell Carlyle. But some of his words of warning apply to what we have now, in the way of insurrection, and of state action, and inaction, of iron man and iron lady.

It might be held that a time like this is no time to be running a fortnightly literary magazine; that the concerns and ill-feelings which it expresses are bound to seem more than usually parochial. Impediments are certainly placed, at such times, in the path of literary journalism. It is difficult for these papers to stay alive financially at such times. But then it is never easy for them to do that; they have generally had to be backed and rescued and charitably supported. And hard times, crisis and apocalypse make good subjects. Even for those journalists who have no desire to act the sage, the past two years and more have been a challenge. Carlyles, as it happens, have not done all that well.

To this challenge the *London Review of Books* has responded as best it could – poorly, I think, in certain respects: but at least we are not the sort of literary journal which prefers to be silent about public matters of this kind. We are now in our fifth year of physically separate existence, after a first six months of sheltering within the *New York Review of Books*. We have always been independent editorially. The readership figures of around fifteen thousand are those of the *Edinburgh Review* in the early years of the last century; in the 1840s, Marx's *Neue Rheinische Zeitung* was read by half that number of people. I mention these influential papers, not to scrape up an affinity, but as a reminder that comparable figures now would be beneath the notice of experts on the press, on 'What the Papers Say', who do not consider the policies and fortunes of weeklies and fortnightlies to be worth their words: I am writing here – in September 1984 – on the assumption that the policies and fortunes of the *London Review* are worth quite as many words as those of the *Daily Mail*.

Looking after a magazine feels different now from what I recall of the times in the past when I literary-edited the *Spectator* and the *New Statesman*, and then edited the *Listener*. The *Listener* was a different animal from the other two journals: it was light on opinion, being in duty bound to deliver the BBC's programmes, which were produced in accordance with the problematical edict of 'balance', and which were already on the slide towards their present miserable condition. The other two were in duty bound to be polemical; on political matters there was the excitement and the fatigue of their always having to take a line and to know better. Such journals are constitutionally polemical, and have often been recruited from young writers with an appetite for controversy and ideology, with a sectional or sectarian outlook, and a wish to dispossess entrenched authority in more spheres than one. It is now harder to know better. The left-wing and liberal constituency is despondent and divided, volatile and unstable. And the young – searching as they are for a steady job – are not prominent in our corner of journalism. This impression, of the abstention and indifference of the young, is likely, of course, to be affected by the fact that I have grown old in controversy myself. The *London Review* has had to lean heavily on past associations, and a younger editor would have known and introduced more writers of his own age, and that would have been a good thing. But it is a good thing, too, that the writers we have, many of them venerable, have done, as it seems to me, so well. There is no need to get out the sackcloth and ashes. I haven't the slightest doubt that this is a better paper than any other I have worked on.

These lines are being written in the Tuscan hills, which go up and down like circulations outside my window. The other night I saw my first firefly dancing through the woods, like some midsummer night's dream. The hills have taken something from my power to sit down and describe the policy and progress of the *London Review*: but I have agreed to try, and I hope I am able to avoid any gross display of the journalistic ill-feeling which I find I want to write about in the course of doing so. We are privately financed, and we have also been aided, over the years, by the Arts Council. Policy is formed by a tiny staff of three persons, two of them part-time, who are assisted by a board of editorial advisers. It was apparent to the three of us at the outset that times had changed since we'd last been editors. What were we to say now? Who should say it? Where were the young? It was being said that literary journalism, and that literary journals, had been blown up, and that literary theory had accomplished this. Here, we thought, was some kind of polemical claim. Running a paper like ours had to be an attempt to disprove it.

Criticism has to make enemies, and to believe that it knows better. It expresses, and is betrayed by, ill-feeling. It also has to speak up for things. The back half of the *New Statesman*, when I worked for it, spoke up, among other things, for the goals of the democratic Left, for the socialism of Crosland (no socialism at all, according to the front half), for the poetry of Larkin, the fiction of Kingsley Amis, V. S. Naipaul, Dan Jacobson, for the criticism of Leavis, and for that of Empson, the most intelligent British literary theorist of modern times and a writer remarkably free from malice, whose death we now mourn. A coterie within a coterie, the back half opposed the control of cultural outlets by public-school and other inimical coteries, and it opposed the assumption that taste and money were in love with one another. The *Edinburgh Review* was founded by the unemployed Whigs of a Tory town, and it went on to traffick in guilt and reproof. '*Judex damnatur*,' ran its motto, '*cum nocens absolvitur*.' Criticism was to push the claims of 'wealth and sense', as against those of hereditary right. Such was their bid for power. The *New Statesman*'s bid at this time was in a manner of speaking its opposite. Wealth and sense were to be divorced. By 1979, however, that strategy of the 1960s could be considered out of date. New arrogations were on the agenda. Leavis had been unmasked as an élitist by those who had come forward as theorists.

It can be suggested in all good feeling that this rejection is in some measure generational, part of what it is to be young and ambitious, that theory is a weapon, and a mask, favoured by those in whom a new form of the old criticism, in whom the old critical practice of hostility, can be identified. These new judges can behave in a manner to which we are not unaccustomed, as their language indicates. Leavis had 'demolished' and 'dislodged', though most of the monuments due for removal are still standing. Now there is a movement which entitles itself Deconstruction and which uses words like 'wound' and 'fracture'. Criticism (like trade-unionism) could well be lost without its injurious terms. It is probable that the monuments assailed by Deconstruction – the literary text, the literary tradition, authorship – will also survive. But that is not to say that they will have escaped alteration, that the exciting work of destruction will have been wholly in vain.

It was plain to us that the usable, understandable meanings which had been discovered in literature by the canonical Leavis and the ambiguous Empson alike were still there for the seeking. But it was equally plain that the new theoretical writings should also be understood. For my own part, I have found them hard to understand. But I have found them interesting at times, and some of them have come to be published in the *London Review* – not always to the satisfaction of its readership. Deconstruction is a form of philosophical scepticism from which literary critics and historians can learn to think harder about the determination of meaning in literature, about the debatability of canon and curriculum, and about the complacency of standard views concerning the significance for poetry and fiction of their features of contradiction and uncertainty. Whether Deconstruction will ever serve as a principle of action, whether it will ever emerge from the academy, where it would appear to have been a comfort in hard times, is another question. There is an esotericism here to which it must have been convenient to retreat. Much of what I have read in this vein strikes me as silly-scholastic, or merely rancorous, and I wonder whether there is anyone who really believes that there are more than a very few writers in this country who have put the method to rewarding use.

When the first number of the paper was being assembled – only a matter of days after the project had been thought of, let alone settled – it was decided to risk stating an editorial position, rather than fight shy. The position that was stated referred to the new theory in a way that looks old-fashioned now and must have looked old-fashioned – like a reference to the old Structuralism – even then. To some, it must have looked like a piece of stranded and demoralised late-Leavisism. It must have pained Frank Kermode – a member of the advisory board who has done a great deal to carry the paper forward – as being simply impervious to the efforts that had been made in several related fields. The statement of intent explained that this paper of the democratic Left would be against 'the elimination of the author from his work'. But the paper was to prove, as I have observed, less impervious than readers may have been led to expect.

This was an outcome, though, which had in a sense been foreseen. For whatever it was that we did not know, and should have known, we did know that an editorial position is all the while changing, on the move – in response, for one thing, to the motions of the writers it wants to print. We knew, moreover, that it could be seen to be the business of a paper like ours to be hospitable to writers whose opinions differed from those of individual editors. I remember a remark which came at this early point from Robert Silvers, editor of the *New York Review*, to the effect that he saw himself as giving people the chance to have their say. In former times, I had gone for contributors in the hope of a united front. Now that I was having trouble in finding out what was being said, and in figuring out what it meant when I had found it, there seemed to be a merit in letting people say it. Now that people seemed to be having trouble in reaching agreement, there might be a merit in publishing their debates. I need hardly add that the commitment to hospitality and diversity was a long way from boundless. I am talking about a fairly small matter of degree.

We are not the *Neue Rheinische Zeitung*, but we have a political position. It is a position to which this idea of hospitality has been especially applicable, at a time of disagreements, of new directions and lost tracks. But it is a position which our readers have had no trouble in recognising. Some of them have reproached us for, as it were, a premature anti-Beginism, others for joining the SDP. That party began when the paper did, and it was indeed to raise people's hopes. Recently, however, it has given them little to support – apart from the leader-like self-confidence of David Owen's performance in the House of Commons and on platforms. I believe myself in a Social Democratic Party which has yet to happen, or to be fulfilled: one which says clearly what it means to do, which looks less like a career vehicle for its leading politicians, which is pledged to protect the welfare state and the public interest, and to reverse the Thatcherite use of the depression to enrich the rich, pledged to a controlled economy and a governed country. By the SDP which is happening now we have been flung the bone of the 'social market economy' – an item of stultifying jargon which is said to have been associated both with the Christian Democratic economic 'miracle' of the Fifties in Germany and with the subsequent success there of the opposing SPD, and to which we can be morally certain that no one outside the court of David Owen's political advisers will ever be able to attach a meaning. In this sign conquer? Meanwhile, in showing itself unable to deal either with a vulnerable government or with the violence and conspiracy supported or countenanced by sections of the Left, the Labour Party has lost the ability to make sense to the electorate as a whole, and it is doubtful whether its inadequate leader will find among his many words the ones that will restore this ability. 'Our people' against theirs – the slogan is Tony Benn's. It is also that of Margaret Thatcher, who has yet to pay the price for it, and who will avoid doing so for as long as her opponents are what they are now.

The paper's politics, then, are those of none of the political parties. 'Mr Scargill must be defeated, but so, in a sense, must Mrs Thatcher' – given her 'arbitrary decisions', her breaches of democratic principle. This was the conclusion reached by Michael Stewart in an article on the miners' strike, published in the *London Review* in early September, 1984. If we had supposed that the article might appeal to the readership as an acceptable specimen of the paper's politics, we would soon have been disabused. Michael Stewart's views have divided the readership, and feelings, as I write, are running high. Letters have directed at Stewart an obloquy which is equal to that of Scargill himself, and which makes conspicuous their exemption of Scargill from serious criticism. It is as if, since Mrs Thatcher has been in the wrong, Mr Scargill must be in the right. This is the most consequential of the rows we have had, and we have not heard the end of it.

It is worth admitting and examining how much almost any journal must owe to its adversary function, to its strategies of destruction, suppression and reproof, its judicial, magisterial or sanitary styles, to its 'our people' element of putting other people in the wrong, which can then force divisions within the community of its own writers and readers. I don't suggest that a journal should be proud of, or content with, its ill-feelings, though there can be cases – such as that of *Private Eye* – where these can be the secret of a success. Nor do I suggest that we would be happy to be judged solely in terms of the offence we have caused. But there may perhaps be an interest in the mention of three previous occasions when offence was caused, three previous rows, since they indicate the character and extent of the hostility, and of the hospitality, exhibited by the paper. These rows do not describe the paper, which is often peaceful. But journalistic rows, when they can be penetrated and understood, are rarely uninformative, and it may be that these three are revealing of what we do. For some who are unfamiliar with the paper they may place us in a bad light: but they also give an idea of our subject-matter and editorial range.

The paper would rather that the Falklands war had not been fought, while recognising that the British victory produced some fortunate results – among them, the disgracing of Galtieri and the accession of the Alfonsin government in Argentina. At the time when the fighting on land was about to begin, we argued for further negotiations, while recognising that there could well be military reasons for starting the fight at that time. The Armada sailed on, and in, and the *Belgrano* had already been sunk, despite the British Government's undertaking not to attack outside the exclusion zone which they had appointed for the islands. The *Belgrano* was officially stated, for a while, to have been itself on the attack. The Government's present position is that the *Belgrano* was sailing away from the islands – the aptly named Sir John Nott was reported on 21 September 1984 as saying that 'if I had known at the point of time when she was sunk that she was steaming in another direction I would not have used the word "closing"' – but that there is reason to think nonetheless that she was part of a pincer movement converging on the Task Force. The true relation between this event and the Peruvian peace proposals and the expiry of the Haig initiative is currently under dispute, and may never emerge from the dark and reek of recrimination and denial: a sizeable public row is belatedly in progress on this and other aspects of the war. But it seems clear that there could have been further negotiations at the time the ship was sunk, and that the sinking helped to prevent these – whatever it may have done, or been intended to do, to initiatives that preceded it or coincided with it. The sinking of the *Belgrano* was to sink the *Sheffield*, and by the time this small war was over many hundreds of lives had been lost on both sides.

The Labour MP Tam Dalyell was responsible for part of what we had to say, over the following months, on the subject of the Falklands: so that the paper has extended a willing hospitality to what we take to be an honourable course of opposition – until recent times, virtually single-handed so far as its Parliamentary expression has been concerned – to the Government's conduct of the war. David Owen, who was all for the war at the time, now talks of the enormity of the Government's subsequent lies to the House of Commons (which has so far found itself unable to debate the miners' strike). He is objecting to the Government's cover-up of actions which he appears to have no way of knowing why they should have wanted to cover up. Why *did* they want to cover them up? If it was all right for them to fight when they did, it can hardly have been all wrong for them to sink the *Belgrano*. But then Ministers may since have feared that the decision might look precipitate and underhand, and they cannot now wish it to appear, in a world which is defined by the enlargement of nuclear arsenals, that they were in a hurry to make war. Their fears, if these *were* their fears, have not been misplaced. There must be people who will take a lot of persuading that Mrs Thatcher may not have wanted a small Falklands war for the same reasons which, in the view of some of her opponents, have led her to favour, and to fix a favourable time for, a miners' strike.

This, at any rate, is the account I would offer of the paper's handling of what happened in the South Atlantic. We are a literary journal which sees itself as having to say what it can, according to its abilities and by an exercise of hospitality, about such matters. We are not a pacifist paper. We are, as I have said, a polemical paper. But we are also a pacific paper, and as such always more or less uneasy about the battles in which we feel we have to take part, and about the errors and excesses we may commit there. We do not believe that the suffering which came about because of this 'neat' little war – as one patriotic contributor privately characterised it – was justified by what the country has had to show for its victory. As I write, a vote overwhelmingly in favour of the Argentinian claim to the islands is expected in the General Assembly of the United Nations.

Reviewing these controversies, I can reveal that the most formidable, from the paper's point of view, arose with Norman Stone's examination of the life and work of the historian E. H. Carr. This was a discussion which Stone had had it in mind to write several months before Carr's death, and which was then rapidly completed. So far as the discussion related, as it largely did, to Carr's work on the development of Soviet Communist society, I remain of the opinion that Stone was entitled to pursue the arguments he chose to pursue, though I would add that the long letter of criticism which Carr's collaborator R. W. Davies sent to the paper seemed to me, as an outsider in these matters, to be an exemplary performance in respect of polemical tone and in other respects besides. As for the description given in the article of Carr's personal life, I am of the opinion that there is a place for biography in the kind of obituary retrospect which the article had by then become, and that there is a place for a decent candour in obituaries. Such a candour is difficult to achieve, and I would accept that Norman Stone did not manage to sustain it. The possibility that this might be so should have been more thoroughly investigated at the manuscript stage, and I take the blame for the paper's inaction here.

But I am unable to take the species of blame which Eric Hobsbawm, a friend of mine and a historian sympathetic to Carr, assigned to the paper for printing the piece. *Why* did we print it? 'It', I recall his saying, not 'all of it', which would have been the harder question. Eric spoke of the 'yellow press', though I don't suppose he thought we'd been *hired* to throw this stone. Presently Eric published in the paper a review of a book by Carr's aggressor, which said that it was the work of a good historian, while regretting the attack on Carr which he had earlier blamed on the yellow press. Not long afterwards, for what it is worth, this good historian was made Regius Professor of Modern History at Oxford. The episode of the Carr critique is instructive, and one of the things it teaches is that a justified suspicion of the press runs sufficiently deep for it to appear natural to visit on one section the practices of other sections to which it is constitutionally hostile. No doubt it will continue to be evident to some that the article represented a lapse into the kind of journalism which we allege that we dislike.

The third of the controversies, unlike the others, did not include letters for publication, and might seem to some people to have been more of a storm in the teacup of the paper's internal editorial relations. A. Alvarez had brought out a book on divorce, which has a chapter telling of his own, and of his dealings with his first wife, Ursula Creagh. That first wife reviewed the book for us, declaring her interest. One of the editorial advisers strongly complained about the impropriety of the decision, while another remarked that we should not review books which are sure to elicit an emphasis on personalities and private lives. As in the other two cases, I don't wish to insist that we were altogether right to proceed as we did. But it is interesting that in this case the *readership* did not complain, and that they showed an ample appreciation of the point of having someone who is not a professional writer comment on a version of her life which has figured in a professional writer's book – always provided that the review furnishes a rational account of the book. We thought that we had acted without malice, and for literary reasons. But we did not think that we had set ourselves a precedent for the coverage of autobiographical material.

Those who never have any regrets, and those who are prone to them, should both stay away from editing, which makes you sorry, and sore, or impervious. Never sorer than when hospitality obliges you to carry a piece which you dislike – something that happens about once a fortnight. Editing has, of course, its pleasures, and it may be appropriate to adduce, as a further item of description, my sense that the greatest of these are the printing of a piece which moves you with the truth it succeeds in telling, and the directing of attention to a book which deserves it. These are the fireflies in your wood. I have been reading, in the Tuscan hills, Alice Walker's novel about the American South, *The Colour Purple*, and thinking of the pleasure there would be in publishing a piece which explained that this is a feminist tract, of high quality, which is also a marvellous work of fiction; it is a work in which character changes, almost out of recognition and perhaps controversially, in apposition to a process of self-discovery. The adversary pleasure of arguing against some harmful and pretentious book, some *White Hotel*, which has won over the media, and won over the public which takes its cues from the media, can also be freely admitted. There is a place for what Francis Jeffrey of the *Edinburgh Review* called the 'wholesome discipline of derision', and the pity is that we have not exercised it more.

KARL MILLER
September 1984. Tuscany

One

London Review OF BOOKS

VOLUME 6 NUMBER 20 1 NOVEMBER TO 14 NOVEMBER 1984 85P

Peter Pulzer

The Oxford Vote

The last ten years have seen a major expansion in the education service. The next ten will see expansion continue – as it must, if education is to make its full contribution to the vitality of our society and our economy.

Education: A Framework for Expansion, presented to Parliament by the Secretary of State for Education and Science (Mrs Margaret Thatcher), December 1972.

I do not think that irrevocable damage has yet been done, but I do regard the situation as alarming in the sense that the contribution made by Britain to world science will be severely reduced if the factors now operating are allowed to continue for a number of years.

Sir Andrew Huxley, Presidential Address to Royal Society, 30 November 1984.

A lot has happened in the 12 years that separate these two pronouncements, much of which can be summed up as the revolution of declining expectations. Few now assume that the world will continue to supply more of everything and that each of its inhabitants can count on automatic increments of welfare. The result is that competition for resources has become fiercer and, in some cases at least, more ill-tempered. That is the context for the vote on 29 January by Congregation of Oxford University, by 738 votes to 319, not to award an Honorary Doctorate of Civil Law to the Prime Minister. The vote was not an end in itself. If it had been, some of the accusations of personal spite that have been levelled at the majority would be justified. It was a means to an end and the end was political: not in the partisan sense of Left *versus* Right, but as a statement of the changing relationship between academia and politicians.

There are two main components of that relationship: the political atmosphere in which we now live, and the universities' own reassessment of their place in it. The atmosphere is that of the politics of conviction, of which Mrs Thatcher is the principal prophet, but not the only practitioner. No one has repudiated more explicitly than she the old consensus that saw Britain – for better or worse – through the post-war decades. Consensus does not mean absence of conflict. There were plenty of strikes and demos, and some violence, in those years. But the social fabric held together, because most people most of the time kept to the recognised rules of the game. Oxford, with Cambridge, had an accepted place in this world, as the principal supplier of civil servants, bishops, judges and prime ministers. As long ago as 1970 the *Times* complained that this cosy world of interlocking acquaintanceship offered the country no real choice: both parties were led by men who had been at Oxford together, along with the civil servants who were to administer their decisions.

To offer an honorary degree to a serving politician in those conditions was therefore not a political act at all, since Oxford and government were parts of the same world. Hence it could be taken for granted that Socialist dons would no more veto an honour for Edward Heath or Harold Macmillan than Tory dons would veto Harold Wilson. Even Michael Foot might have slipped through as a representative of the old order, a Thirties-ish, literary champion of the supremacy of Parliament, who caused offence mainly by mistaking the Cenotaph for the Aldermaston March. But Tony Benn of Westminster School and New College? Not on your life. One of the ironies of the whole episode was that the Iron Lady's champions appealed to a set of conventions that she had done more than any other British politician to consign to the dustbin. Those who sow conviction politics must also reap them. Indeed our vote was not a snub at all, but an accolade, a recognition that we had learned to read the new map of politics.

Yet if the vote was a response to the changed political atmosphere it took a complicated form. Dons have responded to the increased politicisation of education, as of every other sphere of public life, by making their own withdrawal from the old consensus. In the old days they were, like the rest of the country, mainly Labour or Conservative, though in practice that probably meant Butskellite. As the two main parties move off more and more into their ideological cloud-cuckoo-lands, dons – like car workers and bank clerks – have cast off the partisan restraints that kept political conflict stable. According to a revealing opinion poll in the *Times Higher Education Supplement* of 18 January only 17 per cent of academics would now vote Conservative. But that is not because there has been a swing to the left. The Labour share is 28 per cent. Even in the Polytechnics, whatever their reputation may be, the Labour share is 32 per cent. The favoured parties of academics are those of the Liberal/SDP Alliance. Yet this is in many ways an apolitical, even anti-political stance. Few Alliance votes come from the deeply committed; most are a protest against polarisation and elective dictatorship, rather than for this or that item from a largely unread manifesto. The vote against Mrs Thatcher was another go at breaking the mould, or at least that bit of the mould whose motto was 'You vote for my crook, I'll vote for yours.'

There is more to the universities' response to the changed atmosphere than a repudiation of the traditional courtesies, however. The biggest mould-breaker of them all is, after all, the Prime Minister herself. The universities, like the schools, like any number of other long-established institutions, are on the defensive. True reformer that she is, Mrs Thatcher is making us account for ourselves. Perhaps the British record of slow but steady national decline really does call for a great ceremony of public repentance, some auto-da-fé in which we throw off our old, comfortable habits. What we now realise is that universities have in the past hoped to survive by being ignored, either unaware of how weak their base of public support is or keeping their fingers crossed that this weakness would not be exposed. In the light of the substantial backlash against the Thatcher vote we can no longer plead ignorance. We have to ask ourselves what we should do, though the answer will depend on whether we are defending Salford, Essex or Oxbridge. I shall concentrate on Oxbridge, not only because I have more experience of that, but also because its image shows the greatest contradictions. For most of its existence Salford had no image at all. It was the place down the road. More recently, it has acquired a reputation of business-like hard-headedness, of which more below. Essex, which produces excellent research on a number of subjects, is irrevocably caught in a time-warp of rioting students. But Oxford and Cambridge?

Oxford and Cambridge, as anyone working in them knows, are tourist attractions. Visitors regard colleges much like stately homes. They admire the architecture, the paintings, furniture. But the real curiosity is about the daily lives of the inmates: who sits at high table, is chapel compulsory, when do you wear a gown, does the Queen ever come? We are a remote and romantic world, which touches everyday existence at few points. The best-known work by a don at my former college, Christ Church, is not the *Essay Concerning Human Understanding* but *Alice in Wonderland*. Side by side with this deferential admiration there is a strong anti-intellectual populism, as some of my post-bag reveals. Dons and undergraduates alike are parasites who have never done an honest day's work in their lives, but are maintained in their luxury by hard-working taxpayers. This populism is exploited, not only by tabloid newspapers and tabloid MPs, but also by at least half of the quality press. In the present context the populism is right-wing: most dons are assumed to be active agents of the KGB; the only fact known about Oxford is the 'King and Country' debate of 1933, the only fact known about Cambridge is that it produced large numbers of homosexual spies. In a different context the populism could as easily come from the Left, where there is, after all, plenty of anti-intellectual animus and certainly plenty of anti-Oxbridge animus. We'd be CIA agents, not KGB agents, but the general tone would be much the same.

This anti-intellectualism is probably a constant factor in British life, stimulated into sudden outbursts by particular events, but otherwise not fluctuating very much in its level. Since one's chances of converting the hard core with a few well-aimed shafts of reason are rather low, it is best to concentrate on the floating voter. For the fact is that we have to convince rather a lot of people that we are worth spending money on, and the first step towards that is to ask ourselves why we are worth spending money on. Again I want to concentrate on what I know about at first hand, universities, though much of what I say applies to other sectors of education too.

We have to show that we are socially useful. We also have to show that the less government interference there is in our activities, the more effectively we can serve society. This last proposition is not self-evidently valid and is rejected by a great many of our paymasters. Populist anti-intellectualism extends to fear and resentment of research. That penicillin or pocket calculators or meteorological satellites would not exist unless someone had done the basic theoretical research on which they are based is a notion alien to that constituency. Research consists either of mad professors waiting to blow up the world or looking for more animals to torture, or of clueless sociologists asking old ladies their preferred method of crossing the road. Here, too, there is nothing to be done. But there is another line of attack, rather more dangerous because more plausible, and because more plausible more attractive to the present government. It goes like this: by all means research, but make sure it yields results. If the results are what industry or commerce or public authorities want, they will pay for it and you won't need handouts. If not, you had better stop playing about with it. Put briefly, this is the why-can't-you-be-like-Salford argument.

No doubt there are ways of making us be like Salford. If I had been Vice-Chancellor of Salford, faced with the choice of leasing out my university or going broke, I should have acted exactly as he did, though probably with less success. All universities do to a lesser extent what Salford does: i.e. undertake research on contract and teach for vocational qualifications. I am told that Oxford generates between a fifth and a quarter of its research money in this way. But they can only sell on the basis that they – or someone else – do the fundamental research: the sort that private industry's shareholders and bankers are understandably reluctant to take an equity in. They know this very well at Salford, though they may not, in their present shell-shocked state, want to say it out loud. They know it equally well in industry and nothing illustrates this better than the success story of Silicon Fen, the high-technology complex round Cambridge. Explaining its secret recently, one of the whizz-kids, Hermann Hauser, listed three conditions that are essential for take-off. One is a good network of personal relations. A second is that these relations must cut across the industry-university divide. But the most important was 'a top-notch university – a second-rate one won't do: you need access to state-of-the-art research' (*Sunday Times Magazine*, 27 January). In other words, if the university of Newton, Russell and Whitehead had not been there, there would have been no spin-off. This is what is threatened by current cut-backs, and this explains the turn-out of scientists and medics at Congregation and the 70–30 majority against Mrs Thatcher's degree. But it is not the only source of anxiety and not the only purpose of universities that is threatened.

Society needs its science parks and silicon valleys, its surveyors and veterinary surgeons. It also needs its ivory towers. Somewhere where thoughts can be thought and books written without the worry about where next year's support grant is coming from. Somewhere where new, critical, unpopular, even dangerous ideas can be tried out. Somewhere where speculation can flourish even if it does not have any obviously quantifiable 'added value'. Somewhere for Wilhelm von Humboldt's ideal of *Einsamkeit und Freiheit* – solitude and freedom. That is a lot to ask and those who get it are highly privileged. It means that a handful of people, chosen by some not tremendously exact criterion of intellectual merit, are allowed to live in some comfort and –

in the case of Oxford and Cambridge – exceptionally beautiful surroundings as Crown pensioners to pursue their hobbies. (The hobbies include teaching, contrary to the widely held belief that that is the one thing dons want to get out of.) They can do this only if they do not have to look over their shoulder all the time, in case something they say or think loses them points in the competition for renewal or promotion. Ivory towers therefore risk an element of waste. It would be surprising if our profession were unique in having no dead-beats. But the dead-beats are protected along with the geniuses by the tenure system. They are the insurance premium for freedom of thought. In so far as there is a malaise in academia today, in so far as there is a suspicion of politicians and parties in general, and of the politicians in this government in particular, it is because of the fear that solitude and freedom are under attack. It is not the demand that we should be useful that we resent, but the insistence that politicians alone define that usefulness, and the use of fiscal stringency to make us come to heel. No government in living memory has established such detailed supervision over what we teach and where, who researches on what and where. That is true of the 'New Blood' posts; it is true of research grants, which are subject to the Secretary of State's veto if over £25,000; it will, according to newspaper reports, apply to schools as well, through special earmarking of the block grants to local education authorities.

Those who founded the University College of Buckingham in the 1970s as a countervailing force to state control have been conspicuous by their silence in the face of this creeping nationalisation. Anyone wondering whether education and science are exceptional victims of this detailed scrutiny need only look at changes in the administration of grants to the arts, or the Secretary of State's proposed discretionary powers in the Local Government Bill now going through Parliament. Indeed, one illustration of how seriously the Government takes the need to control our thoughts on policy questions is the curious matter of the spending figures which appeared in friendly newspapers (the *Times*, *Daily Telegraph* and *Daily Express*) a day or two after the Congregation debate, as well as in speeches during the debate itself. They were carefully tailored to suggest that Government spending on education had actually increased, although presented in a form that differed from that available in any published source. Their brief career ended on 6 February, when the Under-Secretary of State, Mr Peter Brooke, agreed in a Written Answer that, even when expressed in real terms, these figures are not comparable from year to year.

What one does about all this is a different question. The universities have in the past been lazy about defending themselves, relying on friends in high places. Now fewer high places are occupied by friends, and those that remain are tarnished by past associations. Still, there are some who advocate a softly-softly approach. There are others who advocate a defeatist prudence, fearing that only disaster can come from collision with as immovable an object as our Prime Minister. As one of my colleagues put it, 'you throw a tigress a hunk of meat, you don't stick a pin up her arse.' This is a superficially attractive strategy. Its weakness is that there is no evidence the tigress is satisfied with one hunk. Indeed, she has had her hunk in the form of a much-disputed and much-resented FRS. It does not seem to have turned her into a herbivore.

Having been politicised against our wills, we have no choice but to act politically, for all the risks that that entails. We are in much the same position as the Frenchman during the revolutionary turmoils who protested, on his way to the guillotine, that he had never interested himself in politics. That, he was told, was why he was about to be executed. There are two political conclusions that I draw from the debate in Congregation and from many casual conversations, telephone calls and my fairly voluminous post-bag. The first is that the response from anyone even remotely involved in education, especially outside Oxford, was overwhelmingly positive. It may even – though this was not our intention – have done the image of Oxford some good in those quarters. One lady from Peterborough wrote: 'Universities, particularly Oxford and Cambridge, are sometimes accused of leading a cloistered existence, shut away from the realities of the outside world. This action by the academic staff of Oxford University shows that this is not the case.' A couple from Malvern wrote: 'We have two 18-year-old children studying for A-level examinations in a comprehensive school. Your vote was a vote for them.'

There lies the strength of our case. Its weakness is that it looks self-interested. If we were merely asking for more for ourselves, as the down-market editorialists implied ('Greedy grow the dons'), if we were simply another lobby in 'the long welfare handout queue' (Digby Anderson in the *Times*, 6 February), we should deserve nothing. There is only one purpose for which we want more money: so that we can work better, harder and for longer hours. Having your project cancelled is, after all, a great way of getting more leisure.

The second conclusion is that there is undoubtedly a large Thatcher constituency in the land that is hostile to all but strictly vocational and practical education. That this constituency is Thatcherite rather than Conservative is evident from my letters. The Prime Minister is compared favourably, not only with Wilson and Callaghan, but with Heath and Macmillan. She comes second only to Churchill and Queen Elizabeth I. Her supporters condemn, as she does, the whole of the post-1945 regime. It is this constituency, more than any other, that was deeply offended by our vote. However, this constituency is not as big as the noise it makes would imply. The most recent MORI poll (*Sunday Times*, 10 February) indicates that only 34 per cent of electors are satisfied with the way Mrs Thatcher is running the country, while 51 per cent think she is out of touch with ordinary people. Mrs Thatcher's camp is organised, disciplined and determined. That, not overwhelming support, is its mainstay. The non-Thatcher camp (and it would be misleading to call it anything else) is heterogeneous, divided and directionless, although on many issues and in many places – including such non-radical institutions as Christ Church and All Souls – it is in the majority. It would be extravagant to claim for the vote in Congregation any great national significance, for all the publicity it received. What it does indicate, yet again, is the re-alignment Mrs Thatcher has brought about in political loyalties. It expresses her success. But it also defines the limits of that success and the composition of the army that could launch a counter-attack.

Michael Neve

Opera Mundi

Out of Order by Frank Johnson
(Robson, 1982)
Frank Johnson's Election Year by Frank Johnson
(Robson, 1983)
Enthusiasms by Bernard Levin
(Cape, 1983)
Poem of the Year by Clive James
(Cape, 1983)
The Original Michael Frayn by Michael Frayn
(Salamander, 1983)

Opera and opera-going proliferate at very strange times. The opera revival of the last decade is a matter of considerable interest, since in some ways it seems so inappropriate, so profligate, when all the talk is about tightening belts. Opera booms when the expense of it is most ruinous, and events seem most 'operatic' when they are huge, scary and very much for real. Opera as a cultural form lays bare the fact that there is money to sustain it while at the same time – the same Wagnerian time, one might say – it calls into question the base that supports it. Something was changed utterly when the children of Switzerland decided a few years ago to seek out and destroy the national opera house. Opera in Switzerland had become the symbol of an EEC style of bloatedness, of financial mismanagement on a scale that only the financing of opera could rival. After the riots in Switzerland, punks against Puccini, it really did seem that Herbert von Karajan was a Nazi; that Luciano Pavarotti was the ultimate Italian mother's boy, bent on world domination, and that opera would be subsidised in the industrial wastelands of a Europe unable to employ vast numbers of its own citizens. History repeats itself, appearing first as tragedy, then as farce, and then as opera.

The social history of opera is instructive in other ways – above all, in the way people talk and write about it. There seem to be two positions: a modest one, a way of liking opera, as Frank Johnson does, on the quiet, without shouting about it, and an orgiastic one, where one is cosmically-life-affirmingly-overwhelmed by it, as Bernard Levin is. What we are talking about when we talk about opera becomes an intriguing moral moment. People who talk about it well seem to do it very well, to be able to be large-minded and yet sceptical at the same time. (True Wagnerians do not think that everything Wagner wrote was wonderful.) If talked or written about badly, opera wreaks a terrible revenge, and everything seems pompous and deranged. Talking badly in this way also becomes a way of not really thinking: we may, for example, call Parliament a 'soap opera' simply because we are staggeringly uninterested in what is happening in our own seat of government. Calling something 'operatic' is one way of avoiding finding out about it.

Opera sits at the centre of a now visible two-class society – Britain in the 1980s. As we sit idly by, a small élite of quite extraordinary wealth rediscovers opera. 'The middling sort' of citizenry may, of course, find their way into the upper circle. But the language of opera, rendered histrionically, invades other places, and the culture of opera can quite suddenly seem the province of the stinking rich. And, if we say this, if we dare to propose that opera in this version may be unacceptable, we have Mr Levin on hand to condemn us as life-hating-pleasure-loathing-Marxist-tainted-little-shits. *Verbum sat.*

As these successive collections of his political journalism indicate, Frank Johnson obviously quite likes opera. In fact, his own sense of opera helps one see why he has a deserved reputation for Parliamentary reporting: he doesn't boast about opera, and he doesn't underestimate Parliament. I make this point about Johnson not boasting about opera because he actually spent some part of Maria Callas's performance in *Norma* at Covent Garden in 1957 with the diva's right tit thrust into his eye, and 'it remained there throughout the subsequent duet with Stignani.' Mr Johnson, who was born in Hackney, was playing an urchin in the opera uptown, and there are programme notes to prove it. But Johnson is a sceptical empiricist, putting in the long hours, with a good sense of ordinary foolishness. He avoids the larger questions, in order to study the minute language of political life. He eschews the cosmic. It seems that Mr Levin's life was changed by discovering *Moby Dick*. Mr Johnson, as a young man, found it 'unintelligible'. Now of course Mr Johnson in some sense took over from Mr Levin at what one is tempted to call the late London *Times*. He was a little worried, following on in this line: 'Politics was my trade, not the universe.' No doubt it was a *diminuendo* devoutly to be wished. Johnson is not indefatigable compared to Levin, but he is, in the best sense, prosaic. He likes how elections feel, out on the streets. He inhabits the cruddy world of politics and sees hilarity in its tiny events. He knows his subjects ('James Callaghan, the Harold Wilson of politics'). He knows that Mr Healey is clever, and will therefore lose the argument. And he reminds us that Mr Heseltine is 'a blonde'.

Johnson quotes his namesake, the good Doctor, on taking care to see 'that the Whig dogs should not have the best of it.' This doubting conservatism informs Johnson's political writing, and when he's being funny it works. When he resorts to mere facetiousness, it doesn't. He is wrongly uninterested in any Wilsonian legacy, silly about Dennis Skinner, bad on Enoch Powell and crass about gays and feminists. There is no necessary connection between being a political commentator and having no capacity for praise. Mr Johnson's lack of ostentation is fine, but sometimes the large thing, well said, is the right thing. *Out of Order* is inevitably full of Falklands triumph, but it's hard not to feel that Mr Johnson is too easily impressed, while, in his account of election year 1983, he seems deliberately underimpressed by Roy Jenkins holding Glasgow Hillhead, as he had been when Jenkins took it in the first place. It is the facetiousness that annoys. Is John Pilger really so dreadful? Can the Stephen Waldorf affair be taken *lightly*? Does Johnson have to talk about Greenham women as if he were an agent of Lord Gnome? The British Library will catalogue him under 'Anecdotes, facetiae, satire etc' – which is fine. But he should allow himself the chance to state a principle, as well as having the wit to hint that Lloyd George is the last PM one can imagine having a fuck. At one point he evokes Callaghan in Cardiff on 4 June this year – 'perhaps the last Labour Prime Minister'. Callaghan is offered an umbrella against the rain. '"Thank you, but no. I prefer to keep both hands free when I'm working," he replied, slightly chillingly.' Johnson then takes a chance at a larger statement which is exact and chilling: 'The whole effect was of a proletarian or lower middle-class version of the Third Marquis of Salisbury – wary, experienced, loathing ideological fervour.' That is very good, and shows that Johnson should extend himself: he has earned the right to overwrite, because he has read his Trollope, knows his Goethe, but modestly. The index to *Out of Order* has the imposing body of G. W. F. Hegel interposed between Heffer and Heseltine, so you see my point. My feeling is that Johnson could do better still – and that he is not seen to best advantage between the hard covers of an anthology. It would be a pity if he were to end up as a footnote in the important story of how the Peterhouse approach has penetrated the metropolitan press – with the exception of the *London Review of Books*.

With Bernard Levin all the opposites hold. *Enthusiasms* could be read as an innocent saga of how a lonely schoolboy came to love life, but that doesn't work. Levin's odyssey through his own greed is aggressive and ridiculous. He may see himself as busy slaying the New Puritans, but it is the story really of his own appetite that concerns him. His review of *Nicholas Nickleby* undoubtedly helped that show to its later success, but Mr Levin claims that he himself '*legitimised enthusiasm*' (his emphasis). I am drawn to his hope of glimpsing into transcendental things, but most of this offensive book is accusatory: if you don't talk big, and think big, like Levin, you are somehow anti-life. Why should we be told about his eating something, stuffed with something else, sauté'd in some other bloody thing, and dished up in some unreachable village in Provence that no one else knows about? Does it matter that Bernard Levin is surprised that he didn't discover (or is it invent?) Shakespeare until he was 11? He tells us that 'a man of modest means' may not 'be able to eat at the Gavroche, but he can eat at the Gay Hussar.' You have only to ponder what a family of modest means would make of that to see it for the baloney that it is. Books like this drive one to class warfare, simply as a way of answering back. Levin is of course swift with his famous double-bind, that if I invite him to 'tell the inhabitants of Dalston about your *mousseline de rascasse* in Cannes', then I must be a pleasure-loathing-creep. After this gross cultural, gastronomic, literary and musical display, maybe I'll become just that. The world, poor battered thing, is Mr Levin's oyster. He has seen into the Infinite and, not least, Wagner (who, as Levin well knows, would not be grateful). I have to plump for Frank Johnson's deliberate philistinism, where he talks about Amfortas, in *Parsifal*, 'doing nothing but moan all evening'. I see that *Enthusiasms* has driven one reviewer to R. A. Knox's classic Catholic work, *Enthusiasm*, of 1950, a critique of illusionist visions. Well, to play the game, I was driven back further, to Meric Casaubon's *Treatise concerning enthusiasme, as it is an effect of nature: but it is mistaken by many for either divine inspiration, or diabolic possession*, of 1655. So there.

I thought I'd never say it, but thank God, after all that, for Clive James. *Poem of the Year* is not a great success, partly because it is worried about itself, and the presence of one of its best antecedents,

MacNeice's *Autumn Journal*. James goes for a 'sprightly' ottava rima to write about 1982 as it was happening. Lebanon, Falklands, space shuttles. As a result, we get a curate's egg, hatched under pressure. Take Thatcher on public spending:

She can't trim bureaucratic overmanning.
She cuts the social services instead.
You needn't be as wise as Pitt or Canning
To see how malnutrition lies ahead.

Now the decency in this is to propose that malnutrition does lie ahead. The cock-up is 'wise as Pitt or Canning', where the demands of the rhyme bring in on the side of deep perception two of the least wise leaders of early 19th-century Britain. This nervousness in James's public style is not a fault, except when it leads on to Levinesque, name-eating conspicuous consumption. And leads to howlers such as the discussion, at the beginning of Section VIII, of something called 'the British World Cup football team':

A goalless draw with Spain wipes out the chance
Britain was in with.

Hey Clive, you're going to need a bodyguard after that.

Poem of the Year is best when most about private things, and private hopes. Even if it is Biarritz, there is a lovely glimpse of his children, happy on a beach, oblivious to the various distant horrors. James too often quotes to show off, but here Auden's line from 'Taller Today' – 'Something fulfilled this hour, loved, or endured' – is right. And James can be shrewd, even Audenesque:

The artist when he claims the Right to Fail
Just means the risk he takes is a sure bet.

Tucked in towards the end of James's poem is an optimistic aside – a glimpse of China, a future China, perhaps, of relative freedom, bicycles, safety, a place, maybe, where children could be brought up, without heroin, or *paté de foie* on a bed of caviar toast. James disliked the regimental side of China, looked clumsy on a bike, and also felt in Hong Kong, by his father's grave, that freedom should have 'a sharper taste'. James sees China as a place which is neither Australia nor America, where the biggest ambition of all seems to be a chance to see the masterworks of European grand opera.

Vague expectations of the SDP, a sense of how the world is joined together in networks of horror, images of that horror, the need to believe in a continuing struggle in Poland – these are features of the poem, features that seem overtly political when compared with the collection of satirical essays by Michael Frayn. As James Fenton suggests in his Introduction, Frayn's satire, even when concerned with wordly matters, seems to come from a slightly unrecognisable recent past. Frayn's is a style that is wry, conversational, non-operatic, and closer to Beachcomber than we can now afford to be. Some of the pieces are hilarious, but also ineffectual in a way that is hard to pin down. It may be to do with how the world changed after 1968 (when Frayn ended his stint as an *Observer* essayist), but Christopher Smoothie MP does seem to come from a different time – as do titles like 'I said "My name is Ozzy Manders, Dean of King's"'. The recent past, as Alan Bennett has suggested, is a puzzling time and Frayn's innocence and wit share in that puzzle.

E. D. Hirsch, Jr

Derrida's Axioms

On Deconstruction: Theory and Criticism after Structuralism
by Jonathan Culler
(Routledge, 1983)

Deconstruction, the subject of six new books reviewed in a recent issue of the American journal the *New Republic*, must be judged, simply by virtue of the commentary it has generated, an important cultural phenomenon. Although it originates in the philosophical writings of the French writer Jacques Derrida, deconstruction has exercised its main influence upon the teaching of literature in American universities. Just a few years ago, Derrida's work was introduced into the American academy by Professor Paul de Man; it was then taken up by his students and colleagues; and for the past five years it has been at the centre of academic literary debate. Intellectual culture thrives upon debate. Although opponents of deconstruction may accuse it of nihilism and anti-humanism, nothing could be more humanistic than vigorous arguments about the nature and aim of literature. Deconstruction has forced traditionalists to look to their assumptions and protect their theoretical flanks. Defensive critics have responded to its challenge by denying the importance of literary theory altogether. That manoeuvre will not work, for anti-theory is itself a theoretical position, and a particularly vulnerable one at that.

But deconstruction has itself benefited from cultural impulses that are anything but theoretical, and has served as an outlet for emotional and institutional needs that have no logical connection with Derrida's philosophy. Indeed Jonathan Culler rightly says in his workmanlike book that Derrida has not dealt with the 'task of literary criticism' and that 'the implications of deconstruction for the study of literature are far from clear.' In fact, Derrida's philosophy has no special implications for literary study or any other subject. As a general philosophy, it entails no specific program in politics, literature, or anything else – though by accident of history it did imply for Paul de Man a scepticism that happened to suit his temperament as a literary critic. But deconstruction as a philosophy holds no more implications for reading books than does, say, the philosophy of Bishop Berkeley. Nonetheless, deconstruction has been applied to literary study, and because of its elusiveness and difficulty, graduate students and others interested in literary theory will wish to have a reliable guide to Derrida's philosophy from a literary point of view. This Jonathan Culler has suplied in *On Deconstruction* with his customary lucidity and care. He does not address the non-literary, cultural question as to why Derrida should have caught on in the American academic scene. (This baffled even Derrida, as he told me some years back.) Nor does Culler place Derrida in a wider philosophical context. Culler sticks to the literary applications of deconstruction and he speaks as a disciple and advocate.

In this review I shall pay rather less attention to Culler than to his master. For Culler is mainly an accurate transcriber of Derrida's views and an acute observer of their uses in de Man and others. Moreover, it is easy to get lost in the details of Culler's account, despite its lucidity, and I shall use material in his book as a starting-point for rather general observations about Derrida's philosophy. The sanction that Derrida gives to deconstructive literary criticism must in the end derive from his adequacy as a philosopher. And we will not get very far in gauging his philosophy if we approach deconstruction either as acolytes who accept Derrida at his own (high) estimation or as antagonists who demonise him as a nihilist and anti-humanist. Derrida deserves to be taken seriously – but perhaps not as seriously as either his epigones or his opponents have taken him.

He belongs to a school of modern philosophy that has representatives in both the Anglo-American and Continental camps and includes such diverse names as Wittgenstein, Heidegger, Quine and Sellars – all of whom, despite their diversity, are united in their repudiation of the idea that knowledge can have a firm foundation in *anything*. Not in sense data, nor intuition nor divine revelation. Everything we know is already theory-laden, imprinted with foreknowledge, already an interpretation rather than a given. (The best description of this theme in modern thought is Richard Rorty's *Philosophy and the Mirror of Nature*.) Derrida, in criticising 'presence' and 'Western Metaphysics', is, along with Wittgenstein, Heidegger, Sellars and Quine, criticising the 'myth of the given' – the myth that knowledge can be based on something to which we could have direct access. I believe that this attack on the given has succeeded, and that it marks a genuine advance in the history of philosophy. But I don't by any means accept the idea that it therefore puts an end to 'truth' or 'Western Philosophy', or does anything as portentous as Derrida and others claim. (It simply marks the end of the myth of the given.)

Derrida's version of this modern theme makes claims that are open to challenge, but one must concede him both the basic seriousness of his effort and the basic correctness of his attack on 'presence' and the given. What raises doubts about the adequacy of his philosophy is its reduction of thought and experience to 'textuality'. ('*Il n'y a pas de hors texte*,' there is nothing outside text.) This, the most distinctive element in Derrida, is of course the element that has appealed to some of the experts about texts – literary critics. It is also a theme in his philosophy which deserves careful scrutiny.

1. Axioms of Deconstruction

Only the central section of Jonathan Culler's work is devoted to Derrida's philosophy as such, the rest being concerned with literary criticism. And even the philosophical section of Culler's book refers constantly to Derrida's relevance for the activities of professional critics. This weighting of Culler's exposition towards the literary domain makes perfectly good sense for the audience he has in mind. But it also creates a certain haziness of focus for those interested in understanding and evaluating Derrida's thought. Culler's emphases on 'iterability', 'marginality' and 'hierarchical oppositions' identify points of contact with literary criticism, but these deconstructive fruits have roots that lie elsewhere. If, in seeking those roots, I were to avoid Derrida's lingo and were to describe his underlying ideas in ordinary terms, something like the following axioms would emerge:

Axiom 1. Everything can be given at least two equally cogent explanations.

Axiom 2. In the temporal process of thinking about anything, one explanation collapses into its contrary.

Axiom 3. This entire process occurs within a linguistic-semiotic structure of thought.

From these three axioms and the critique of the given mentioned above can be derived all of the chief doctrines of Derrida's writings.

1. *The Antinomies of Thought.* 'Everything can be given at least two equally cogent explanations.' Derrida does not *argue* that everything has at least two equally cogent explanations: he assumes it, and makes it the basis of his second axiom, which is the central principle of his philosophy. But this first assumption should be brought into the light, not only because it is true, as Hume demonstrated in his *Treatise of Human Nature*, but also because it exposes the hidden connections between Derrida and the traditions of Western philosophy he rejects. Here I refer not only to such traditions as the Cretan liar paradox and Kant's antinomies (which disclose irreducible bafflements of understanding) but, more particularly, to Hume, the deconstructionist *par excellence*, who bluntly stated his version of deconstruction as follows: 'The understanding, when it acts alone, and according to its most general principles, entirely subverts itself and leaves not the lowest degree of evidence in any proposition.'

2. *The Instabilities of Thought.* 'In the temporal process of thinking about anything, one explanation collapses into its contrary.' This collapse into the contrary is the characteristic movement of deconstruction. What we thought to be present turns out to be absent; what we thought to be marginal we discover to be central. This movement is the hallmark of Derridean criticism. Culler states the critical implications of the principle: 'to deconstruct a discourse is to show how it undermines the philosophy it asserts.' We know in advance that this interpretative manoeuvre will succeed, because it is founded upon Hume's inviolable principle that 'the understanding entirely subverts itself.'

This collapse into the other has its antecedents in other pre-Derridean philosophers, particularly Hegel. Hegel explored how the here and now, the given, is subverted by the passage of time: 'The Now is pointed out; this Now. "Now": it has already ceased to be when it is pointed out. The Now that is, is other than the one indicated, and we see that the Now is just this – to be no longer the time when it is.' Hegel observed that it is the same with any 'This': 'A *This* is set up; it is however rather an other that is set up; the *This* is superseded: and this otherness, this cancelling of the former, is itself again annulled' (*The Phenomenology of Mind*, Chapter One). A brilliant development of this Hegelian insight is to be found in Heidegger's introduction to *Being and Time*, where he meditates on the concept of 'phenomenon' – the given that is not given. In still other writers – Blake, William James – this collapse into the contrary is conceived as a cyclical process within intellectual history. Certainly, in this central feature of his philosophy, Derrida has not broken with 'Western Metaphysics'.

3. *The Textuality of Thought.* 'The collapse into the contrary occurs within a linguistic-semiotic structure of thought.' Like the structuralists his predecessors, Derrida accepts as a starting-point the idea that thought is language in some sense of the term 'language'. Both structuralists and post-structuralists hold that thought is dependent upon language, and that the structure of thought is like the semiotic structure of a language. Derrida's originality lies in his further development of this idea. The normal view had been that speech is the basis of language, and thus of thought. Derrida reverses this. He argues that 'writing' (in a special sense) is prior to speech. Derrida reasons that since nothing in speech is truly *present* we must interpret speech as a 'trace', an iterable 'engram' in memory, which is just what writing is, an engram. Hence writing founds speech, not vice versa. But having made this point (which properly understood is less paradoxical and significant than first appears), Derrida goes on to treat writing as the structuralists treated speech – that is, as a 'system of differences'.

This notion of language as a 'system of differences' started with Saussure, whose original account – from Part One, Chapter Four of the *Course in General Linguistics* – is worth quoting for its clarity:

> Psychologically, our thought, apart from its expression in words, is only a shapeless and indistinct mass. Philosophers and linguists have always agreed in recognising that without the help of signs we would be unable to make a clear-cut, consistent distinction between two ideas. Without language, thought is a vague, uncharted nebula. There are no pre-existing ideas, and nothing is distinct before the appearance of language . . . In language there are only differences. Even more important: a difference generally implies positive terms between which the difference is set up: but in language there are only differences *without positive terms*.

Since thought is a language-like system dependent upon language, and since language is a structure of differences without positive terms, it follows that thought will also exhibit this structure of differences. But from Axiom Two (the collapse into the contrary) we know that when a thought arises from a momentary play of differences it will never be available as a stable *present*. 'Now' constantly becomes 'Then', and is constantly deferred. The meaning that arises from the play of differences is therefore never present, but is always being deferred. By combining Axiom Two (deferment) with Axiom Three (Saussure's 'difference'), we join deferment with difference, yielding the punning neologism 'differment', or in Derrida's original French,

Différance. This neologism and the metaphor of 'writing' are twin features of Derrida's philosophy.

2. One-Sidedness of Deconstruction

Unfortunately for the coherence of that philosophy, deferment and difference do not fit together harmoniously. The principle of difference as enunciated by Saussure requires a *stable* system of oppositions: Saussure is very clear that the system must be momentarily stable in order to give rise to meaning and the play of differences. That is the basis for his discrimination between 'synchronic' (stable) states of language and 'diachronic' changes of language over time. The principle of deferment, however, is a principle of constant instability for the system as a whole. Deferment creates a system in which nothing stands still, in which nothing is synchronic. Hegel memorably describes such a system as a 'bacchanalian revel, where not a member is sober'. One is here compelled to choose between Hegel and Saussure.

That choice ought to be in favour of Hegel. For one thing, it was empirically wrong of Saussure to claim that meaning in language arises exclusively from the systematic play of differences. Although Saussure rightly stressed the autonomous character of language systems, and rightly opposed the view that language is *just* a set of names for extra-linguistic realities, he was wrong to state his point so absolutely. Language is partly an autonomous system and is partly a set of names that derive their meaning from outside the system. Saussure's purely internal conception of a language system encouraged him to state flatly that ideas cannot exist before language, but the truth is the other way round. First we have ideas (object concepts), and then we name them. For a recent account of empirical work on names and the function of language in the development of concepts and vice versa, see *Language Acquisition*.[1] Saussure was a great and original linguistic theorist, but his idea of language as purely a system of differences is incorrect, and is a very weak foundation on which to erect the whole edifice of modern French thought.

But even if the concept of 'difference' were not based on an overstated linguistic theory, it would still consort badly with the concept of 'deferment'. Difference is a kind of pan-lingualism (in Derrida, it is a pan-textuality – *Il n'y a pas de hors texte*). Difference is thus monistic, even idealistic, in flavour. But deferment – the collapse of one thought into its contrary – is dualistic in flavour. Hegel overcame this inherent dualism by positing an Absolute at the end of the process – an end to deferment. Derrida does not end in an Absolute, not even an Absolute Text. Deconstruction, by coming to a stop in a monistic conception of difference à la Saussure, is at odds with its own genuine insights.

Derrida's literary followers are even less careful than Derrida on this score. Here is a statement by Culler (the italics are mine):

> When one attempts to formulate the distinction between reading and misreading, one inevitably relies on some notion of identity and difference. Reading and understanding preserve or reproduce a content or meaning, maintain its identity, while misunderstanding and misreading distort it; they produce or introduce a difference. But one can argue that in fact the transformation or modification of meaning that characterises misunderstanding is also at work in what we call understanding. . . We can thus say, *in a formulation more valid than its converse*, that understanding is a special case of misunderstanding.

In a similar vein, Culler argues that for the opposition literal-versus-metaphorical, the latter is foundational: a literal expression is a 'metaphor whose figurality has been forgotten'. Such tendencies to monism are a persistent danger for deconstructionists, and a danger that they rarely avoid in practice. Yet to be a monist is precisely *not* to be a deconstructionist! One ought therefore to distinguish between authentic deconstruction and capital-D Deconstruction, which in its monistic forms is a very inconsistent philosophy indeed.

As an example of the one-sidedness of Big-D Deconstruction, we may consider how it treats the following list of contraries:

1. part — whole
2. percept — object
3. signifier — signified
4. temporal — spatial (non-temporal)
5. difference — sameness

Big-D Deconstruction characteristically chooses the left-hand side of this list. It reduces the right-hand side to an illusion whose reality is on the left. The collapse into the contrary seems to go just one way and come to a halt. Of those contraries listed above, perhaps the fourth, the non-temporal versus the temporal, could be viewed as the basis for Deconstruction's other leftward-tending preferences. Temporality, after all, is the ground for 'deferment'. Derrida holds that mental life is purely temporal, is just one-thing-after-another; one moment is always different from another moment of mental life. Husserl's profound argument against this temporal conception of mental life led Derrida to devote a whole book (*Speech and Phenomena*) to attacking Husserl. But Derrida never touched Husserl's key argument favouring a dualistic, i.e. a temporal-nontemporal, conception of mind. Derrida concentrated instead on Husserl's admittedly vulnerable conception of Presence, as though by thrashing Husserl on that peripheral issue he could also defeat his other ideas. But to the extent that empirical psychology has any say in the matter, Husserl's dualism is a correct, and Derrida's monistic temporality an incorrect, account of mind. Even if that were not so, Deconstruction would be inconsistent in accepting temporality as an adequate description of mental life. On this point, as on so many others, Hume showed himself to be the more authentic deconstructionist when he admitted that the persistence of self-identical objects over time cannot be either confidently asserted or denied. Hume also said in similar vein that 'a true sceptic will be diffident of his philosophical doubts, as well as of his philosophical conviction' (*Treatise*, VII). That is the authentic principle of deconstruction – not Derrida's '*différance*' but Hume's 'diffidence'.

3. Deconstruction and Formalism

Derrida's weaknesses as a philosopher are somewhat beside the point, however, when we enter the realm of literary deconstruction as Culler describes it. Culler seems to admire the success of Deconstruction in sanctioning and continuing the professional occupation of writing about writing. His account suggests that Deconstruction has a self-sustaining effect on university publication. An academic institution, like any other, adopts an ideology that preserves the institution as it is. This is the powerful principle of institutional homeostasis.

No harm in that. But the cultural question that needs to be asked is whether we *want* to sustain the institutions of textual analysis that have dominated academic literary criticism in the past forty years. The trouble with keeping that tradition going under a new deconstructive guise is not that it is wrong or radical, or inhumane, but that the tradition of academic literary analysis is uncommitted to any cultural values at all. Literary Deconstruction is another version of formalism. It is quite unconcerned, for example, with choosing a new canon. (The old canon will do fine, Culler informs us.) Deconstruction stresses the *how* of criticism rather than the *what*. And like the New Criticism before it, Deconstruction claims that the how *is* the what of literature. Similarly, just as the New Criticism tended to find that the subject of literature was literature, Deconstruction finds that the subject of literature is Deconstruction. In exposing this feature of Deconstruction, Culler's account exhibits the twin virtues of clarity and explicitness: 'When considered at the first level, literature is remarkable for the diversity of its themes . . . At the second level, a powerful theory with literary implications seeks to analyse those structures which it takes to be most fundamental or characteristic, and thus emphasises repetition . . . Although deconstructive readings work to reveal how a given text elucidates or allegorically thematises this ubiquitous structure, they are not thereby promoting one theme and denying others but attempting at another level to describe the logic of texts.'

'To describe the logic of texts' is to describe their form, logic being the study of form *par excellence*. Such preoccupation with form in the American academy is part of a general tendency in American education to inculcate reading and writing skills without committing one to any preference for particular cultural contents. Recently we have discovered that this educational formalism will not work even in teaching elementary reading skills. To think that formalism could suffice in teaching a literary tradition is an even more obvious mistake. Deconstruction as practised in America is part of a pervasive educational formalism that avoids advocating specific values and contents. But in literary education such formalism is an evasion.

Nothing could be more illustrative of this evasive, American use of Deconstruction than Culler's treatment of feminist criticism. Culler deserves praise for treating that subject at all, and he is right to say that feminism is 'one of the most significant and broadly based critical movements of recent years'. But after spending twenty pages in analysing recent work on the subject, he summarises feminist criticism as follows:

> From these varied writings a general structure emerges. In the first moment or mode, where woman's experience is treated as a firm ground for interpretation, one swiftly discovers that this experience is not the sequence of thoughts present to the reader's consciousness . . . In the second mode, the problem is how to make it possible to read as a woman . . . In the third mode, the appeal to experience is still there . . . But experience always has this divided, duplicated character; it has always already occurred and yet is still to be produced.

In short, the logic of feminism follows the general logic of Deconstruction. Whether or not that is so, this abstracting of feminism to its Derridean 'logic' or 'structure' seems to me to express no significant truth at all about the feminist movement in criticism, and provides no basis for calling it 'one of the most significant' critical movements of recent years. That it certainly is, because of its content, not its form, and because it has encouraged a change in our canon, and in our estimate and use of particular works.

In my view, the most glaring weakness of American Deconstruction is not its intellectual incoherence but its cultural evasiveness. 'English' in American schools and universities has always been a cultural, not a progressive, intellectual subject. Although 'English' does have connections with the genuine disciplines of history and philosophy it came into being for cultural rather than disciplinary reasons. Every attempt to show that 'English' is a discipline with a logic and method of its own has so far proved specious and unenduring. Such narrow approaches to literature do not butter any intellectual or cultural bread. The function of 'English' is to help sustain or change traditions, to help provide the myths and values we live by, and to help create a culture that is worth living in. Formalism has seduced American literary study away from these authentic and original cultural purposes. Is it too much to hope that Deconstruction, the *reductio ad absurdum* of formalism (and also a very inconsiderable philosophy), may be the last gasp of this evasive tradition?

1. Edited by Eric Wanner and Lila Gleitman (Cambridge, 1983).

John Bayley

Superchild

The Diary of Virginia Woolf. Vol. V: 1936–1941
edited by Anne Olivier Bell, assisted by Andrew McNeillie
(Chatto, 1984)
Deceived with Kindness: A Bloomsbury Childhood
by Angelica Garnett
(Chatto, 1984)

To read Virginia Woolf when young is, or was, to have the feeling of entering a new world, to realise with sudden ecstasy that this was true being, where words and consciousness and the solitary self melted into one. 'She gave me eyes, she gave me ears,' wrote Wordsworth of his sister Dorothy. Virginia Woolf gave more than that: she gave, or seemed to give, the pure Private Life, quite separate from the contingent miseries, anxieties and rivalries of adolescence, a free-floating poetic awareness, an otherness wholly and excitingly up-to-date. Such at least was the experience of many young persons in the years following her death; and such still seems to be the experience of young readers who discover her today.

But there is something wrong, very wrong, somewhere: there is contradiction at the heart of it all. Her *Diary* shows what it is. For its appeal is quite different; to a different audience, a different expectation, a different sensibility. In very few writers does there seem such a gap between the sensibility projected by the art and the atmosphere generated by the personality. The style is the woman, because the woman needed the style, needed to make words for everything and to turn everything into words. All writers do that, and need to do it, and very often their readers who follow them do too. But Virginia Woolf's relationship with words is particularly direct, like a child's relation to things. It is this which captures the young and releases them into a whole consciousness of words, words they seem to be writing even as they read them. And yet the writing has nothing behind it – sometimes worse than nothing – and the *Diary* shows it. Superchild could also be a nasty child.

The paradox is certainly an odd one. Her art releases us, as it were, from school, and from all its banal miseries, anxieties and rivalries. But her *Diary* reveals that she was herself their source and embodiment. It appeals to just the kind of people and situations from which her art delivered us. She is revealed as the toady and confederate of such people, their *semblable* and anxious hanger-on, having no nature but the communal one of those on whom she sharpened her malice and whose good opinion she sought. Typical of the kind of school atmosphere Bloomsbury discloses that the two activities were really the same: its boys and girls proved their solidarity, their unified self-approval, by being nasty about each other.

There is, however, pathos in the wretched sense of all this which the *Diary* too reveals. Her awareness of her own lack of being, except in words, and at the same time her own utter determination to become one of the great ones of the school community and excel in its social and sporting activities – this is what caused Virginia Woolf to feel herself condemned 'to dance like a cat on hot bricks till I die'. The feeling of depression the *Diary* arouses is not that of the spectacle of madness, which seems almost peripheral, and certainly not causative of its general atmosphere, but rather that of a sensibility in an impossible situation, unable to achieve any proper self-confidence of its own. It is the sensibility the first novel, *The Voyage Out*, turned triumphantly into art with the character of Rachel. But this Rachel does not die, as at the end of the novel. Losing that selfhood, she drags on interminably and unchangingly through all five volumes of the *Diary*.

There is the gossip; the unending need to impress, the unending contempt for those who fail to do so. Rachel Vinrace (significant name), the heroine with whom all we outsiders identify, turns out to have been Head Girl all along. She compiles secret reports, sees that standards are kept up, throws herself into all the school activities. Diffident, defeated, dead she might be in the novel, but the real Rachel Vinrace was determined to succeed in life. The *Diary* records how she did so, and how she revenged herself on any who doubted her abilities and status as a writer. Katherine Mansfield is both rival and despised friend, a member of the same set, almost alter ego. The compulsion of words united them, and Mansfield's *Journals*, like Woolf's *Diary*, are a way of practising that compulsion and keeping it in constant exercise.

In some degree it is a matter of period and the idea of a feminine style: Gertrude Stein was also laying down words compulsively, and rearranging them like patience cards. More important, it is a matter of trying to make the words add up to somebody. Katherine Mansfield writes in her journal what Virginia Woolf's *Diary* continually implies: 'I must not forget that.' She must not forget the way the hens looked, and how the rain soaked her thin shoes. A few days before her death Virginia Woolf recorded the haddock and sausage meat. 'I think it is true that one gains a certain hold on sausage and haddock by writing them down.'

And the reader also gains a hold. That is or should be the virtue of the business, as if the reader were helping – co-operating – in keeping the thing going, the writers existent. The reader is flattered to be participating, but he also gloats: his own share continues, whereas theirs is over. They have been abandoned by the words with which they gained a hold over the haddock and the sausage. The reader is of course also proud to be in at a death. He knows how all this word business is going to end, and the diarists who needed the words so much did not.

Readers will look in any case in the last volume of Virginia Woolf's *Diary* for signs of disintegration and madness, the words spinning out of control. They will not find them. Words had always helped Virginia Woolf to keep a hold on the haddock and the sausage meat, and they continued to do so till the end. She uses them in her usual way on the sights of Brighton, in the month she died, March 1941, and then considers what for her was obviously a totally strange idea: introspection. What is the point of it? Her words are only there for her to see herself as she sees others.

> Observe perpetually. Observe the oncome of age. Observe greed. Observe my own despondency. By that means it becomes serviceable. Or so I hope. I insist on spending this time to the best advantage. I will go down with my colours flying. This I see verges on introspection, but doesn't quite fall in. Suppose, I bought a ticket at the museum; biked in daily, and read history. Suppose I selected one dominant figure in every age and wrote round and about. Occupation is essential.

Occupation had always been her standby as it had been that of her father, Leslie Stephen. And words provided it. But if the words of the *Diary* prove one thing it is that, for a creative artist, they were no substitute for introspection. Turning back a volume or two we come to the dinner party in January 1930 with the Harrises. Bogey Harris was apparently quite a character. In her account, unerring as it clearly is, he ceases to be one, as do his womenfolk and the Prime Minister, Ramsay MacDonald, 'an unimpressive man; eyes disappointing; rather heavy; middle-class; sunk; grumpy; self-important; wore a black waistcoat'.

> They all called each other Van, Bogey, Ramsay, Eadie, across the table; engaged in governing England . . . Bogey has the glazed stuffed look of the well fed bachelor. Is evidently one of those elderly comfortable men of taste and leisure who make a profession of society; a perfectly instinctive snob. Knows everyone; lunches with Lord Lascelles; has taken the measure of it all exactly; nothing to say; proficient; surly; adept; an unattractive type, with all his talk of Lords and Ladies, his belief in great houses; something of a gorged look, which connoisseurs have; as if he had always just swallowed a bargain.

This is much the same kind of person who is met with in *The Years*, the idea of which was beginning to form in her mind at the time. The novel shows little difference in method from the principle of observation in the *Diary* itself, and this may have been deliberate policy on her part. She would write as she observed, and in the first plan for *The Years*, to be called 'The Pargiters', she envisaged something 'leading naturally on to the next stage, the essay-novel'. That is what all her novels are in some sense, even *The Waves*, and it was in the air from Gide's synchronisations of the journal with the novel form. After doing a draft of 'The Pargiters' Virginia Woolf professed to find, as she put it, that the genius of fiction and of the essay were not compatible, and yet all her writing is essentially of the same kind, the kind suggested so well in her very touching entry on the last day of December 1932.

> . . . why not simply become fluid in their lives, if my own is dim? And to use one's hands & eyes; to talk to people; to be a straw on the river, now & then – passive, not striving to say this is this. If one does not lie back & sum up & say to the moment, this very moment, stay you are so fair, what will be one's gain, dying? No: stay, this moment. No one ever says that enough. Always hurry. I am now going in, to see L. and say stay this moment.

Her going in to see Leonard, and murmur to him her version of the line from *Faust*, moves us more than the idea itself. Ever since the Romantics the notion of being a passive recorder, a chameleon, a Proteus of the fire and flood, a vessel of negative capability, had not ceased to beckon like a siren to the aspiring artist. As an ideal it seemed to have everything. Had not Coleridge and Keats seen it in Shakespeare, greatest of exemplars to the English creator in words? They had, and rightly, but a deep misconception nonetheless crept in. The new passivity, the new truth, had made an end of inventiveness. So it might be supposed, so in many sects it was supposed, although in practice a writer of talent went on using his unconscious powers of construction and transformation to create a new thing in art out of what had been experienced in life. The eternal moment might beckon seductively, but the novelist knew it was not his job, in this so seemingly effective direct sense, to record it.

Of course Virginia Woolf was continually being told, in her lifetime, that she could not 'make things up', and of course it irritated her. She hated what Forster called the novelist's 'faking' and the death of Rachel in *The Voyage Out* can be seen as a protest against the way death is managed in fiction. Of the death of Milly Theale in *The Wings of the Dove* she wrote in her *Diary* that 'There is a great flourishing of silk handkerchiefs & Milly disappears behind them.' Yet she had no self-confidence, none of the lordly conviction of Henry James or James Joyce; she awaited both reviews and the comments of her friends in a perfect pathos of fear and trembling, and each new attempt at a book was wholly tentative and unsure. Her ideas were all in the form of an attack on existing fictional practice, and only an occasional comment in her *Diary* reveals her awareness of connection in her own method. 'In truth the Pargiters is first cousin to Orlando, though the cousin in the flesh: Orlando taught me the trick of it.' That is very revealing. *Orlando* may be a 'fantasy', but it is just as much a matter of observation – using one's hands and eyes – as is the novel that was to become *The Years*. No true imaginative process has occurred. Virginia Woolf simply looked at Vita Sackville-West as she looked at Bogey Harris, however much the former may be dressed up in a style and a fancy. There is nothing to be done with Orlando, beyond seeing her in this way, just as there is nothing to be done with Bogey Harris beyond seeing him at the dinner-table.

Surprising, in view of this, that so perceptive an admirer as Stuart Hampshire should have remarked of the first volume of the *Diary* that it gave 'an almost unequalled account of the imagination working'. Is not the impression of a different process, of writing and seeing as a substitute for imagining? Her imagination is enchanted into the paralysis of the eternal moment: there is no feel of its undergoing progression throughout the years of the *Diary*. The Romantics thought of Shakespeare as the passive creator with no personality of his own, and Keats aspired to the same state, but it would be hard to find two more graphic instances of imagination's sheer powers of organisation and transformation than are afforded by the plays, the Odes. Going back again to Bogey Harris, what is effective about his presentation, but also very depressing, is the sense of accuracy without the mediation of the introspective mind. He is not *created*. No more than Bernard and Louis, and the characters in *The Years* and the rest of her novels, is Bogey Harris transformed into a work of art.

That is his point, she might reply: that is what I am aiming at. 'Of course this is external,' she says, as she meditates the Pargiters ('pargiting' or 'pargetting' is facing with cement the surface of a wall) – 'But there's a good deal of gold – more than I'd thought – in externality. Anyhow, what care I for my goose feather bed? I'm off to join the raggle taggle gipsies oh! The Gipsies, I say: not Hugh Walpole & Priestley – no.' The names show what she was reacting against. It was against characters in books, which formed a convenient target and Aunt Sally, disguising the fact that what she really repudiated was the imaginative and introspective organisation which produced the character as a work of art. 'If they didn't feel a thing why did they go and pretend to?' asks Rachel in *The Voyage Out*. Her attitude to life is her creator's attitude to art. For the first time the Romantic doctrines of wise passiveness and negative capability were being pressed to their logical conclusion.

'*Madame Bovary, c'est moi*,' said Flaubert, and the obviousness of the point does not conceal its importance. In the same sense Shakespeare is Hamlet and Falstaff, Desdemona and Miranda; Dickens is Quilp and Mrs Gamp; Anthony Powell is Widmerpool; Henry James is Isobel Archer and Gilbert Osmond. The character as work of art has the closest possible relation with his creator's projected being. He is an embodiment of all that is present in his author, but which his author – being the ordinary bundle of responses that sits down to breakfast – can never become. Between them stretches the mysterious factory in which knowledge, self-awareness, observation, humour, love of art, are all hard at work at their business of chemical processing. Virginia Woolf wants to pull down the factory, to operate face to face in the open air. Christopher Isherwood, in some ways her most affectionate and enthusiastic disciple, went through the motions of restating her formula at the outset of some of his own fictions. He is the passive recording camera. Of course nothing could be less true of the process which creates Mr Norris, Sally Bowles, Herr Issyvoo, Christopher himself. But the bow to her method shows both how much Virginia Woolf's philosophy of creative writing had caught on, and how it was being quietly, probably even unconsciously, set aside in practice. Isherwood's world is as essentially *made up* as that of any other good novelist, and it is of course for this reason that it gives the reader so much and such varied satisfaction. Art, thus cunningly made up, '*makes* life, makes interest, makes understanding', in Henry James's noble words, and, as he went on, 'I know of no substitute whatever for the force and beauty of the process.' Art, in this sense, also makes truth. The truth of art is a question of harmony, and of the deeper kinds of wish-fulfilment which arise out of the artist's deep and prolonged identification with the character and pattern of the work. Madame Bovary and her fate is Flaubert's wish-fulfilment in this sense.

For Virginia Woolf wish-fulfilment was in words themselves, that protected her from herself and from society. She could make no harmonious pattern out of either and did not want to. Other diaries, like Isherwood's again, combine the real and the invented in ways natural to art: the diarist is creating himself, even if unknowingly, in the same way that the novelist is creating his characters in the novel. But there is nothing of that in Virginia Woolf's. In novels and *Diary* alike to set down the haddock and the sausage is for her the equivalent of what for other artists would be the metamorphosis of self into a larger social and artistic whole. It makes her and her *Diary* unique: it creates that world of words which fascinates us when we first read her: it makes that strange contradiction I noticed at the beginning between that world and her ignobly competitive, childishly unattractive self. It is a platitude that the artist is a feeble and dispersed creature in comparison with his creations, and yet the artist is present in his creations, shapes them, makes and remakes himself through them. With her there is nothing to be made – hence no point of contact between herself and the words she depended on. It is this gap which unwittingly fascinates us when young, because we can fill it up ourselves, being the 'Virginia Woolf' that she was not. No other writer is so wholly alienated from the works with which she apparently seems so completely identified.

There is a uniqueness here certainly, even a kind of genius, but not one of a kind normally associated with the processes of art. Many readers came to see this in their own way, and she knew they did and resented it. She dreaded the discovery that the Vestal of Bloomsbury, the High Priestess of the new aestheticism, might be seen to have no clothes, at least none of the clothes she had deliberately put on. Desmond MacCarthy's thoughtful and friendly review of *The Years*, which 'as usual depresses me beyond reason', said she knew 'nothing of the drama of the will in action out of which stories are made. What an extraordinary, what a fatal, limitation you would say, in a novelist! And yet (it is the mark of the artist to make his limitations also serve his end) she succeeds in being one.' That is true enough: what is not true is the implicit counter-claim that she was inventing a new form. The form of *The Waves* is a sham: it is simply her *Diary* by other means. It is often said that the characters are all aspects of herself, but that is not true either, for she had no self in the sense that the novelist divides his potentiality of being among his dramatis personae. Like Mrs Dalloway or the Pargiters, the voices in *The Waves* talk about themselves as if they were observations in the Diarist's world, and the poetry in italics is simply stuck on. The same is true of the figures of the Stephen parents, the Ambroses in *The Voyage Out* and Ramsays in *To the Lighthouse*. Many moments of malice and despair in the *Diary* suggest her awareness that she was not finding any substitute for the 'force and beauty' of the old artistic process.

Where fiction was concerned she once had a self – that of Rachel Vinrace in *The Voyage Out*, whose illness and death is the most memorable sequence in any of the novels. That self had to die, together with the uses that fiction could make of it, and it was not replaced. The private self, the wraith-like 'Virginia Woolf' that beguiles her readers, became the emptiness of the *Diary*. She was released from the father figures who tyrannise Rachel, but just as rigorously if more subtly controlled by the new kinds of social and aesthetic domination, and by such bogus concepts as Clive Bell's 'significant form'. As Diarist, she had an assiduous zest for social goings-on of any kind, and for the places where things were happening. But she had the snob's fatal lack of independence, of the ability, essential to most good writers, to get on secretly with what they know to be best for them. Having killed the budding heroine of *The Voyage Out*, she reverted to an earlier and more amorphous condition, the dependence of childhood.

It might be objected that all this is beside the point, that the *Diary* is a wonderful repository of events and personalities. It is indeed beautifully edited, and the notes and 'Biographical Outlines' are as invaluable to students of the period as they are to amateurs of fashion and connection. The appeal is to a world from which the art once seemed to deliver us. That would not matter if it were not for what seems to me the gravest drawback of all. Everything seen and recorded becomes in the process boring, meaningless, uninteresting. That's life, you might say, but where are we then? It is the function of art to make life delightful, to make eternally memorable and entertaining what in life was boring, transitory, confused, insipid, banal. Dickens and Thackeray and Proust, Scott Fitzgerald and Elizabeth Bowen and Anthony Powell – they are all packed with lunches and dinners, balls and parties, which one would much rather not have been at, but which art has contrived to make glorious for us by proxy. Unfair to compare diaries with this? No, because diaries intended for publication (and there is no doubt hers was, as was everything she wrote) give us pleasure in vicarious experience channelled through the diarist's personality.

The reason hers does not must again be linked with her lack of such a personality. Our pleasure in what a writer describes – ragged and contingent as it may have been at the time – is also our pleasure in getting to know the writer. And we may come to know him all the better if he seems unaware of the fact. In the *Diary* we get to know neither Virginia Woolf nor the people she meets. There is none of that reflexive concentration on making up a story, a story which shapes the writer for the reader in involuntary depth, and makes the writer the part of the tale which most gives it interest and meaning. Pepys does that, and Rousseau, and Chateaubriand, and Stendhal in *La Vie de Henri Brulard*, and Newman and Ruskin and Hardy – all the way down to Anthony Powell in his Memoirs and the just published diaries of Barbara Pym. Indeed this contribution to the state of the art by a humbler sister in the fiction business – and appearing posthumously in the same way – might well have aroused Virginia Woolf to envy and admiration.

Even when she was an undergraduate overwhelmed by shyness and silliness, longing to be noticed and loved, falling head over heels for handsome young men, Barbara Pym created herself in her diary; and in so doing creates the people about whom she was absorbed and passionate. They come as much alive in the diary as they were to do later in her novels. What does it is sex, and all it entails, the element absent in Virginia Woolf, though the two women have a remarkably similar view of maleness. 'There is something maniacal in masculine vanity,' says Virginia Woolf, noting the antics of Partridges, Stracheys etc ('stupidity, blindness, callousness, struck me more powerfully than the magic virtues of passion'). But her own magical powers of seeing, and making us see, human creatures driven by their various devils, depend on her detachment. Where Barbara Pym is a willing victim of the emotions and needs she is afterwards so funny about, Virginia Woolf only sees that 'the truth is people scarcely care for each other. They have this insane instinct for life. But they never become attached to anything outside themselves.'

Yes, the sense of living, which she can get by so vividly and incessantly recording it, is different from that 'instinct for life' which plunges the ego into unexamined situations of which it cannot escape the consequences. The *Diary* is like the business record of a miser, the ledger of a tycoon who, having taken over everything he can, at last plunges to his death from a window on the fiftieth floor. Writing, talking, meeting, the aesthetic life, are a frenetic business activity, devouring every moment of the day. Would Virginia Woolf have been surprised to be told that she had no more time than has a very busy businessman for the life of culture and the mind? Much in the texture of her diary embodies the frenetic routines of the high-powered entrepreneur, the obsessional lunches and dinners and committees, the balance sheets and the being seen at the best places. It would have tickled her sense of humour, no doubt, to have realised that she led about as spiritual a life as a soap manufacturer, that she was no Margaret Schlegel but a Wilcox of Wilcoxes.

There is something unnerving about the way the masterful goes with the helpless, the career woman with the child. This in itself may not be uncommon – a part of human nature: but here it is displayed with the honesty which is a technical aspect of her diary method, an honesty both willed and involuntary. She distrusted Forster but he was intimate as a 'schoolfellow', who was not to be shown her Wilcox side; and she enjoyed the way her husband Leonard put them both right, told them what to think about modern politics and the current situation. One of the results of not making up a story about herself is that she does not value her own shrewdness, kindness, humour. They are as inconsequential as her sense of others. None of her views or attitudes, like those on the feminist question, strike one as things which she feels she should feel, responses she owes to herself. Bloomsbury has bequeathed us a special type of *bien pensant*, but she was certainly not one, and when she tries to be, as in *Three Guineas* (which Forster, who hated female independence, disliked so much), the tone goes wrong.

This may be because she was really what her friend Desmond MacCarthy used to call a 'leprechaun', a being without a sense of moral order, without the endowment to accept or cultivate a responsible social and moral stance. Insatiably sociable as she was, she remained on the outside of the social structure. In contrast with her own, one is struck by the sheer pomposity of other diaries and memoirs of the period, their involuntary tone – as paramount in André Gide as in, say, Harold Nicolson – of helping to run the world, of being confident that one counted in its councils. A leprechaun is an honest being because it lacks the norms and instincts by which honesty is judged and valued, attributed or found wanting. Unlike Dr Johnson's butcher, Virginia would *not* have been free of any uneasy sensation if she said or wrote that her heart bled for her country. Uneasy sensations were coincident with dancing on hot bricks and putting the dance into words. There is no contrast in her between an inner life of more or less comfortable egoism, and an outer one of proper utterance and action.

That contrast has been, in general, of immense importance to literature. It is both the principle of incongruity and the basis of storytelling. We make up stories as we make up virtues, conventions, personalities; the goal of art is to give us a deliberate and fascinated consciousness of the artistry in the process. But no more than de Sade could Virginia Woolf 'imagine virtues for herself', or imagine a story about herself. Her reputation and that of her *Diary* – both seem to be ever on the increase – is not entirely due to the academic industry, or to social interest in her world and circle. Her consciousness as a writer still seems exceptionally modern today because of the way she emancipated fiction from its own arts, from the 'willing suspension of disbelief' which was taken as much for granted by readers of Proust and Henry James – of *Ulysses* too – as by the reader of popular romance. The novelist for whom 'art *makes* life, makes interest, makes importance' is bound to invent a great deal more than he knows, to take the merest crumb or clue of appearance in order to build up, round off and complete a situation, story, character. In her *Diary* as in her books, Virginia Woolf stuck resolutely to appearances, trying to make words themselves make up for the shortcomings of appearance, its scrappiness and lack of meaning, comprehending no more than she can see and note down – Violet Tree and her sudden death, the women at Brighton, the rash on Leonard's back which he thought might be to do with his prostate but which the doctor said was caused by new pyjamas, Clive Bell glimpsed for a second at his dining-room window as they leave his house after a lunch-party.

'One life, one writing,' as Robert Lowell was to say. Words must be as inconsequential as talk, which she could not have enough of, and yet as imperishable as stones. The anxiety present on every page is: would the paradox succeed? The reputation of Tom and Morgan is higher than her own? Brief despair – will she always be an outsider? Certainly Eliot and Forster had inner and outer selves, a persona which pretended, and an inner art which made life, made interest. And in October 1938 she is lamenting the fact that Cyril Connolly in *Enemies of Promise* has called her one of the 'Mandarins'. Absurdly wide of the mark this now seems, for her vision and method as a writer have proved to be wholly and pervasively democratic. Her ghost is behind TV features, tapes and discussions; her influence instantly recognisable in the impressions of themselves and their situation which beginners send to publishers. Every sort of instant literary art, even the bed descriptions she would so much have disliked, can still call her their inspiration and patron.

And her appeal is still to the young. She still gives them eyes and ears, and enhanced awareness of what Wordsworth in another poem calls 'the pleasure that there is in life itself'. Even her hesitations reassure them. ('Have I the power of conveying the true reality? Or do I write essays about myself?') The immediacy in every phrase still shoots at us – the *ding dong* of the Rodmell church bells outside the window, coming between her and the words as she writes, and so clambering into the words; the German planes passing overhead and their sound of sawing as she and Leonard lay flat on the grass.

It is significant that she had a secret bond of understanding with Hugh Walpole, whom she patronised in public as everyone else did. And he understood her. She carefully copied out an affectionate letter from him which claimed they were opposite ends of the same stick. He too was a child – 'half of me is very mature, half has never grown up at all' – but the ordinary kind who told himself endless stories, while she had a quite different though related genius, a superchild indeed, as he seemed humbly to recognise. In terms of art they had a curious sibling bond – hers sexless, his homosexual – and the same zest for life, always haunted by the fear of losing it – not life, that is, but the zest for it. Although zest is as great as ever, the fear is strong in the last volume of the *Diary*, as she feels her friends may be losing their appetite for life, and thus for herself and her books. Even Clive Bell. 'Poor old Clive even, a little on the bare wheels; no blown up tyres. That is to me very ominous – if Clive's spirits should give way – if he were to give up his enjoyment of life.' Other friends have a similarly 'damping' effect, especially if they express any reservations about what she is writing, if they beat her at bowls, or speak well of other writers.

We are all young some of the time, and she grips us the most when we most feel young, when we are least at home in ourselves and most vulnerable. She enjoyed her sister Vanessa's resentment of her success, and was fascinated by her niece Angelica, a fascination in which she seems the child and the child the adult. Angelica's elopement with David Garnett deeply upset her. Angelica Garnett's book about her childhood, *Deceived with Kindness*, shows a quite exceptional understanding of the whole environment. Tolerantly and without malice she analyses the ways in which Bloomsbury licensed and indulged the grossest egoisms as if they were the finest flower of civilised and rational behaviour. Of these she was herself the victim.

For her aunt Virginia 'seeing' was itself a form of egoism – the pure child's-eye view – which she contrasts in her *Diary* with what she calls 'fiction'. 'Seeing' is life, and the awareness of one's own life is 'fiction', a dichotomy more openly dwelt on in the final entries.

On Saturday I 'saw'; by which I mean the sudden state when something moves one. Saw a man lying on the grass in Hyde Park; newspapers spread round him to keep off the damp. Ought one only to write about what one 'sees' in this way? These sights always remain.

Mrs Dalloway 'sees' when during her party she looks across into the lighted window of another house, where an old woman is going to bed. Virginia Woolf connects such moments with memories of her mother. This is how to write and it excites her to think of the flattering request by Christopher Isherwood and John Lehmann for a short story for *New Writing*. But a day or two earlier she had feelings she described as 'fiction', when she had a sudden urge to go to Paris and Leonard said he would rather not. 'I was overcome with happiness . . . after twenty-five years can't bear to be separate . . . you see it is an enormous pleasure, being wanted: a wife. And our marriage so complete.'

Then she 'returns to facts (tho' this "fiction" is radiant still under my skin)'. One sees why she regarded settled self-satisfactions – always criticised in others – as 'fiction', and her 'seeing' as life: her own life in writing as such 'seeings'. The contrast is used in the form of *Between the Acts* and might have been explored further in later novels. Always immanent in what she wrote, it became more marked with the passing of time, with her worldly and literary success and the solidity of her marriage. Had she lived she might have grown up in her last years and moved us in the more considered ways that older writers do. There is plenty of evidence for this in the last volume of her *Diary*, even in such a throwaway entry as during that terrible pause in the spring of 1940 before the war got going. 'Not a sound this evening to bring in the human tears. I remember the sudden profuse shower one night just before the war wh. made me think of all men & women weeping.' Even that darting birdlike gaze comes to rest in the end on old clichés – sad ones or happy. Like some lady in a Victorian novel or sentimental melodrama she would say to Leonard, 'Do you ever think me beautiful now?' in order to hear him say: 'The most beautiful of women.'

Ian Hamilton

Diary

Years ago, when I was serving as an anonymous hack on the *Times Literary Supplement*, one of my duties was to pen sprightly paragraphs for a weekly books column. The idea was to mop up publications which were not considered worth full-scale reviews but which nonetheless had to be 'covered' by a journal of record such as ours. Things like: *A Dictionary of Spy Writers* or *The Balladeers' Handbook* or *Henry Williamson: My Friend*. Usually, there was a brisk supply of such material and it was easy enough to knock out the required eight or nine paragraphs per week.

Sometimes, though, there would be nothing: no *Murderer's Who's Who*, no Yorkshire verse, no New Zealand little magazines. To guard against such barren stretches, we invariably had one or two 'timeless' items on the go: foreign stuff, mostly, since no one knew when that was out of date, but now and then something solidly domestic – jokey items on the philosophy of crossword puzzles, or shrewd, relaxed meditations on what ought to be done about the Regions/Writers-in-Residence/The Open University. You could always find a current peg for material like this – 40 per cent of 'on the one hand', 40 per cent of 'on the other', and a final, plangent 20 per cent of 'It is to be hoped that . . . ' Child's play, really, provided that you remembered to change the names and dates.

To liven things up (it must have been a Friday, after lunch) we decided to compose a spoof poem and submit it to one of those 'Poems Wanted' publishers who advertise in all the weeklies. To a literary editor, the phrase 'Poems Wanted' has an outlandish, almost eerie twang. I can't remember how our poem went but it was made up of extremely well-known lines out of, I think, the *Faber Book of Modern Verse*. It might even have read:

April is the cruellest month
Because
It makes me think
Continually of those who were truly great

So it's no go
My honey love, it's no go my poppet.

It might even have been titled 'Do not go gentle into that good knight'. The point is, we were almost begging to be rumbled.

Anyway, we sent the thing off under a daft pseudonym and, within days, back came a cordial acceptance. The publisher (call him Arthur Daley) would be glad to include our 'splendid' composition in *Best Poems of 1969*, or whatever year it was. The catch (described by Daley as the bonus) was that we would be expected to purchase eight copies of the book when it appeared. Although it wasn't spelled out, the deal was clear: no purchase, no publication. We calculated that with, say, two hundred poets buying eight copies each, this rather shoddily printed anthology would chalk up a decent profit before a single copy reached the shops; if shops indeed figured in Mr Daley's plans.

So we wrote it all up, mingling tired mockery with almost prim reproof, and bunged it into the column during a slack week. There was much applause all round, as if we had dealt the philistines a telling blow. For my part, I was at first simply glad to have filled the space with something that had been quite fun to do. Later, though, I did begin to wonder. After all, who had we damaged, if damage had been done? Not the publisher, certainly: poetry might be a tidy little earner if you play it right but Arthur could as easily switch to monogrammed nappy-liners or one-legged tracksuits. By the time our piece appeared, he had probably already diversified, moved on. No, the most likely victims of our little jape were the two hundred 'poets' who had no doubt been quite happy with the way things were – only too eager, probably, to fork out for eight copies of a book they could pass on proudly to their grannies, ex-husbands, and the like. These sensitives were now exposed as shoddy self-deluders. Auden understood about the real, the hidden and depressed, readership for poetry: these poets of 1969 were even more hidden, more depressed and very likely ate in even nastier cafeterias than the types Auden had in mind. They had probably never even heard of Auden. Who were we to bully such harmless dabblers into rough self-knowledge?

After a day or so spent musing along these pious lines, it dawned on me that I must surely be suffering from hoaxer's backlash, that sour and anxious sensation I remember seeing on the faces of a gang of bloods at my Oxford college just after they had finished booby-trapping a swot's room, and on the less well-bred faces of my barrack-mates in the Air Force when they sent the weediest of our colleagues out on a fake-date with the CO's daughter – what fun it had been watching the poor slob dab after-shave into his armpits, and how blissful the moment when, with a chuckle that could only be described as 'debonair', he decided finally to wear the flowery tie and not the striped . . .

Do all hoaxers end up feeling a bit wretched, after the event? Did the inventors of Ern Malley experience a few spasms of discomfiture after their spoof poet had taken the Australian literary scene by storm? I suppose not – after all, this was a high-minded hoax, an act of Criticism, really: its authors could boast that there was nothing in it that was petty or vindictive. And what about Dr Johnson's pal, the awesomely resourceful George Psalmanazar whose fraudulent study of Formosa got him a job at Oxford, teaching missionaries to master his faked-up Formosan tongue? George was made to suffer for his cheek, and in time he did repent – but he too could surely have pleaded that his jests had served a highish purpose.

Higher, certainly, than the purpose served by our own most recent literary hoax. I have before me a press hand-out from the firm of Michael Joseph:

WE BELIEVE THAT NEVER BEFORE HAS A CELEBRATED WRITER OF FICTION SO SUCCESSFULLY DISGUISED HER IDENTITY AND CREATED SUCH AN EXPERIMENT IN PUBLISHING. AND NEVER BEFORE HAS A WRITER AT THE HEIGHT OF HER POWERS WRITTEN TWO SUCH POWERFUL AND MOVING BOOKS IN ANOTHER PERSONA.

The story is now well-known. In 1982, a writer who called herself 'Jane Somers' submitted her 'first novel' to three London publishers. Two of them – Cape and Granada – turned it down. The third, Michael Joseph, published it in 1983 – under the title *The Diary of a Good Neighbour*; they said that Jane Somers had already written some romantic fiction and was well-known as a journalist. The book got 'mild reviews', according to my hand-out, and 'sold moderately'. It was published in America, and translated into three languages. Earlier this year, Jane Somers's second book appeared, entitled *If the Old Could*, and shortly afterwards it was revealed that Jane Somers was just another name for Doris Lessing. Now both books are reissued in a single volume under Lessing's name – with a rather dotty introduction explaining why she had gone to all this trouble.[1]

The explanation is in two halves: one half is severe and public-spirited, the other is girlish and bewildered. On the public front, Lessing contends that she has revealed important truths about the state of publishing and reviewing: it's all so mechanical and yet it's all so name-fixated – by means of her hoax, she has established that a known author gets more respect than an unknown. Well, thanks for telling us. She also wanted to help these said unknowns by demonstrating that even somebody as gifted as herself could, when rendered nameless, be treated with institutional disdain. And, as if all this were not sufficiently confusing, she (parenthetically) rather liked the idea of exposing the shoddiness of her regular reviewers. 'Some reviewers complained they hated my Canopus series, why didn't I write realistically, the way I used to before; preferably *The Golden Notebook* over again? These were sent *The Diary of a Good Neighbour* but not one recognised me.' *That*'s pretty shoddy, you might think; after all, these people are supposed to be her fans. A sentence or so later, though, Lessing herself lets these (and, I should say, all other) dunces off the hook: 'it did turn out that as Jane Somers I wrote in ways that Doris Lessing cannot . . . Jane Somers knew nothing about a kind of dryness, like a conscience, that monitors Doris Lessing whatever she writes and in whatever style.' And it is here that the girlishness intrudes. What she seems to be saying now is that when Doris Lessing becomes Jane Somers she stops being Doris Lessing; it is only afterwards that she becomes Lessing enough to blame people for thinking Somers is not her:

> Some may think this is a detached way to write about Doris Lessing, as if I were not she; it is the name I am detached about. After all, it is the third name I've had: the first, Tayler, being my father's; the second, Wisdom (now try that one on for size!), my first husband's; and the third my second husband's. Of course there was McVeigh, my mother's name, but am I Scots or Irish? As for Doris, it was the doctor's suggestion, he who delivered me, my mother being convinced to the last possible moment that I was a boy. Born six hours earlier, I would have been Horatia, for Nelson's Day, what could that have done for me? I sometimes wonder what my real name is; surely I must have one.

This is territory remote from the public-spirited, and rather more interesting, but Lessing doesn't linger there for long. The drift of her preface is that she has somehow done everyone a favour. But what, in the end, has been achieved? Publishers and reviewers can hardly be reviled for not having 'heard' the authentic Lessing cadences. As she admits, she wasn't using them. Nor can they be blamed for not doing well by the aspiring Somers. Having now read both novels, I am surprised that the fledgling didn't have a rougher ride. In fact, if Lessing has proved anything, it is that she has a gift for manipulating the very machine she has laboured to 'expose'. In hype terms, thanks to the hoax both titles are now doing very nicely.

Far better, certainly, than they deserve. The first novel has some arrestingly beastly descriptions of old age, but creaks horribly when it tries to describe the innards of a swinging woman's mag. And the heroine's stylish metropolitan know-how is registered with gauche unease. The second book takes a few wild swings at feckless youth, but its main artery is Mills and Boon:

And then, my life with Richard. It really is another life, and I fly into it, my heels winged. Sometimes I arrive at our rendezvous with my hands full of flowers, somewhere to put my joy. Richard laughs when he sees them, straight into my eyes, so that my eyes dazzle with it, like too strong sunlight. He takes flower after flower, putting them in my hair, my belt, my buttonhole. I stand bedecked and people look, at first ready to be critical, but then getting the benefit of the spin-off of our enjoyment.

It's true that the character doing the talking here writes romantic novels (she is, indeed, called Janna Somers) and it is just possible that we are meant to think that she's gone off her head. But not really – here is another character (the sophisticated magazine's sophisticated editor) on his newborn child:

Janna, this is my fourth, and God forgive me the best! I know you shouldn't like one more than another, and in a sense I don't, they are *miracles*. I simply can't believe it, how utterly amazing and marvellous each baby is, each in its own way . . . When little Caroline was born – although I had seen it all three times before and every time it was just the most *perfect* thing – when this little being appeared, and they put a towel around her and put her *straight* in my arms, because I am afraid poor Phyllis was not with us at just that moment, she opened her eyes and looked at me. She wasn't crying or shocked or anything like that – I know now because after all Caroline is my fourth.

He burbles on like this for four pages – he has forgotten, for four pages, that our heroine is childless; the whole soliloquy is a set-up for Janna to surprise herself with a sudden unstylish burst of tears. 'Then he was up in a bound, and he had his arms about me. "Oh Janna, don't don't, I am so sorry. Of course, I had forgotten, you haven't had children, oh poor Janna, I am sorry, how awful of me."'

It is at moments like this – and there are lots of them – that one begins to wonder if Lessing hasn't perhaps pulled off a hoax within a hoax – a new way of packaging old pulp.

1. *The Diaries of Jane Somers* (Michael Joseph, 1984).

Tony Harrison

v.

My father still reads the dictionary every day. He says your life depends on your power to master words

Arthur Scargill, *Sunday Times*, 10 January 1982

Next millennium you'll have to search quite hard
to find my slab behind the family dead,
butcher, publican, and baker, now me, bard
adding poetry to their beef, beer and bread.

With Byron three graves on I'll not go short
of company, and Wordsworth's opposite.
That's two peers already, of a sort,
and we'll all be thrown together if the pit,

whose galleries once ran beneath this plot,
causes the distinguished dead to drop
into the rabblement of bone and rot,
shored slack, crushed shale, smashed prop.

Wordsworth built church organs, Byron tanned
luggage cowhide in the age of steam,
and knew their place of rest before the land
caves in on the lowest worked-out seam.

This graveyard on the brink of Beeston Hill's
the place I may well rest if there's a spot
under the rose roots and the daffodils
by which dad dignified the family plot.

If buried ashes saw then I'd survey
the places I learned Latin, and learned Greek,
and left, the ground where Leeds United play
but disappoint their fans week after week,

which makes them lose their sense of self-esteem
and taking a short cut home through these graves here
they reassert the glory of their team
by spraying words on tombstones, pissed on beer.

This graveyard stands above a worked-out pit.
Subsidence makes the obelisks all list.
One leaning left's marked FUCK, one right's marked SHIT
sprayed by some peeved supporter who was pissed.

Far-sighted for his family's future dead,
but for his wife, this banker's still alone
on his long obelisk, and doomed to head
a blackened dynasty of unclaimed stone,

now graffitied with a crude four-letter word.
His children and grandchildren went away
and never came back home to be interred,
so left a lot of space for skins to spray.

The language of this graveyard ranges from
a bit of Latin for a former Mayor
or those who laid their lives down at the Somme,
the hymnal fragments and the gilded prayer,

how people 'fell asleep in the Good Lord',
brief chisellable bits from the good book
and rhymes whatever length they could afford,
to CUNT, PISS, SHIT and (mostly) FUCK!

Or, more expansively, there's LEEDS v.
the opponent of last week, this week, or next,
and a repertoire of blunt four-letter curses
on the team or race that makes the sprayer vexed.

Then, pushed for time, or fleeing some observer,
dodging between tall family vaults and trees
like his team's best ever winger, dribbler, swerver,
fills every space he finds with versus Vs.

Vs sprayed on the run at such a lick,
the sprayer master of his flourished tool,
get short-armed on the left like that red tick
they never marked his work much with at school.

Half this skinhead's age but with approval
I helped whitewash a V on a brick wall.
No one clamoured in the press for its removal
or thought the sign, in wartime, rude at all.

These Vs are all the versuses of life
from LEEDS V. DERBY, Black/White
and (as I've known to my cost) man v. wife,
Communist v. Fascist, Left v. Right,

class v. class as bitter as before,
the unending violence of US and THEM,
personified in 1984
by Coal Board MacGregor and the NUM,

Hindu/Sikh, soul/body, heart v. mind,
East/West, male/female, and the ground
these fixtures are fought out on's Man, resigned
to hope from his future what his past never found.

The prospects for the present aren't too grand
when a swastika with NF (National Front)'s
sprayed on a grave, to which another hand
has added, in a reddish colour, CUNTS.

Which is, I grant, the word that springs to mind,
when going to clear the weeds and rubbish thrown
on the family plot by football fans, I find
UNITED graffitied on my parents' stone.

How many British graveyards now this May
are strewn with rubbish and choked up with weeds
since families and friends have gone away
for work or fuller lives, like me from Leeds?

When I first came here 40 years ago
with my dad to 'see my grandma' I was 7.
I helped dad with the flowers. He let me know
she'd gone to join my grandad up in Heaven.

My dad who came each week to bring fresh flowers
came home with clay stains on his trouser knees.
Since my parents' deaths I've spent 2 hours
made up of odd 10 minutes such as these.

Flying visits once or twice a year,
and though I'm horrified just who's to blame
that I find instead of flowers cans of beer
and more than one grave sprayed with some skin's name?

Where there were flower urns and troughs of water
and mesh receptacles for withered flowers
are the HARP tins of some skinhead Leeds supporter.
It isn't all his fault though. Much is ours.

5 kids, with one in goal, play 2-a-side.
When the ball bangs on the hawthorn that's one post
and petals fall they hum *Here Comes the Bride*,
though not so loud they'd want to rouse a ghost.

They boot the ball on purpose at the trunk
and make the tree shed showers of shrivelled may.
I look at this word graffitied by some drunk
and I'm in half a mind to let it stay.

(Though honesty demands that I say *if*
I'd wanted to take the necessary pains
to scrub the skin's inscription off
I only had an hour between trains.

So the feelings that I had as I stood gazing
and the significance I saw could be a sham,
mere excuses for not patiently erasing
the word sprayed on the grave of dad and mam.)

This pen's all I have of magic wand.
I know this world's so torn but want no other
except for dad who'd hoped from 'the beyond'
a better life than this one, *with* my mother.

Though I don't believe in afterlife at all
and know it's cheating it's hard *not* to make
a sort of furtive prayer from this skin's scrawl,
his UNITED mean 'in Heaven' for their sake,

an accident of meaning to redeem
an act intended as mere desecration
and make the thoughtless spraying of his team
apply to higher things, and to the nation.

Some, where kids use aerosols, use giant signs
to let the people know who's forged their fetters
like PRI CE O WALES above West Yorkshire mines
(no prizes for who nicked the missing letters!)

The big blue star for booze, tobacco ads,
the magnet's monogram, the royal crest,
insignia in neon dwarf the lads
who spray a few odd FUCKS when they're depressed.

Letters of transparent tubes and gas
in Dusseldorf are blue and flash out KRUPP.
Arms are hoisted for the British ruling class
and clandestine, genteel aggro keeps them up.

And there's HARRISON on some Leeds building sites
I've taken in fun as blazoning my name,
which I've also seen on books, in Broadway lights,
so why can't skins with spraycans do the same?

But why inscribe these *graves* with CUNT and SHIT?
Why choose neglected tombstones to disfigure?
This pitman's of last century daubed PAKI GIT,
this grocer Broadbent's aerosolled with NIGGER?

They're there to shock the living, not arouse
the dead from their deep peace to lend support
for the causes skinhead spraycans could espouse.
The dead would want their desecrators caught!

Jobless though they are how can these kids,
even though their team's lost one more game,
believe that the 'Pakis', 'Niggers', even 'Yids'
sprayed on the tombstones here should bear the blame?

What is it that these crude words are revealing?
What is it that this aggro act implies?
Giving the dead their xenophobic feeling
or just a *cri-de-coeur* because man dies?

So what's a cri-de-coeur, *cunt? Can't you speak*
the language that yer mam spoke. Think of 'er!
Can yer only get yer tongue round fucking Greek?
Go and fuck yerself with cri-de-coeur!

'She didn't talk like you do for a start!'
I shouted, turning where I thought the voice had been.
She didn't understand yer fucking 'art'!
She thought yer fucking poetry obscene!

I wish on this skin's word deep aspirations,
first the prayer for my parents I can't make,
then a call to Britain and to all the nations
made in the name of love for peace's sake.

Aspirations, cunt! Folk on t'fucking dole
'ave got about as much scope to aspire
above the shit they're dumped in, cunt, as coal
aspires to be chucked on t'fucking fire.

OK, forget the aspirations. Look, I know
United's losing gets you fans incensed
and how far the HARP inside you makes you go
but *all* these Vs: against! against! against!

Ah'll tell yer then what really riles a bloke.
It's reading on their graves the jobs they did –
butcher, publican and baker. Me, I'll croak
doing t'same nowt ah do now as a kid.

'ard birth ah wor, mi mam says, almost killed 'er.
Death after life on t'dole won't seem as 'ard!
Look at this cunt, Wordsworth, organ builder,
this fucking 'aberdasher Appleyard!

If mi mam's up there, don't want to meet 'er
listening to me list mi dirty deeds,
and 'ave to pipe up to St fucking Peter
ah've been on t'dole all mi life in fucking Leeds!

Then t'Alleluias stick in t'angels' gobs.
When dole-wallahs fuck off to the void
what'll t'mason carve up for their jobs?
The cunts who lieth 'ere wor unemployed?

This lot worked at one job all life through.
Byron, 'Tanner', 'Lieth 'ere interred'
They'll chisel fucking poet when they do you
and that, yer cunt, 's a crude four-letter word.

'Listen, cunt!' *I* said, 'before you start your jeering
the reason why I want this in a book
's to give ungrateful cunts like you a hearing!'
A book, yer stupid cunt, 's not worth a fuck!

'The only reason why I write this poem at all
on yobs like you who do the dirt on death
's to give some higher meaning to your scrawl.'
Don't fucking bother, cunt! Don't waste your breath!

'You piss-artist skinhead cunt, you wouldn't know
and it doesn't fucking matter if you do,
the skin and poet united fucking Rimbaud
but the *autre* that *je est* is fucking you.'

Ah've told yer, no more Greek . . . That's yer last warning!
Ah'll boot yer fucking balls to Kingdom Come.
They'll find yer cold on t'grave tomorrer morning.
So don't speak Greek. Don't treat me like I'm dumb.

'I've done my bits of mindless aggro too
not half a mile from where we're standing now.'
Yeah, ah bet yer wrote a poem, yer wanker you!
'No, shut yer gob a while. Ah'll tell yer 'ow . . .'

'Herman Darewski's band played operetta
with a wobbly soprano warbling. Just why
I made my mind up that I'd got to get her
with the fire hose I can't say, but I'll try.

It wasn't just the singing angered me.
At the same time half a crowd was jeering
as the smooth Hugh Gaitskell, our MP,
made promises the other half were cheering.

What I hated in those high soprano ranges
was uplift beyond all reason and control
and in a world where you say nothing changes
it seemed a sort of prick-tease of the soul.

I tell you when I heard high notes that rose
above Hugh Gaitskell's cool electioneering
straight from the warbling throat right up my nose
I had all your aggro in *my* jeering.

And I hit the fire extinguisher ON knob
and covered orchestra and audience with spray.
I could run as fast as you then. A good job!
They yelled 'damned vandal' after me that day . . .'

And then yer saw the light and gave up 'eavy!
And knew a man's not how much he can sup . . .
Yer reward for growing up's this super-bevvy,
a meths and champagne punch in t' F A Cup.

Ah've 'eard all that from old farts past their prime.
'ow now yer live wi' all yer once detested . . .
Old farts with not much left 'll give me time.
Fuckers like that get folk like me arrested.

Covet not thy neighbour's wife, thy neighbour's riches.
Vicar and cop who say, to save our souls,
Get thee beHind me, Satan, drop their *breeches*
and get the Devil's dick right up their 'oles!

It was more a *working* marriage that I'd meant,
a blend of masculine and feminine.
Ignoring me, he started looking, bent
on some more aerosolling, for his tin.

'It was more a *working* marriage that I mean!'
Fuck, and save mi soul, eh? That suits me.
Then as if I'd egged him on to be obscene
he added a middle slit to one daubed V.

Don't talk to me of fucking representing
the class yer were born into any more.
Yer going to get 'urt and start resenting
it's not poetry we need in this class war.

Yer've given yerself toffee, cunt. Who needs
yer fucking poufy words. Ah write mi own.
Ah've got mi work on show all ovver Leeds
like this UNITED *'ere on some sod's stone.*

'O K!' (thinking I had him trapped) 'O K!'
'If you're so proud of it, then sign your name
when next you're full of HARP and armed with spray,
next time you take this short cut from the game.'

He took the can, contemptuous, unhurried
and cleared the nozzle and prepared to sign
the UNITED sprayed where mam and dad were buried.
He aerosolled his name. And it was mine.

The boy footballers bawl *Here Comes the Bride*
and drifting blossoms fall onto my head.
One half of me's alive but one half died
when the skin half sprayed my name among the dead.

Half versus half, the enemies within
the heart that can't be whole till they unite.
As I stoop to grab the crushed HARP lager tin
the day's already dusk, half dark, half light.

That UNITED that I'd wished onto the nation
or as reunion for dead parents soon recedes.
The word's once more a mindless desecration
by some HARPoholic yob supporting Leeds.

Almost the time for ghosts I'd better scram.
Though not given much to fears of spooky scaring
I don't fancy an encounter with my mam
playing Hamlet with me for this swearing.

Though I've a train to catch my step is slow.
I walk on the grass and graves with wary tread
over these subsidences, these shifts below
the life of Leeds supported by the dead.

Further underneath's that cavernous hollow
that makes the gravestones lean towards the town.
A matter of mere time and it will swallow
this place of rest and all the resters down.

I tell myself I've got, say, 30 years.
At 75 this place will suit me fine.
I've never feared the grave but what I fear's
that great worked-out black hollow under mine.

Not train departure time, and not Town Hall
with the great white clock face I can see,
coal, that began, with no man here at all,
as 300 million-year-old plant debris.

5 kids still play at making blossoms fall
and humming as they do *Here Comes the Bride*.
They never seem to tire of their ball
though I hear a woman's voice call one inside.

2 larking boys play bawdy bride and groom.
3 boys in Leeds strip la-la *Lohengrin*.
I hear them as I go through growing gloom
still years away from being skald or skin.

The ground's carpeted with petals as I throw
the aerosol, the HARP can, the cleared weeds
on top of dad's dead daffodils, then go,
with not one glance behind, away from Leeds.

The bus to the station's still the No 1
but goes by routes that I don't recognise.
I look out for known landmarks as the sun
reddens the swabs of cloud in darkening skies.

Home, home, home, to my woman as the red
darkens from a fresh blood to a dried.
Home, home to my woman, home to bed
where opposites seem sometimes unified.

A pensioner in turban taps his stick
along the pavement past the corner shop,
that sells samosas now, not beer on tick,
to the Kashmir Muslim Club that was the Co-op.

House after house FOR SALE where we'd played cricket
with white roses cut from flour-sacks on our caps,
with stumps chalked on the coal-grate for our wicket,
and every one bought now by 'coloured chaps',

dad's most liberal label as he felt
squeezed by the unfamiliar, and fear
of foreign food and faces, when he smelt
curry in the shop where he'd bought beer.

And growing frailer, 'wobbly on his pins',
the shops he felt familiar with withdrew
which meant much longer tiring treks for tins
that had a label on them that he knew.

And as the shops that stocked his favourites receded
whereas he'd fancied beans and popped next door,
he found that four long treks a week were needed
till he wondered what he bothered eating for.

The supermarket made him feel embarrassed.
Where people bought whole lambs for family freezers
he bought baked beans from check-out girls too harassed
to smile or swap a joke with sad old geezers.

But when he bought his cigs he'd have a chat,
his week's one conversation, truth to tell,
but time also came and put a stop to that
when old Wattsy got bought out by M. Patel.

And there, 'Time like an ever rolling stream' 's
what I once trilled behind that boarded front.
A 1000 ages made coal-bearing seams
and even more the hand that sprayed this CUNT

on both Methodist and C of E billboards
once divided in their fight for local souls.
Whichever house more truly was the Lord's
both's pews are filled with cut-price toilet rolls.

Home, home to my woman, never to return
till sexton or survivor has to cram
the bits of clinker scooped out of my urn
down through the rose-roots to my dad and mam.

Home, home to my woman, where the fire's lit
these still chilly mid-May evenings, home to you,
and perished vegetation from the pit
escaping insubstantial up the flue.

Listening to *Lulu*, in our hearth we burn,
as we hear the high Cs rise in stereo,
what was lush swamp club-moss and tree-fern
at least 300 million years ago.

Shilbottle cobbles, Alban Berg high D
lifted from a source that bears your name,
the one we hear decay, the one we see,
the fern from the foetid forest, as brief flame.

This world, with far too many people in,
starts on the TV logo as a taw,
then ping-pong, tennis, football; then one spin
to show us all, then shots of the Gulf War.

As the coal with reddish dust cools in the grate
on the late-night national news we see
police v. pickets at a coke-plant gate,
old violence and old disunity.

The map that's colour-coded Ulster/Eire's
flashed on again as almost every night.
Behind a tiny coffin with two bearers
men in masks with arms show off their might.

The day's last images recede to first a glow
and then a ball that shrinks back to blank screen.
Turning to love, and sleep's oblivion, I know
what the UNITED that the skin sprayed *has* to mean.

Hanging my clothes up, from my parka hood
may and apple petals, browned and creased,
fall onto the carpet and bring back the flood
of feelings their first falling had released.

I hear like ghosts from all Leeds matches humming
with one concerted voice the bride, the bride
I feel united to, *my* bride is coming
into the bedroom, naked, to my side.

The ones we choose to love become our anchor
when the hawser of the blood-tie's hacked, or frays.
But a voice that scorns chorales is yelling: *Wanker!*
It's the aerosolling skin I met today's.

My *alter ego* wouldn't want to know it,
his aerosol vocab would baulk at LOVE,
the skin's UNITED underwrites the poet,
the measures carved below the ones above.

I doubt if 30 years of bleak Leeds weather
and 30 falls of apple and of may
will erode the UNITED binding us together.
And now it's your decision: does it stay?

Next millennium you'll have to search quite hard
to find out where I'm buried but I'm near
the grave of haberdasher Appleyard,
the pile of HARPS, or some new neonned beer.

Find Byron, Wordsworth, or turn left between
one grave marked Broadbent, one marked Richardson.
Bring some solution with you that can clean
whatever new crude words have been sprayed on.

If love of art, or love, gives you affront
that the grave I'm in's graffitied then, maybe,
erase the more offensive FUCK and CUNT
but leave, with the worn UNITED, one small V.

Victory? For vast, slow, coal-creating forces
that hew the body's seams to get the soul.
Will Earth run out of her 'diurnal courses'
before repeating her creation of black coal?

But choose a day like I chose in mid-May
or earlier when apple and hawthorn tree,
no matter if boys boot their ball all day,
cling to their blossoms and won't shake them free.

If, having come this far, somebody reads
these verses, and he/she wants to understand,
face this grave on Beeston Hill, your back to Leeds,
and read the chiselled epitaph I've planned:

Beneath your feet's a poet, then a pit.
Poetry supporter, if you're here to find
how poems can grow from (beat you to it!) SHIT
find the beef, the beer, the bread, then look behind.

Two

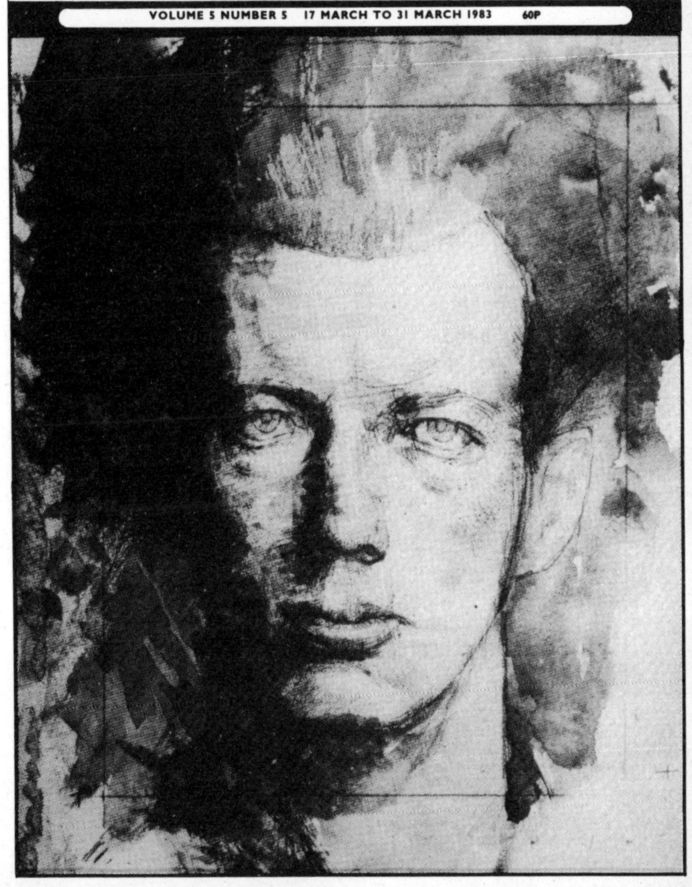
London Review
OF BOOKS
VOLUME 5 NUMBER 5 17 MARCH TO 31 MARCH 1983 60P

Neal Ascherson

Last Leader

Citizen Ken by John Carvel
(Chatto, 1984)

After crossing the river, the little band of Palaeolithic hunters huddled together shivering on the far bank. They were cold and wet, but they still had their flint-tipped spears. Men and women together, side by side, collected dry brushwood at the top of the sandy shore and tried to start a fire. Here at least the ground was firm, unlike the flat swamps of the south bank, and in the distance ahead they could see a line of northern heights, shaggy with forest. There should be deer there, perhaps a mammoth. The fire took hold and warmed them. Soon the group was spreading out and – without regard to colour, sexual preference, age, size or creed – beginning to gather the nuts, berries and tubers and to share them democratically, once more in balance with the environment and with one another. And as the evening shadows lengthened, the first members of the species Homo Erectus to arrive in London fell to their normal diversions, or 'what we would consider a life of idle luxury – music, dancing, relating to each other, the constant flow of conversation'.

So Ken Livingstone might imagine the first inhabitants of the GLC area. They call him a Trot, but there is much more in him of a far older generation of palaeo-socialists. For Livingstone believes in a social version of the Fall, in a State of Nature and – almost – a Garden in which human beings lived with one another, innocently, equally, without private property or surplus, without stress, in balance with nature. In a long conversation with John Carvel, far the most astonishing and winning part of this book, he lays out his own Livingstonian anthropology. These wandering bands did not know war, as the inhabitants of the nuclear-free zone of Lewisham shall not know war. They were 'a very together, well-organised and sophisticated proto-culture'. Everything that we are today has emerged from the hunter-gatherer tradition. 'All of our ability, the development of our intellect, all of our early culture grows out of those kinship groups operating overwhelmingly in a co-operative way . . . The hunter-gatherer is what humanity is.'

So far, so Fourier, or Rousseau or St-Simon. The most interesting question about state-of-nature utopian thinkers is where they insert the Fall and what they consider to have played the serpent. Ken Livingstone has no doubts. It was the introduction of agriculture, the Neolithic revolution 'twenty thousand years ago', which ruined everything. For a start, it accelerated the growth of population until the ecological balance collapsed. 'Hunter-gatherers have a basic diet which means you can't wean children easily. It's all hard, scrunchy stuff. There's no animals' milk or mushy foods.' And with the junk food of planted crops came the creation of wealth, surpluses, hierarchies, technology.

> 'If you look at the way the City of London works, it is operating in exactly the same way as the most primitive of those societies based on agriculture . . . The basic motive force is greed and exploitation, which is there from the start once you move away from that co-operative group. We haven't learned to cope with surpluses and distribute them without greed becoming the major motive factor and the desire for power over others. I do not think that is a natural state for humankind to be in.'

This is all fearful heresy to those – like myself – reared on the work of V. Gordon Childe, whose Marxist version of the natural state was located precisely in the world of Neolithic agriculture, perceived as a non-competitive, co-operative and equal society bonded together by kinship and by the need to give and receive food surpluses to relieve crop failure. For Gordon Childe, the 'origins of inequality' were to be found in the invention of metallurgy, creating, out of the families who possessed the secret, hereditary castes which would eventually develop into a primitive bourgeoisie with all its attendant vices of greed, privilege and war.

But then Gordon Childe, as a Communist, took a basically optimistic view of history. His metallurgical Fall might have wrecked the 'undifferentiated substantive' of primitive farmers. It was, however, the first 'contradiction' in a dialectic which would in the end create equality and co-operation at a higher synthesis – the victory of the industrial world proletariat. What is fascinating about 'Red Ken', so much a child of the Seventies, is his pessimism. A man who does not see history as in at least some sense a progress will never make a recognisable Communist, whether Stalinist or Trot. Talking, or rambling on, to Carvel, Livingstone derides the whole idea of progressive evolution, biological or social. 'It's there in the thinking of a lot of people around Stalin – the idea that man is getting better, that we are part of this inevitable upward progress. We're not really . . . We're still trying to adjust to changes that came over us twenty thousand years ago.' Well, it was there in the thinking of a lot of people around Karl Marx as well. But Ken Livingstone, a man for compassionate issues rather than ideologies who was brought up in South London suburbs rather than among proletarian terraces, simply points to the city around him as evidence of negative evolution. People now live on their own, surrounded by other isolated people. They do not gather tubers with their comrades, neither do they enjoy that 'music, dancing, relating to each other, the constant flow of conversation' which is proper to the species. 'The isolation you get in society, particularly urban society, where people are frightened and embarrassed to turn to other people for support, means that we are living in a way which is completely at odds with the best part of fifteen million years of evolution which turned us into what we are.'

And at this point Citizen Ken brings on the reptiles. Everyone who can read a paper knows that he keeps lizards and salamanders; given the sort of press he gets, millions probably think he uses them to enrich the cauldrons of lesbian separatist covens dancing on Peckham Rye. In fact, he uses them not for food but for thought. Some lizards, he explained to Carvel in the second part of this immortal conversation, reproduce by parthenogenesis – females reproducing themselves without male involvement. (First the Russians discovered such a lizard. The Americans denounced it as a fraud until they discovered one of their own. 'So it's now established that the superpower blocs have parthenogenic lizard parity,' says Livingstone.)

He sees an analogy here with his view of human development. The lizards who developed parthenogenesis at once collected an enormous short-term advantage: by avoiding all the dangers and uncertainties of sexual reproduction, they solved the problem of keeping the species going. But in the long term, the solution must lead to extinction. The gene pool is not mixed, healthy mutation and adaptation cease, and a population of identical, mindless little creatures without an original idea or physical variation among them will be easily wiped out by some catastrophe.

It is not difficult to see what the chairman of the GLC is getting at.

On that cursed day when hunters first broke the soil and threw seed into it, the human race began a parthenogenic leap forward: all the variations and mutations of social relationships were abandoned for the gigantic increase of security and population that agriculture guaranteed. Society lost the capacity to adapt, locking itself into one mould of greed and competition. 'We may be just trundling along on a dead end which suddenly cuts off the whole of the human race very violently and rapidly.' Unrestricted population growth, or pollution, are as likely to bring humanity to that dead end as nuclear war.

And is there no way back? John Carvel inquires. No way back to the state of nature and the pursuit of berries and tubers, the chairman implacably returns. But by establishing little islets of non-competitive association, rafts of co-operative production on the capitalist sea, a start can be made on restoring society's capacity to mutate and adapt. With the help and subsidy of GLEB (Greater London Enterprise Board), humanity can begin retracing the wrong turning taken by the Neolithic revolution.

All this will reduce many archaeologists, many professors of anthropology, probably many GLC ratepayers, to speechless fury. Hunter-gatherers? Lizards? Thoughts like these, even the affectionate John Carvel concedes, 'in the atmosphere of workaday politics . . . sound positively loopy'. So much the worse for workaday politics. Ken Livingstone is a utopian socialist, a man who does not fit most of the categories crammed round his neck by the media. He is anything but a Trotskyist, although he will gladly use small Trot groups for support when it suits his tactics. He is not a working-class politician formed by poverty, but neither – as Carvel points out – is he a 'paperback Marxist' from a 'lumpen polytechnic'. He had no real higher education, and his grasp of theory, as the hunter-gatherer-parthenogenesis hypothesis shows, is wonderfully sketchy and personal. In most ways, he is more of a classical anarchist than a Marxist. His style is to work through a constantly changing series of caucuses, cabals and temporary alliances; one of the reasons why the Parliamentary Labour Party hates him so fervently is that Livingstone dislikes the discipline of permanent political structures, even though he still seems anxious to enter the House of Commons. If there is anyone in European politics whom he resembles, it is Erhard Eppler, the veteran Social Democrat in West Germany, an infinitely graver and more consistent thinker who nonetheless commands a similar coalition of leftists, life-stylers, Green-minded socialists and nuclear disarmers, whose outlook is also pessimistic and who was the first in his party to welcome the 'end of growth' and put forward a sweeping reform programme which did not amount to the mere redistribution of capitalist surplus in years of expansion.

Ken Livingstone complains that the society he lives in has almost killed off the capacity for social 'mutation'. But, as a matter of fact, he himself is a mutation. Citizen Ken is one of the first known examples of a new strain of politician entirely resistant to all known forms of media poison. The last ten years have brought campaigns against the personal and public lives of selected left-wing politicians of a viciousness scarcely seen in Britain since the Victorian period, but none of these campaigns – not even that against Arthur Scargill – acquired the intensity of the hounding of Livingstone. Scargill and Benn, of an older generation, have developed signs of paranoia under this treatment; Tatchell was nearly destroyed by it. But Livingstone actually feeds on pesticide. The more hysterical the abuse, the more provocative he becomes. The quotes about the IRA, the Royal Wedding, gay rights and black pride continue to flow; his wretched Labour group on the GLC have often paid the price, pockmarked by the shower of missiles aimed at their leader and obliged to watch many of their most 'popular' measures obliterated from view by the latest scandal over 'Red Ken' and his big mouth. Meanwhile, Livingstone himself was turning the publicity steadily to his own advantage, emerging as a skilled, unflappable and charming radio and television panellist and interviewee. Increasingly, his case has been heard, and Londoners have developed for him both affection and some respect. Carvel observes that 'Livingstone's crucifixion in the media formed the basis of his subsequent political strength and popularity.'

Most of this book, naturally enough, is about local government and London politics. Livingstone was welcomed to power with the headline 'Red Ken Crowned King of London'. John Carvel shows what a mockery those words were and are. Britain is the most overcentralised state in the Western world, in which local authorities have always been tightly hobbled, and today the Government – through 'rate-capping', through the abolition of the Metropolitan Counties – is engaged on reducing that slight room for manoeuvre even further. Political prejudice against Labour-dominated authorities plays its part, but the real situation is little short of a creeping nationalisation of local government by Whitehall – by the Treasury in particular. The *Daily Express* last year published a cartoon showing 'Red Ken' digging the grave of democracy, but the whole bizarre, impudent, exhilarating history of his administration at County Hall shows that he and his colleagues have been trying to give local democracy the kiss of life on what appears to be its deathbed. The sullen, morose sea of overcrowded humanity that is London has never been encouraged to develop a sense of active community. Who, after all, is remembered as a leader of London? Dick Whittington, perhaps Herbert Morrison. Ken Livingstone has dealt mostly in symbolic politics – there was little else left to deal in – but he will be remembered as the man who gave Londoners their only revelation of common identity since Marshal Goering abandoned the Blitz. He could not be a giant-killer, but he made fools of the giants. Michael Heseltine, as Secretary for the Environment, bungled the legislation to cut the GLC's revenue. The judiciary made imbeciles of themselves in their eagerness to crush the cheap fares policy by pronouncing, in effect, that all forms of subsidy were a misuse of ratepayers' money. The onslaught by the gutter press made Citizen Ken into a folk-hero. Mrs Thatcher, in her eagerness to suppress him and to destroy what remains of local authority freedom, has deeply offended the Conservative conscience in a way which may well contribute to her fall.

Ken Livingstone has also been lucky. Like many obsessive manipulators, he has almost come unstuck on many occasions, saved usually by the blunders of his enemies. He was rescued from taking the consequences of the appalling financial muddle which had developed at the GLC after his first six months as leader only by the surge of sympathy after the judges condemned the fare cuts. The Labour group might well have unloaded him for his 'they are not criminals or lunatics' remark about the IRA bombers, and for his invitation to Sinn Fein to visit County Hall, if the Home Secretary had not changed the focus of the uproar by 'excluding' the two Sinn Fein MPs from the British mainland. He declared that Labour would stay in office and simply refuse to raise transport fares after the law lords' judgment, and was saved from a terminal collision with the law by the mess the Tory GLC opposition made of the crucial debate. And luck has repeatedly frustrated his deplorable hankering to get into Parliament: he was only narrowly defeated at Hampstead, and although he was winning the murderous guerrilla faction war for the nomination at Brent East in 1983, Mrs Thatcher called the election before the sitting MP, Reg Freeson, was finally 'deselected'. Why Ken Livingstone wants to enter the House remains a mystery. The place is full of aging gadflies who achieve nothing beyond turning the Speaker's face purple, and who lack the delicious power to do things like cover London with nuclear-free zone notices and witty posters at the ratepayers' expense.

He is no administrator and, really, no hero. He has a cheerful super-rat gift for dodging upwards through chinks in situations. He is a shameless carpet-bagger and opportunist with a gift for bringing together coalitions of people who all slightly suspect him for different reasons but find his flair irresistible (in this, he has something in common with Lech Walesa, whom he probably regards as a clerical fascist). As a schoolboy, taught at Tulse Hill Comprehensive by the expansive Philip Hobsbaum, he became, in his own words, what he was to remain: 'an argumentative, cheeky little brat'. John Carvel, who obviously admires him, often seems in this book to shake his head with exasperation over the chances Ken takes with his reputation. And yet, if the GLC is to die, Ken Livingstone has ensured as the last leader of greater London that it will perish in a display of vigour, ideas, experiments and sheer entertainment that dims any Lord Mayor's fireworks on the Thames. It may be because he has such a passion for the Irish – seeing them perhaps as hunter-gatherers in arms – that he has turned a sober funeral of democracy into a spectacular wake.

Alan Bennett

The Wrong Blond

Auden in Love by Dorothy Farnan
(Faber, 1985)

On a bitter cold morning in January 1939 Auden and Isherwood sailed into New York harbour on board the SS *Champlain*. After coming through a blizzard off Newfoundland the ship looked like a wedding cake and the mood of our two heroes was correspondingly festive and expectant. On their first visit to New York the previous year Auden had sometimes been in tears, telling Isherwood no one would ever love him and that he would never have any sexual success. True to form on his second visit it was Isherwood who already had a date lined up, Vernon, 'a beautiful blond boy, about eighteen, intelligent with very sexy legs'. From that out-of-the-body vantage-point he shares with God and Norman Mailer, Isherwood looks down on himself and his friend:

> Yes, my dears, each of you will find the person you came here to look for – the ideal companion to whom you can reveal yourself totally and yet be loved for what you are, not what you pretend to be. You, Wystan, will find him very soon, within three months. You, Christopher, will have to wait much longer for yours . . . At present he is only four years old.

If looking for Mr Right was what it was, this celebrated voyage that put paid to a decade, it was lucky that Auden's quest so soon found its object. Otherwise the start of the war might have fetched him home still on the same tack, 1 September 1939 finding him not in a dive on 52nd Street but in some bleak provincial drill hall having those famous bunyons vetted for service in the Intelligence Corps. Auden might (and some say should) have condemned himself to five years as a slipshod major, sitting in a dripping Nissen hut in Beaconsfield, decoding German intelligence with occasional trips to the fleshpots to indulge in those hectic intimacies hostilities notoriously encourage. In the short view this kind of war might at some point have landed him up with the

MO. In the long view it would almost certainly have landed him with the OM. It was not to be. True love had walked in on Auden six months earlier. Henceforth it was to be personal relations for ever and ever.

While Isherwood's man of destiny had not yet made it to playgroup, Chester Kallman had turned 18 and was a junior at Brooklyn College. As Dorothy Farnan describes him, 'he was naturally blond, about five feet 11 in height, slender, weighing about 145 pounds with gray-blue eyes, pale flawless skin, a Norse skull, Latin lips and straight narrow nose' – a description that smacks both of the mortuary slab and (more appropriately) a 'Wanted' poster. In April 1939, Auden, Isherwood and MacNeice gave a reading at the Keynote Club in Manhattan. Kallman and another Brooklyn student, Walter James Miller, were in the audience, with Kallman sitting in the front row giving the two international pederasts the glad eye. Afterwards he and Miller went backstage. Miller was tall, blond, Anglo-Saxon and (a friend who was not a friend) heterosexual. Predictably it was to the unavailable Miller that Auden took a fancy, leaving it to the more realistic Isherwood to chat up the all too available Kallman. Miller had written an article for the college literary magazine and Auden expressed a desire to read it. Twenty years later, when he was Professor of Poetry at Oxford, Auden's desires were still being expressed in the same guileless way, undergraduate poets asked round to read him their verse in the hope that one thing might lead to another. However, on the day appointed it was not Miller who turned up but Kallman. Isherwood was in the next room when Auden came through and said: 'It's the wrong blond.' The rest is history. Or literature. Or the history of literature. Or maybe just gossip. And on that score anathema to Auden himself, who, wanting no biography, would have been appalled to read this blow-by-blow account of his sex life.

Whether Kallman *was* the wrong blond is the whole question of it. The right blond, Miller, would also have been the wrong blond, so maybe the wrong blond was the right one, wrong blond(e)s after all having some tradition in literature: Lord Alfred Douglas, Zelda Fitzgerald, Marilyn Monroe, to name but three who were all wrong, all right. This account of the relationship between Auden and Kallman is written by the blond's late-in-the-day stepmother, Dorothy J. Farnan, also blonde, who, if not wrong, is not always right, but very readable for all that. (I don't want to beat this blond business to a bloody pulp but in his biography of Auden Humphrey Carpenter gives Kallman's fancied companion as the poet Harold Norse. Norse thinks Auden was expecting him. The right blond and ready to be just as obliging as Kallman, Norse was a better bet all round. This is one of those moments when three, possibly four lives go rattling over the points. But Norse or Miller? Auden studies are still in their infancy and it is perhaps too early to say. The fact that Ms Farnan describes Kallman's skull as 'Norse' is neither here nor there. Or is it?)

Auden now wore a wedding ring, bought one for Chester and moved in on Chester's life. There was a honeymoon at Taos in New Mexico, weekly visits to the opera in rented tuxedos and dinners in Auden's Brooklyn household, where, among others regularly passing the (obligatory) potatoes, were Benjamin Britten and Peter Pears, Carson McCullers, Lincoln Kirstein and Gipsy Rose Lee. When love comes to the confirmed bachelor old friends find it difficult to take. Chums winced to see T. S. Eliot spooning with wife No 2, smirked when they brazenly held hands, and there was a bit of that with Auden. Look at it from the friends' point of view. They have to budge up to make room for the new companion, knowing as they do so that they will be seeing less of the great man. Pretty college boy introduced to glamorous world by famous writer in return for services rendered, is he, they telephone each other, on the make? A male lover is judged more harshly than a wife (wives are women, after all), the likelihood of children somehow a safeguard. If the lover comes on too strong in company he is thought to be pushy, if he keeps mum he is put down as just a pretty face. Oh well, the friends shrug, it won't last. Boredom will drive him back to us. But it did, and it didn't. Chester wasn't just a pretty face, he was an amusing companion and better company than Auden because less full of himself ('less of himself to be full of,' said the friends). Still, Chester stayed the course and thirty-odd years later walks behind the coffin in Kirchstetten as Siegfried's Funeral March gives way to more comfortable strains of the village band, the medley of the two just about summing it up.

Back in 1939, Auden is typically bold, not to say boastful about his affair. Even nowadays, with parents the stunned and submissive onlookers at their children's lives, a middle-aged man would think twice about meeting the family of the 17-year-old son he's knocking off. Auden had no such scruples, but then he liked families, particularly those belonging to other people. Casting no spell, they always exercised a powerful attraction. Auden was a practised (if not always accomplished) *ami de maison*, homing in on comfortable domestic set-ups and establishing himself as a frequent and not undemanding guest. Several families of academic sparrows were flattered, if slightly startled, to find themselves playing host to this celebrated cuckoo, who scattered his ash as liberally as he did his aperçus. If one wanted to entertain Auden the first requirement was a good Ewbank.

In this matter of family Chester was well-supplied. He was the son of a Brooklyn dentist, Edward Kallman. His mother Bertha was a cultivated woman, who had acted in Yiddish theatre. She died when Chester was small, his father remarried, and the boy was largely brought up by his grandmother. His grandmother's name was Bobby. His stepmother's name was Syd. (In their choice of names the Americans have always been more eclectic than we are: a girl in *Dynasty*, for instance, is called Kirby, a name hitherto confined to a grip.) These Kallman names can't have helped. With a grandmother called Bobby and a stepmother called Syd it's not surprising Chester turned out to be a nancy.

Edward Kallman sounds an engaging character, even allowing for the fact that this book is written by his wife: Ms Farnan succeeded the terrible Syd as the third Mrs Kallman, though more or less a contemporary of her stepson. Syd had been the bane of Chester's life and tales of her appalling behaviour never failed to fascinate him and (reportedly) Auden too. The tales of Kallman *père*, on the other hand, suggest a cross between Phil Silvers and S. Z. ('Cuddles') Szakall.

Before Auden came on the scene Chester had taken the fancy of a New York financier, Robert King ('not his real name'). King duly enrolled as a patient with Dr Kallman, and after a little bridgework had broken the ice, invited the dentist to supper at the Astor Roof. There was presumably some routine orthodontic small talk ('How's the bite?') before King levelled with his guest. 'I want to adopt Chester,' said King.

> I can do a great deal for him. Send him to Harvard. Take him to Europe. I just want to be near him. Travel with him. Sleep next to him.

Apart from some poisoned remarks from hissing Syd ('That boy is a hothouse flower'), this urbane proposition was the first hint the dentist had had that Chester was not all set to be a model of heterosexuality. Cut to the surgery where the patient is now a psychiatrist. Dr Kallman puts the problem to him ('So my son is a faggot, where did I go wrong? Rinse please'). The psychiatrist recommends another psychiatrist whom Chester dutifully sees, but finding he has never heard of T. S. Eliot, leaves in disgust. It is at this opportune moment that Auden, who *has* heard of T. S. Eliot, appears on the scene. No more is heard of Mr King.

Both generations were incorrigible lechers, the father as active on one side of the street as the son was on the other. Chester was not without girlfriends, though whether Anything Happened is not clear. At one point he had an apartment above his father's and his female callers sometimes knocked on the wrong door, whereupon Edward Kallman would waltz out onto the landing, clad only in a bathtowel, saying 'Won't I do?' Ms Farnan calls him a pragmatist. 'He knew one must make the best of what cannot be changed.'

One comes to like this father, whose adult education must have come from coping with the vagaries and enthusiasms of his wayward son and the increasingly unsympathetic behaviour of his ex-officio son-in-law. He and Auden seem to have quarrelled finally over a kitten which Auden was trying to entice into his house at Kirchstetten. Old Kallman, now deaf, banged a door during the wooing process and the not so cosy poet blew his top. The old man left the house next day. 'Forever after he was quick to tell all who would listen that W. H. Auden had lost his temper because of a cat. What kind of cat? "One hundred percent alley."' Presumably he is still telling whoever will listen, for, twenty years later and in his nineties, he seems to be still around.

It was two happy years after he had met Chester (and back in the world of telegrams and anger, a month after the Germans invaded Russia) that Auden discovered he was not the only one laying his head human on Chester's faithless arm. The first (or at any rate the first known to biography) was Jack Lansing ('not his real name') who 'despite his Latin eyes' was 'as English as cricket. He could trace his ancestors back to the Saxons in the Domesday Book while his father claimed a distant kinship to William the Conqueror.' Ancestry soon got confused with dentistry as Chester would meet Lansing on the quiet at his father's surgery ('Wider please'), and on one occasion their antics kept Edward Kallman waiting over an hour outside the locked door. When Auden found out about the affair his rage and jealousy were murderous. These were emotions he seems not to have experienced before and the effect on him was profound. It's not just the confusion of heartache and toothache that makes Auden's grief less than tragic. It's hard to understand how Auden could have lived with Kallman for two years without cottoning on to the younger man's character, or how he had reached the age of 34 without finding himself in this situation before. Here was one of the most acknowledged of unacknowledged legislators who had laid down the law about love with seemingly no experience whatever of its pains and penalties. There is a powerful impulse to say: 'Well, serve you right.'

That the friendship survived is taken by Ms Farnan to be somewhat unusual and a tribute to Auden's strength of character: a lesser man, she implies, would have packed his bags. But a period of exclusive physical attachment followed by a close friendship in which each party goes his own (sometimes promiscuous) way is not uncommon. Or wasn't. These days homosexuals are having to do what the people the other side of the fence call 'working at the marriage'. Auden had the sense to realise that sharing a joke is rarer than sharing a bed, which, according to Chester, they ceased to do. Whatever it was they did together (and Ms Farnan is not unspecific on the point) they didn't any more. This does seem unusual. Ms Farnan puts it down, if not to principle on Chester's part, at least to his romantic temperament. There seems to be a streak of wanton cruelty in it . . . or the cruelty of a wanton. Chester found nothing so easy as attracting company to his bed, a quality, once he had come to terms with it, in which Auden took pride. With the world's fighting men lining up eagerly for Chester's favours did Auden *never* get a look in, even if not on quite the one-to-one basis with Chester that he wanted? Well, maybe. Ms Farnan chooses to see Auden's love life from here on as tragic, the short-lived affair a lifelong heartache. It doesn't seem to have been too bad, particularly when one remembers that for some people sexual intercourse only began in 1963. He certainly didn't want for consolation. Unhappy but not unhappy about it just about sums it up.

The cast of the sex lives of Auden and Kallman is large. It is also coy. Since this is the love that dares not tell its name, the sex, when it is not anonymous, is pseudonymous, with over a score of the participants footnoted 'not his real name'. Nor are the names under which they do appear of a noble simplicity. Here is no Chuck, no Rick, no Lance. Ms Farnan has lavished much art on these fellatious appellations. They include Royce Wagoner, Dutch Martell, Peter Komadina, Mr Schuyler Bash and (a real ball of fire) Lieutenant Horace Stepole. Francis Peabody Magoun, on the other hand, *is* a real name as also is Giorgione, who is footnoted as 'famous Venetian painter', presumably to distinguish him from all those other Italian boys who went down on posterity but not to it.

The Baring family coined the phrase 'Shelley plain' to mean a personal glimpse of a great man – from Browning's

And did you once see Shelley plain,
And did he stop and speak with you?

In Philip Roth's superb novel *The Professor of Desire* the professor visits Prague and is taken to meet the aged whore once fucked by Kafka. She had had a 'Shelley plain' and would for a consideration reveal to visiting scholars its central location. To have gone down on W. H. Auden is a lesser 'Shelley plain', not so exclusive perhaps, but it's interesting that so many of those who had the experience are still reluctant to admit it. It's a narrow niche, one must admit, but still fame of a sort.

In the early days Auden was proud of Chester and this is still touchingly obvious in the photograph of them taken in Venice in 1950. To begin with Auden had shown the boy off to his friends, but shut him up when he tried to join in the grown-ups' conversation. But as Auden came to acknowledge, Chester was funny and clever in a way Auden was not. A visiting New York publisher was telling them that he was bringing out an autobiography of Klaus Mann, and thinking of calling it 'The Invisible Mann'. No, said Chester (and it's a joke such as Nabokov would have made), you should call it 'The Subordinate Klaus'. Nobody believed Auden when he said Chester had the quicker mind, but he would not have come to opera without Kallman or written libretti, a debt Auden always acknowledged, and where the ascription of credit was concerned he was scrupulous. At the second performance of *The Rake's Progress* at La Fenice, he left early because Chester was not there to take the curtain call with him. In other reviews of this book that I have read Kallman has got some stick because he couldn't hold down a job or wasn't a better poet, never made a success of his life. Wives, which is to say female wives, don't get told off in quite this way, aren't weighed in the same scale. The first Mrs Eliot has been taken to task, but not because her verse wasn't better or because she didn't make her own way in the world. She was a woman so that was only to be expected. Even a literary wife as talented as her husband, like the second Mrs Lowell, Elizabeth Hardwick, finds her work calibrated on the scale of accomplishment not achievement, and the sincerest recognition still hints at the escape from the washing-up or stolen hours while children sleep. Whether you call this condescension or consideration, men who marry men don't get it. They're expected to be career girls besides.

To his credit Auden never tried to make Chester his housekeeper. Chester answered the telephone and when he was around produced meals with digital accuracy, but the households on Ischia and at Kirchstetten were a far cry from I Tatti. Chester never played the role of the great man's wife or the guardian of his talent, rationing visits, anticipating needs, turning away friends, still less hiding the bottle. He was too interested in himself for that. Wives of the proper gender play this role without comment, or without comment in biography, with 'To my wife, without whom etc' reckoned to make up for everything.

Chester was more fun to have around than Auden, less likely to go into a huff for a start, and if he was always hellbent on bed, at least it didn't have to be on the stroke of nine o'clock like his lover. With Auden in bed and Chester still in shrieks with his chums next door, there must often have been something of 'We're having a whale of a time below stairs' to the menage. Auden made touching attempts to be more lighthearted, swapping genders ('Who shook *her* cage?') and trying to come on as a bit of a queen himself. But it didn't really work and he always seems to get it slightly wrong: his famous 'Miss God', for instance, doesn't exactly pinpoint the deity. Camp is no substitute for wit, and Auden wasn't especially good at either.

Luckily for the peace of their various households they were both sluts. If Auden had been as big a stickler for tidiness as he was for punctuality he would never have had his pinny off. Chester was an inspired cook, though wasted on Auden, who preferred good nursery food and lashings of it. A toilet innocent of Harpic, a sideboard barren of Pledge, the New York set-up on St Marks Place was not an apartment for the fastidious. Those who are not as other men are often like a place just so, and the wonder is that none of the visiting bits of fluff didn't nip round and do a spot of post-coital dusting. One who did lend a hand, though very much not a bit of fluff, was Vera Stravinsky. Chester's working surfaces included the bathroom floor, and paying a call of nature, Mrs Stravinsky spotted what she took to be a bowl of dirty water standing there. In a forlorn attempt to give the place a woman's touch Mrs Stravinsky emptied the contents into the wash-basin, only to discover later on that this had been the pièce de résistance of the meal, a chocolate pudding. The basin was incidentally the same basin in which Auden routinely pissed. Where, one wonders, did one wash one's hands after one had washed one's hands?

Auden was wise to want no biography written. The more one reads about him, the harder it is to see round him to the poetry beyond, and he grows increasingly hard to like – for one's thinks to be all thanks. In the tribute that came out the year after his death, edited by Stephen Spender, much was made of how cosy he was. He grows less cosy by the memoir, even allowing for the fact that one like Ms Farnan's is less than fair. Particularly hard to take is the 'All do as I do' side of him that early on bullied off Britten. It's a masculine characteristic and it stands out so painfully because he happily lacked other masculine characteristics that often cluster round it. He didn't care much for fame, for instance, or go in for self-advertisement, was careless about his reputation and was unmoved by criticism. So much about him is mature and admirable he seems a bigger baby for what is not. It was Kallman who found Auden dead in 1973, lying in his hotel bed in Vienna after a poetry recital the night before. Kallman knew Auden was dead because he was lying on his left side. He never lay on that side. It is just this side of him that's hard to take, the rules he made for himself but which others were expected to know and observe. If he hadn't in his later work made such a point of domestic virtue and the practice of loving kindness it might not matter so much. 'You're not the only pebble on the beach,' one wants to say. 'Grow up.' Grow up, or don't grow old.

There will be other memoirs. There are currently at least three published in America that haven't yet appeared here. In one of them, *Auden: An American Friendship* by Charles Miller, the peculiar gouging of his face is put down to 'a medical condition known as the Touraine-Solente-Golé syndrome, which also affected Racine'. The skin seemed to divide up into clints, like the limestone Auden praised, the best remark about that coming, I think, from David Hockney. Auden sat to Hockney, who after tracing those innumerable lines, remarked: 'I kept thinking, if his face looks like this, what must his balls look like.' At this rate it can only be a matter of time before we are told that too.

W. G. Runciman

Henry and Caroline

The Official Sloane Ranger Handbook: The First Guide to What Really Matters in Life by Ann Barr and Peter York
(Ebury, 1982)

Anthropological method, as classically practised by Malinowski among the Trobriand Islands, depends in the first instance on patient scrutiny of the details of the daily life of the community under study. But it depends also on the detection in, or behind, those details of what Malinowski himself called 'the natives' *Weltanschauung*' – that is, the whole unspoken complex of myths, prejudices, values and assumptions through which they interpret the meaning of the world to themselves. It is not easy to do as well as Malinowski did (and he wasn't perfect). It depends, not on compiling statistics or transcribing official documents or handing out questionnaires, but on knowing how to identify and dissect the archetypal codes and customs, the revealing turns of speech and manner, and the almost imperceptible nuances of life-style, by which the community defines itself in relation to its environment and its past. Where the anthropologist is working in an exotic and alien culture, the task, however daunting at the outset, is made much less so at the point of publication by the simple fact that the audience to whom the reported findings are addressed has no means of checking them against what the natives themselves might have to say. But where the fieldwork has been done in the anthropologist's very own milieu for dissemination to, as well as about, the natives themselves, publication is a much more hazardous affair. How can you dare pretend to be telling it like it is if the natives are going to turn round and tell you it isn't?

This test is, however, triumphantly passed by Ann Barr, Peter York and the intrepid and diligent team of assistant fieldworkers with whom they have penetrated far and deep into the rose-red canyons of SW3, 1, 7, 10, 6 and 5 – correctly ranked in that order – and the near- and far-flung outposts where there continue to flourish the eponymous Henrys and Carolines and the eternal state of mind by which Sloane Rangerdom maintains its undying faith in What Really Matters in Life. The observations that, for example, Henry and Caroline never cry at funerals, but only at carols, that Sloanes never 'go' anywhere but always 'whizz', 'toddle', 'rush', 'beetle', 'tear' or 'zoom', and that 'Hooray Henrys' Get Pretty Pissed, not to show they can hold their liquor, but, on the contrary, to get drunk enough to do some crazy thing which will go down in the Hooray annals as a Historic Act of Hilarity, command instant recognition and assent. The tones of voice are meticulously registered: to this reviewer's ear, at least, Caroline's cry of 'absoLOOtly' is ABsolutely right. The favourite jokes are well chosen: 'scene but not herd', 'in the days when England was a White's man's country', 'christened her Marigold and hoped she would'. So are the photographs, particularly of Sloanes at play. The maxims are both valid and pithy: 'A Sloanie has a pony,' 'Anyone who has read Proust is not a Sloane Ranger.' Best of all, in its way, is the opening map on which the symbolic geography of Rangerland is set out in accordance with the best structuralist principles. Rangerland extends in longitude from Vancouver ('Just like England') and Martha's Vineyard ('Edward's boss has a boat') to Delhi ('Where we lost Johnnie during his hippie phase') and Hong Kong ('Dumfries on Sea'), and in latitude from Cape Town ('Henry's cousin has a farm here – wonderful black people bringing cold drinks!') to '"The Dreaded North of the Park", Yorkshire Moors, Dumfriesshire, Inverness (in that order)'.

But dedicated fieldwork by itself is not enough. Ungenerous as it may seem to carp at the fruits of so much painstaking scholarship, it has to be said that the *Handbook* rests on solider empirical than theoretical ground. The back cover suggests that it can be read as a guide to 'upper-class' life. But this is misleading. As the text itself makes clear, Henry and Caroline are not, and are not about to become, either owners or controllers of any significant proportion of the means of production. Sloane Rangers are the subalterns and field officers, not the major-generals commanding, of the fortress heights of the economy and the state. They are not the rapacious financiers or the galvanic industrialists or the power-hungry politicos. Henry's job in the City or the wine trade and Caroline's little Trust can keep them safely afloat at the level of public-school fees, a (Dreaded) Au Pair, Supertravel skiing holidays, Hermes scarves, General Trading Company ice-buckets, engraved writing paper, hunt bollock tickets, teeny silver thimbles for the dowryette, and the Volvo Estate car with bars for the Labrador. But it's

Blanquette de Limeaux, not Moët, in the Buck's Fizz, it's the Royal Thames, not the Squadron, for Henry's boat, the 12-bore is a Spanish AYA, not a Purdy (unless Henry's been lucky enough to inherit his grandfather's), and the cost of maintaining the Old Vicarage, Blogton, Berkshire (which is really the Old Vicarage, Tiggleton Road, Blogton, Hungerford, Berkshire RG17 0TL) is almost, although never quite, ruinous.

In any case, Sloanes are not, in the technical sense, a class at all. They are a classic example of a *Stand*, or 'status-group', as defined by Max Weber himself – that is, an amorphous but exclusive community distinguished by a common life-style whose characteristic features are both positively evaluated and strictly ritualised. Status-group differences are, of course, closely bound up with class differences. But they are not to be equated with them. Status-groups seek to acquire and defend monopolies of consumption, not production, and the barriers by which they surround themselves are barriers of standing, not wealth. Superiors are openly acknowledged as such, and inferiors are excluded by avoidance, ridicule, refusal of hospitality, and, above all, the denial of intermarriage. On every one of these criteria, Sloane Rangers are an almost pure example of a *Stand*. They are no more patrician than they are bohemian. They are not to be located anywhere in the raffish circles where Arts, Barts, Smarts, Tarts and Upstarts meet and mingle for mutual exploitation and pleasure. They worship the Royals, revere the Aristos, detest the Parvenus, despise the Charlies, ignore the Bolshies and take a positive pride, as the *Handbook* correctly points out, in refusing to acknowledge as real whole TV regions of Britain and regarding as wildly humorous and unlikely such things as social work departments and computer graphics. Above all, they deploy what the authors rightly acknowledge to be an 'extremely subtle and secret verbal culture' to keep safely at bay any threatened intrusion by trendies, tradesmen, swots, pooves, ponces, proles, peasants, Jews, media types, lefties, yobbos, jerks, Mayfair Mercenaries or International White Trash.

Yet it would be unfair to the authors to judge them innocent of theory altogether. If in method they are the disciples of Malinowski, in approach they are the disciples of Veblen. This is not because they are satirists, any more than Veblen was: although Veblen's *The Theory of the Leisure Class* is widely supposed by people who know it only by its title to be a denunciation of the conspicuous consumption of the idle rich, it is in fact an earnest social-Darwinian exercise in the analysis of the survival and function of archaic behavioural traits. But this approach is exactly what is needed to account for some of the most distinctive characteristics of Henry's and Caroline's life-style. Take shooting, for example, about which Veblen observed that 'even very mild-mannered and matter-of-fact men who go out shooting are apt to carry an excess of arms and accoutrements in order to impress upon their own imagination the seriousness of their undertaking.' Isn't this precisely Henry in his plus-fours and Husky and flat cap and cartridge bag and what the *Handbook* calls 'military/historical/symbolic' accessories, toddling up the moor to enact 'the ritual perfected for the defence of men against birds'? Even better, take Henry's walking-stick. Here is the *Handbook*: 'watch Henry with his stick – how he likes to lightly change his grip on it, tap the ground as he walks along, point things out with it, slash at a weed. You can see it's a sword.' And here is Veblen: 'taken simply as a feature of modern life, the habit of carrying a walking-stick may seem at best a trivial detail; but the usage has a significance for the point in question . . . The walking-stick serves the purpose that the bearer's hands are employed otherwise than in useful effort, and it therefore has utility as an evidence of leisure. But it is also a weapon, and it meets a felt need of barbarian man on that ground.' Snap!

The fundamental sociological point that the *Handbook* makes, and Veblen would wholeheartedly endorse, is that Sloanes are 'a living museum of old modes of behaviour'. The authors have rightly discerned that what the accoutrements and appurtenances of Sloane life unwittingly reveal is a 19th-century view of the 18th century, sustained and exemplified by token symbols of warrior/landowner gentrydom, which would be quite unrecognisable to a real Fielding squire. The obsession with the ubiquitous Horse Motif, the quasi-military trophies and table-mats, the taste for archaic breakfast food, the staunch preference for Georgian wood and silver, the too-prominent placing of the dog-basket, the *Fields* and *Horse and Hounds* in the downstairs loo, Caroline's incurable addiction to *Debrett*, Henry's thin, gold, oval, engraved, *not* swivel-backed cufflinks, the nostalgic love of dhurries and Mogul hangings and Indian bedspreads (even if Grandfather *wasn't* in the Indian Army or ICS), the silk shirts 'copied by Sam on a business trip to Hong Kong', even the Sloanes' 'keen as bloodhounds' sensitivity to the smells of boats, bonfires, leather and high-octane petrol (good) and aeroplanes, old vase-water, imitation leather and diesel oil (bad), are all symptoms of a half-conscious ideology whose deep structure is explicable only by reference to an unbreakable attachment to tradition: 'Sloanes put tradition top because it keeps them top' – or near enough to it to keep them happy.

There is, to be sure, a Darker Side. But true to the spirit of Malinowski, the authors do not shrink from revealing it, too (if only because it turns out to be almost touchingly harmless). Sloanes do commit a lot of traffic offences, and not infrequently cheat on their income tax. A few Henrys are unmistakable 'four-letter men', even if they seldom qualify as roaring shits on the full-blooded patrician and/or bohemian scale. There may well be a naughty uncle living in Marrakesh with *'others of his ilk'*, and another being dried out at the Priory in Roehampton or the Crichton in Dumfries. Sloane marriages do quite often come unstuck, whether just because Henry's 'moved into his dressing-room' or because he's decamped with his secretary, the nanny or his best friend's wife, in which case Caroline (unless she's the best friend's wife in question) goes vengefully off on a Serenissima culture tour. Sloanes are not, on the whole, very charitable. Caroline can be not only meaninglessly gushing, but unpleasantly callous. (The authors are a little ambivalent about this: they are right that Ranger understatement is sometimes misinterpreted by outsiders as callousness, but they also recognise that 'other Sloanes can be cruel if someone's "a bit of a mess"' – i.e. a 'fermented boozy' who's gone 'well and truly off the rails'). More of them than are aware of it themselves are intermittent and sometimes chronic depressives, but it's out of the question to go to a Shrink in (Dreaded) Hampstead or even to admit to the possibility of a need for one ('You would be a behaviourist – if you knew what it meant'). The real trouble is that Sloanes are not merely ineducably complacent, but indefatigably resistant to any remote possibility of seeing themselves as others see them.

So come the Revolution, what then? Nothing recorded in the *Handbook* will redeem Henry and Caroline in the eyes of Bolshie Scargill, class-traitor Benn and the *enragés* of the Lumpen Polytechniat. Hauled by Red Guards before a People's Court, they will at once be condemned as parasites, exploiters, racists, sexists, imperialists, warmongers and lackeys of international capitalism. The Old Vicarage will be taken over by a free-loving trade-union commune of braless women and bearded men in gungey dungarees, growing ecological vegetables and Marching for Peace. Gone will be the income from Caroline's (badly-invested) little Trust, gone Henry's salary from the merchant wank, gone the hard-earned joys of the ski-slope and the hunting-field, gone Ludgrove and Lady Eden's and the St Andrew's Day Wall Game ('No goals have been scored since the First World War, but Henry is always hoping'), gone the Bullingdon point-to-point, gone Glyndebourne, gone the Norland Nannies, gone the teeny silver thimbles, gone the favourite watering-hole 'where Toby practically lives', gone Turnbull & Asser and Swaine Adeney, Brigg & Sons and the Burlington Arcade. Will posterity shed a tear? Probably not. But then posterity only keeps a soft spot for the seriously grand, the romantically wicked and the authentically doomed. Henry and Caroline are neither saints nor sinners. Their ambitions are modest, their snobberies venial, their vices innocuous, their loyalties genuine, and their tastes as much their own affair as are the tastes of those either richer or poorer than they.

In any case, none of that come-the-Revolution business is ('*act*ually') going to happen. Like it or not, Henry and Caroline have a long innings ahead of them during which to savour the *Handbook*'s authoritative account of their sacred passion for the Status Quo ('*not* the pop group'). Indeed, the only mystery is that such perspicacious participant-observers apparently failed to realise, or to persuade their publisher, that they had a bigger bestseller on their hands than even Malinowski's *Sexual Life of Savages in NW Melanesia*. Did they really not foresee how many eager students of form both inside the stable and outside the fence would be queuing for copies of the Ranger Guide to WRM in L?

Anthony Pagden

Being a Benandante

The Night Battles: Witchcraft and Agrarian Cults in the 16th and 17th Centuries
by Carlo Ginzburg, translated by John and Anne Tedeschi
(Routledge, 1983)

In the mountainous district of Friuli in Northern Italy there were good witches and bad, 'good walkers' (*benandanti*) and evil ones. On certain nights of the year during the Ember Days, in the valley of Josaphat, the two met and did battle for the crops. The *benandanti* came armed with stalks of fennel, the witches and warlocks with sorghum and sometimes the wooden palettes used for cleaning ovens. Ranged like armies with their captains and their banners, they fought all night long. If the *benandanti* won, then the harvest would be safe, but if the witches won then there would be famine. The *benandanti* could also on occasion cure the bewitched and protect people's homes from the vandalism of the witches: as one of them explained, the witches 'go into the cellars and spoil the wine with certain things, throwing filth into the bungholes'. Unlike the witches, who had sold themselves to Satan in exchange for their supernatural powers, the *benandanti*, who fought only for 'Christ's faith', were born to their profession. Every man whose mother had preserved the caul in which he was born and who wore it about his neck was compelled to 'go forth' when called to defend the crops. These night battles did not, however, take place in this world but 'in the spirit'. The soul alone 'went out', sometimes in the form of some small animal, leaving the body behind inert and as if dead. In the morning, before dawn, the spirit returned, but if someone should attempt to turn the body or 'come and look for a long time at it', the spirit would never again be able to re-enter its former home and would be compelled to join the horde of those who had died 'before their time'. Being a *benandante* was clearly a risky business.

Carlo Ginzburg's account of this Friulian 'fertility cult', as he calls it, first appeared in Italian as *I Benandanti* in 1964, and has now been skilfully, even elegantly translated into English by John and Anne Tedeschi. *Night Battles* follows the fortunes of the *benandanti* through a series of Inquisition trials from 1575, when they first appear in the records, until 1676, when both they and the witches had ceased to be of much interest to the Church authorities. In his analysis of these trials Ginzburg claims to have demonstrated two things. First, that the *benandanti* formed part of a widespread fertility cult traces of which could be found all over Central Southern Europe; and second, that under constant pressure from the Inquisitors, who could see no difference between good and evil witches and believed that the *benandanti* were merely attempting to cover up the true nature of their activities, the 'good walkers' were slowly assimilated into the evil ones, so that by the 1670s their cult had lost all but the most superficial traces of its original rituals and had largely forgotten its purpose.

Since the appearance of his best-selling *The Cheese and the Worms*, whose material, the trial of a 17th-century Friulian miller with highly idiosyncratic cosmological beliefs, comes from the same archive as the *benandanti* trials, Ginzburg has acquired an international reputation as one of the most interesting living historians of popular culture. In Italy *I Benandanti* has also appeared, much modified, both as an adult comic-book and as a play. Ginzburg himself is unhappy with the uses to which his work has been put: but to be oneself made into an object of popular interest is surely the highest tribute a historian of popular culture can have paid to him. The reasons for this popularity, both in and outside the academy, are not hard to find. The material he has discovered is truly exciting; it offers a glimpse into a wholly alien world which historians have only recently begun to take at all seriously; and it possesses an immediacy which appears, though this may be a delusion, to allow, as he claims, 'the voices of these peasants to reach us directly, without barriers'.

Carlo Ginzburg is also a highly sensitive and imaginative historian whose prose style reproduces much of his mother Natalia's clarity and precision. He has been able, as few others would have been if presented with the same material, to make his historical characters live. *Night Battles*, like *The Cheese and the Worms*, is also a *tour de force* of reconstruction, building out of scattered and fragmentary sources a whole world for the reader to inhabit. Ginzburg's well-merited success, together with the increasing professional interest in the social history of 'lesser people' in general, has, however, obscured the sometimes shaky nature of the arguments and assumptions which underpin many of his reconstructions.

The most obvious problem is to be found in the documents he has used. We know little about the daily lives of peasants for the simple reason that the so-called 'dominant culture' took very little interest in them. Of their mental world we know next to nothing, and most of what we do know comes from a single source: the records of the trials of the Inquisition. Since the Holy Office was concerned with maintaining the orthodoxy of the entire population, the common people, believed to be much given to 'dangerous novelties', came in for a great deal of careful scrutiny. Before the late 18th century at least, the Inquisitors were the only members of the dominant culture who made any attempt to discover what peasants and artisans believed. Trials for heresy and blasphemy, recorded with all the precision of Europe's first efficient bureaucracy, thus provide the historian with an enormous wealth of information on the 'mentalities' of the 'common' man. They also present him with considerable difficulties. In the first place, the Inquisition was, obviously, *only* concerned with what it held to be doctrinal deviance. Not of course that all of its victims were deviants: but since the Inquisitors were astute, intelligent, well-trained men who were frequently well-informed about the curiosities of popular 'superstition' and generally tolerant of them, most of those whose trials lasted long enough to be of any interest to the historian were, at best, unusual. Nor should it be supposed that the Inquisition's view of what constituted orthodoxy was not shared by the majority of the people. Most of its victims, and in particular most of the poor (who did not broadcast their beliefs), only came to its attention because they had been denounced by their neighbours, and this was the case with most of the *benandanti*.

The 'trials' were also, in fact, extended interrogations, frequently carried out with the use of torture. Their transcripts record the suspects' responses to questions posed by men who were only concerned to establish quite specific things. Sometimes other information leaks through, particularly when the Inquisitor is not entirely sure what species of heterodoxy he is dealing with. In the case of the *benandanti*, what the Inquisitors wanted to know, what indeed they seem to have set out to establish, was the association between these supposed anti-witches and the witches themselves. For, on the evidence which Ginzburg provides, what seems to have worried them most was the *benandanti*'s claim to be able, indeed destined, to act as God's champions, and their potentially heretical belief that their spirits could depart from, and then return to, the body at will. The victims, for their part, knew full well that they were in considerable danger, possibly of death and certainly of torture, confiscation, humiliating public penance, exile or excommunication. In every trial, the Inquisitors suggested, and finally persuaded the *benandanti*, that what they were doing was in fact not so very different from the activities of 'ordinary' witches. In every trial, too, and this is something which emerges very vividly from Ginzburg's narrative, there seems to have been a crucial point at which the victim realised that he had implicated himself so far that his only way out was to offer a full 'confession'. These confessions inevitably tended to contain everything the Inquisitor was believed to want to hear. Some of the *benandanti*, particularly in the earlier trials, when their case was still a subject of some bewilderment to the authorities, persisted in their claims that they were not witches, that they had not attended the sabbat and were only doing God's – and by implication the Church's – work. Some were believed and released or had their cases suspended. Some made minor confessions. Later suspects, like Olivo Caldo, a peasant from Ligugnana, and one of the last cases with which Ginzburg deals, confessed to having attended the sabbat, to having ridden on a billy goat, to having sold his soul to the Devil. (The Inquisitors themselves, however, came to suspect the veracity of these statements, all of them extracted under torture, and Olivo, who then denied everything he had previously said, claiming the only act he had ever committed was to have once 'made a sign over some people who came to him', was finally pronounced to be only 'lightly' suspect of apostasy and banished from the parish for five years.)

Ginzburg sees in these varying responses to the Inquisitors' demands evidence for the steady transformation of the *benandanti* from anti-witches into witches. There would seem, however, to be a lot wrong with this idea. It supposes, what Ginzburg assumes throughout, that the *benandanti* were, in fact, a true sect whose members were capable of passing on information about the changes which had taken place in their beliefs and practices – and about what the Inquisitors had made of those beliefs and practices – from one generation to the next and, since the *benandanti* came from different parishes, from one region to another. Yet as Ginzburg admits there is little evidence that most *benandanti* did know each other; nor, except during the night battles themselves, do they seem to have thought of themselves as a group, much less as a sect with clearly prescribed rituals. Their beliefs, as they emerge from the records, are simply too vague, too uncertain in the face of determined and precise questioning – and torture – to be subject to wholesale transformation. Certainly the Inquisitors did attempt to persuade the *benandanti* that they were closet witches, disguising, perhaps even in ignorance, diabolical activities as 'God's work'. But what the *benandanti*'s reply to these accusations would seem to reveal is less a shift in a body of coherent beliefs than a number of individual responses to a common, though varied experience: the experience of fighting for survival against skilled interrogators whose purpose is never entirely clear. For these peasants had only an imprecise idea of what was heterodox and what was not. They had to choose their words with care. Little wonder, then, that in this overwhelming darkness many chose to follow the lead offered them by their accusers. In Ginzburg's brilliant reconstruction of the ordeal of one of the last of the 'good walkers', Michele Soppe, whose case even came to the personal attention of the Pope and Cardinal Francesco Barberini (though primarily because it confirmed their suspicions that 'hardly a single trial can be discovered in this matter that has been correctly and legally instituted'), we can watch the behaviour of a man on the run, turning this way and that, first denying and then affirming, and finally accepting nearly everything the Inquisitors put into his mind, in his efforts to save himself from the stake.

There is another significant change between the earlier and the later trials. It is one which Ginzburg barely notices, but it may help to explain why the later *benandanti* appear in a far more obviously diabolical light than their predecessors. For the earlier victims, though they do speak of being able to cure the bewitched, were primarily concerned with their role as defenders of the crops – an activity which, since it took place at night, and then only in the spirit, and might just do some good, could have caused little offence to their neighbours. As the trials progress, however, we hear less and less about this aspect of their calling, and more and more about their powers as healers, as the undoers of the spells cast by witches. Here they came up against the uncertainties of the community's attitude towards magical doctors, an attitude which could rapidly change from wary acceptance to outright hostility if the practitioner either failed to cure, refused to cure or demanded too much for his services. Michele Soppe was originally denounced from several sources on this account because, as one of his accusers put it, 'I thought it was right to denounce this one so that these clever swindlers get the punishment they deserve.' Although Soppe confessed to being a *benandante*, he was never involved in night battles with witches. His relationship with them was indeed a close one, for he was a healer, and one of the ways he healed was 'to find the witch who has cast the spell and beg her to break it'. This is certainly a far cry from the claims of the earlier *benandanti* such as Paolo Gasparutto and Battista Moduco, but it is not sufficient evidence that Soppe, Gasparutto and Moduco were all members of a single cult whose common body of beliefs had suffered a sea-change in the face of Inquisitorial hostility. They may as well have all been single individuals aware, as the entire community was clearly aware, of the existence of a number of beliefs which linked the possession of the caul to an ability to protect the crops and to cure those who had been bewitched; and they each exploited this knowledge – and confessed to their exploitation of it – in their different ways. Primarily, though their motives were clearly complex, they did so in an effort to eke out a living. As one witness observed of a female *benandante*, 'she wants to be paid and well paid at that . . . and can tell at a glance those who are able and unable to pay.'

Ginzburg's other claim that the *benandanti* of Friuli were members of a fertility cult linked to others throughout the whole of Central Southern Europe, seems to be even more dubious than the transformation thesis. It derives in part from Margaret Murray's frequently discredited claims that the nocturnal rites described by those accused of witchcraft did actually take place, and that they were the remnants of a pagan fertility cult hostile to Christianity. Ginzburg is sceptical about the first of these claims (though he rightly insists that the *benandanti*'s night battles were real enough to *them*), but accepts that the second contains a 'kernel of truth'. Certainly the principal concern of the *benandanti* was with fertility, and they clearly did have some tenuous links with those who could 'see the dead', with the German belief in Diana or Holda or Perchta, as goddess of fertility and leader of the 'Furious Horde' of those who had died prematurely, and with the cult of the Livonian werewolf who claimed to be one of the 'hounds of God'. Given, however, that we are dealing with peoples who all shared similar economic and material preoccupations, lived under the aegis of the same set of (orthodox) religious beliefs and in very similar communities, given, too, that theirs was a culture which was slow to change and transmitted orally by groups who migrated widely in search of a livelihood, it would be surprising, particularly in frontier regions like Friuli, if Slav and German beliefs did not crop up. But the fact that some who were, or claimed to be, *benandanti* also claimed to be able to 'see the dead' on Ember Days does not of itself demonstrate that they and those who could see the German 'Furious Horde', or followed the goddess Diana, belonged to the same cult.

There is also something slightly worrying about the method Ginzburg occasionally uses to establish these links. On page 35 one Anna la Rosa who claimed to be able to 'see the dead', and to have learnt things from them she dared not tell to anyone lest she be beaten with stalks of sorghum, is linked, tentatively, with the *benandanti* although Anna never claimed to be one and the word was never mentioned at her trial. On page 41, however, the same Anna is referred to simply as 'Anna la Rosa – one of the *benandanti* who claimed she could see the dead.' And Anna's presence among the *benandanti*, though it is not crucial to the argument, is nonetheless used to establish a link between them and the followers of the *dame Abonde* of the *Roman de la Rose*. This is not an accusation of wilful distortion. Any social historian working with such fragmentary evidence is compelled to attempt to 'get inside' his subject and in order to do so he has to employ a great deal of sympathetic imagination – what Vico, describing a not dissimilar enterprise, called *fantasia*. Ginzburg's historical imagination is of a very high order and most readers will be prepared to give him the benefit of the doubt. After all, Anna may well have been, or believed herself to be, one of the *benandanti*. What *is* disconcerting is that what Ginzburg claims for his reconstruction is not one possible world among many, or even the mind-set of a number of individuals with similar or overlapping beliefs: it is nothing less than 'in a broad sense the mentality of a peasant community'. And however much weight we are prepared to give that 'broad', it is clear that Ginzburg believes these men and women to stand, in more than a metaphorical sense, for the collective mentality of the entire community. What we may expect to find in this house of inferences is, we are told, not the 'individual in his (presumed) non- historic immediacy', but the 'force of the community's traditions, the hopes and needs tied to the life of society'.

The *benandanti* are surely too marginal a group to carry the burden of such a claim. All too often they appear to have been regarded by their neighbours in much the same light as they were by the Inquisitors. 'Some of us think she is crazy,' remarked one woman of the self-declared *benandante* Florida Basili. Few seem to have had an established place in the community. Most were poor, some destitute or women afflicted by domestic problems. Even their name, *benandanti*, seems sometimes to have become conflated with 'vagabond'. We know that peasants in this period were highly eclectic in their beliefs, that they were prepared to use Holy Water or the Host to cure the sick or ease the birth of a calf together with 'white magic' – or even black – if the need arose. But we have no evidence to suggest that they belonged to large-scale cults practising elaborate and controlled rituals, cults which could reasonably be said to constitute their 'mentality' and which they sustained, as best they could, in the face of opposition from the dominant culture. Most peasants seem to have been somewhat hazy about the exact nature of much Christian doctrine. The *benandanti* were, for instance, genuinely surprised that the Inquisitors should have found their claim that their souls left their bodies so worrying. But the 'superstitions', many and confused, which made up the peasant versions of the Christian faith owed their existence largely to the ignorance of their priests and the lack, in most of rural Europe, of any adequate religious education. When the Calabrian peasant (or the Asturian or the Sardinian or the Polish, for the story is repeated again and again) who, on being asked by a Jesuit missionary how many Gods there were, replied that he was uncertain but he thought possibly nine, he was not asserting his belief in an ancient polymorphic mystery cult. He was simply mistaken. A true 'peasant mentality' cannot be reconstructed from a handful of cases concerning persons whose very unusualness was what marked them out.

Ginzburg's claims for the centrality of the *benandanti* to the 'hopes and needs tied to the life of society' is also weakened by the apparent attitude of the Inquisitors towards them. Few *benandanti* were actually convicted, and when they were, the sentences were generally light. In most cases, however, the proceedings were, as so often happened with Inquisition trials, merely abandoned. True, the Inquisitors were, at this period, more preoccupied with other matters: with the belief in justification by faith or predestination or the spiritual authority of the Papacy. They were looking for real heresies, not mere 'superstition' or 'mild apostasy'. But since the *benandanti* claimed nothing less than the power to act as independent agents of Christ, it is unlikely that the Holy Office would have treated the whole matter so lightly if there had been any substantial evidence to suggest that these people were, in effect, members of a secret sect, an integral part of 'the community's traditions'.

There is another question which this book raises but never asks. For even if the *benandanti* were marginals, perhaps even in some cases 'a little crazy', even if they do not, in the end, add up to a cult or a sect, we still have to ask what did it *mean* to hold such beliefs? What, for instance, do their nocturnal journeys, the procession of the dead, the belief that if the body was turned while the spirit was absent it would 'remain dead', tell us about their understanding of the relationship between body and soul. In their starkly Manichean world where is the redeeming grace of Christ – or was that too alien a notion for a society to grasp which had so little hard evidence of God's benevolence? However heterodox the beliefs of the *benandanti* may have seemed both to their neighbours and to the Inquisitors, they were clearly not incomprehensible; and in the interstices of their more straightforward statements other more worrying phrases come bubbling to the surface. What, for instance, did Gasparutto mean when he invited the Inquisitor and his parish priest along on one of the nocturnal journeys? Where in the mind of this man did the frontier between the world of the body and the world of the spirit lie? When another spoke of 'crossing several great bodies of water and . . . at the river Iudri one of his companions became afraid because a great wind had come up,' how is the geography of Friuli (the Iudri is a local river) laid over an imaginary Biblical terrain which reaches all the way down into the Valley of Josaphat and into the 'centre of the world' itself? These men were not, as Le Roy Ladurie absurdly seems (or seemed) to believe of the peasants of the Languedoc, merely pre-rational minds struggling towards enlightenment; nor were they clearly the mouthpiece for some Durkheimian articulation of the community's traditions (the interpretation which I suspect Ginzburg would favour). The beliefs of the *benandanti* – their 'rites' – are surely grounded somewhere in a set of 'absolute presuppositions' (to use Collingwood's phrase) about precisely such matters as the crucial relationship between body and soul, between this world and the next, between past and present, the living and the dead. Though they are couched in a language the historian has still to learn how to read, these did indeed articulate the community's traditions by providing the 'common man' with an explanation – or explanations – for precisely those things for which his priests could offer none he could understand, and usually none at all beyond the simple injunction to accept the Church's rulings and believe.

To ask what it means to have a belief, and to regard the believer as, in some measure, a conscious agent, is alien to the *mentalité* of most historians of *mentalités*. Yet it is surely wrong to suppose that even the most 'ordinary' men and women were merely the unthinking mouthpieces of a mind-set not of their own making, of beliefs which could be so easily manipulated by the institutions of the dominant culture. It may be a long time before we find satisfactory answers to questions of meaning. But if we want to reconstruct a *mentality* those are the questions we *must* ask.

Mary-Kay Wilmers

Hagiography

Difficult Women: A Memoir of Three by David Plante
(Gollancz, 1983)

One evening in December 1975 David Plante called on his friend, the novelist Jean Rhys, who was staying in a hotel in South Kensington: 'a big dreary hotel', she said, 'filled with old people whom they won't allow to drink sweet vermouth'. She was sitting in what the receptionist called 'the pink lounge', wearing a pink hat. She was then in her eighties. He kissed her and told her she was looking marvellous. 'Don't lie to me,' she said, 'I'm dying.' After supper and a great deal of drink, they went up to her room: 'sometimes her cane got caught between her legs and I had to straighten it.' They drank some more and talked about her life. Five hours later, David Plante got up, took a pee and told her he had to leave. '"Before you go," she said, "help me to the toilet."' He took her there and left her, in her pink hat, holding onto the washbasin. Sometime later she called to him.

I opened the door a little, imagining, perhaps, that if I opened it only a little, only a little would have happened. I saw Jean, her head with the battered hat leaning to the side, her feet with the knickers about her ankles, just off the floor, stuck in the toilet. I had, I immediately realised, forgotten to lower the seat . . . I stepped into the puddle of pee all around the toilet, put my arms around her, and lifted her.

'I'll try to walk,' she said when he offered to carry her to her bed. So he propped her up against a wall and 'took off her sopping knickers'. When he got her onto the bed, he rang Sonia Orwell, who arrived to take charge of the situation: 'For God's sake, David,' Mrs Orwell said, 'don't you know when someone's drunk?'

A few days later, he again visited Jean Rhys, who in the meantime had been moved by Mrs Orwell to another hotel, one which no doubt allowed its guests to drink sweet vermouth. She was feeling better. 'Now,

David,' she said, 'if that ever happens to you with a lady again, don't get into a panic. You put the lady on her bed, cover her, put a glass of water and a sleeping pill on the bedside table, turn the lights down very low, adjust your tie before you leave so you'll look smart, say at reception that the lady is resting, and when you tell the story afterwards, you make it funny.'

David Plante has little trouble making his stories funny: he could probably have made them even funnier had he wanted to, but telling funny stories about your friends is a tricky business if you intend to go on having friends; and on the evidence of this book, Mr Plante, an American novelist who lives in England, has quite a busy social life. Sonia Orwell once said to him that the life he led was 'very chic': too chic, she thought, for a writer. But he has got his own back on her now. *Difficult Women* is a memoir of three women whom it was once very chic to be friends with, and the one whom it was most chic to be friends with was Mrs Orwell, though she told Mr Plante that in Paris she knew some 'very very ordinary' people. It's an unflattering book, especially in its account of Mrs Orwell, but whether Mr Plante has any sense that he might have betrayed their friendship is hard to determine since, while making her sound entirely unlovable, he keeps telling us how much he loved her.

Jean Rhys died in 1979; Sonia Orwell, George Orwell's widow, a year later. Mr Plante's third subject is Germaine Greer, who, as well as being a friend with a house near his in Italy, was his colleague for a term at the University of Tulsa ('from Tulsa I wrote letters to Sonia, one long one about Germaine Greer'). Of the three, Germaine Greer seems to have been the one he liked best, but now she thinks him 'a creep' for having written this book. Former friends of the other two will have worse things to say of him: indeed, some hard things have already been said (in print) by people who didn't know either of them, and it seems possible that a lot of dinner parties of the kind he describes will now be taking place without him. As a foreigner, Plante claims in self-defence, he is unable to grasp the distinctions the English make between public and private life – which sounds convenient but could, I suppose, be true. No one who records everything he sees his friends do and hears them say does so without malice, yet something besides malice must have prompted Mr Plante to write up his diary for publication, especially as he can't make his friends look silly without looking pretty silly himself.

Mrs Orwell, being a sociable woman, gave a great many dinner parties ('Sonia is knowledgeable about and gives a lot of attention to her cooking, which is mostly French'). He didn't enjoy these parties. 'I would get home from an evening of being victimised, angry and depressed, and swear I'd never see Sonia again. The next morning, however, I'd ring her to say what a lovely dinner party . . . and how I longed to see her again.' Mr Plante, of course, is a snob for whom there was pleasure in the thought of being an intimate of the well-connected Mrs Orwell, or a personal friend of Jean Rhys or a close companion of the electrifying Ms Greer; and pleasure, too, in being the kind of nice young man who can get on with everyone, however rich and famous. He is also a homosexual, though he doesn't precisely say so; and like many homosexuals, he has a weakness for unaccommodating women – the kind actors call 'outrageous'. He often refers to this weakness in explaining his affection for these 'difficult' women but says little to elucidate it. 'You could jump to a Freudian conclusion that this had to do with my mother,' he said in an interview. And then added: 'But I absolutely reject that.'

It may be that 'difficult women' are a luxury that only homosexuals can afford in their lives. But if there is some truth in this (men who have to live with women, if they have any sense, must prefer them to be easy-going), there is none in its converse: lesbians don't sing any songs in praise of difficult men. It would be against their code of honour to do so, and quite unnecessary since heterosexual women do it all the time. Given that the history of the world can in a sense be seen as a history of the difficult men who have run it, it seems appropriate to register a protest against Mr Plante's title. No one has yet written a book about three moderately famous men who happened to have known each other and called it 'Difficult Men'. (Or even 'Nice Men: A Memoir of Three'.) Still, there's no sense in being curmudgeonly, or in pretending that there's no such thing as a difficult woman – the chances are that if you aren't 'difficult' no one will write a book about you. Mr Plante is very good at describing some of the ways in which women can make life hard, while insinuating that no merit attaches to being friends with someone it's easy to be friends with. 'Difficult women', it turns out, can make you like yourself better for liking them.

Take Jean Rhys. Of the three relationships Mr Plante describes this was the one that troubled him most, largely because he knew that he wanted something from it that wasn't just friendship, and he didn't like this in himself. 'I wondered if my deepest interest in her was as a writer I could take advantage of,' he reflected at an early stage in their relationship. 'I did not like this feeling.' The feeling recurred when she accepted his offer to help her write the autobiography she wanted to write but could no longer manage. ('I can't do it myself and no one can help me,' she said, as she always said.) Their collaboration was long and painful. The same material was gone over again and again: sometimes she liked it, often she hated it; she would drink, become confused, shout at him, say it was worthless, that there was no point going on. He would put a thousand disparate fragments into chronological order and she would drop them on the floor. Then, looking at what she had done, she would again say: 'I don't know if this will ever be finished, it's in such a mess.' After Jean Rhys died, Sonia Orwell explained what Mr Plante had no doubt understood all along: that Jean Rhys was overcome with terror at the thought of another writer taking over her book. Her fears are easy to sympathise with. Unfortunately, they tie in all too well with the paranoia of a woman who, while always asking for help, never ceased to find fault with those who helped her; who would say, 'I don't want to see anyone,' and ten minutes later: 'No one ever comes to see me.' It's clear from David Plante's account of her, as it is from everything she wrote both when she was young and when she was an old lady, that she depended on, and was inspired by, a sense of being treated badly.

Mr Plante describes a tearful afternoon when she tried to dictate a passage about the loneliness of old age:

> She said no one helped her, she was utterly alone. She said she had had to come up to London on her own, when in fact Sonia and her editor had gone to stay in the village for three days to get her ready, and drove her up to London to the flat they had found for her. She asked me to read the whole thing out. She said, afterward: 'Well, there are one or two good sentences in it.' I wondered how much of the 'incredible loneliness' of her life was literature, in which she hoped for one or two good sentences – all, she often said, that would remain of her writing, those one or two good sentences.

She was always incredibly lonely because in her own mind no one else existed. Sonia Orwell told David Plante that she wished he had known how charming Jean Rhys had been when she was younger, but the charm is there for everyone to see in the heroines of her novels, all of whom are versions of herself and all of whom are charming and very pretty. 'I don't think I know what character is,' she admitted to Mr Plante. 'I just write about what happened.' By which she meant what happened to her. And it wasn't only as a novelist that she found the notion of character elusive: everyone she knew in life was a mystery to her. 'I don't know much about my husbands,' she told Mr Plante, confessing that she had no idea why her first and third husbands had spent time in prison. Max Hamer, her third husband, was married before, she said, 'but whether he had any children or not I don't know.' She herself had two by her first husband, Jean Lenglet. After they divorced, the daughter (prudently) stayed with her father: the son had died in early infancy. 'What did it die of?' Mr Plante asked. '*Je n'sais pas*' was her reply: 'I was never a good mother.'

It was characteristic of her that while she talked a great deal about her writing and writing in general, both of which seemed to matter a lot to her, she was prepared to turn her back on everything she had done for the sake of a couple of sad sentences: 'I'll die without having lived . . . I never wanted to be a writer. All I wanted was to be happy.' What is hard to understand is the part Jean Rhys's obsession with herself played in other people's affection for her. 'For some mad reason, I love you,' David Plante said to her one day and then wondered, not why he had said it but why he loved her. 'The most enormous influence on me in the four and a half years since I met her,' Scott Fitzgerald once remarked of his wife, 'has been the complete, fine and fullhearted selfishness of Zelda.' Perhaps there is something unfailingly attractive about pretty women whose self-absorption makes them unable to cope with anything. 'It took me three visits to teach her how to open a compact she had been given as a gift,' Mr Plante writes in passing about Jean Rhys: maybe it was the gallantry her selfishness inspired that made him think he loved her.

David Plante had first met Jean Rhys at a 'luncheon party' at Sonia Orwell's house; and when he was working on her autobiography he liked to discuss her with Mrs Orwell. Heaven knows why, since Sonia could not bear to let him think that he knew anything about Jean that she didn't already know: 'Everything you've said about Jean that she's told you I've known, in greater detail, from her and there is a great deal she has told me which she hasn't mentioned to you.' That's the way Sonia Orwell, who thought, perhaps rightly, that 'most people' didn't like her, talked to her friends, as if telling them anything that didn't make them feel awful would encourage in them a terrible sense of well-being. 'When I was with her,' Mr Plante writes, 'her effect was to make me see my life as meaningless, as I knew she saw her own life.' It's a funny reason for wanting to be someone's friend. 'I was in love with that unhappiness in her,' he continues. Mrs Orwell, who had more common sense than David Plante, thought it was self-indulgent to say that kind of thing about oneself – and she had a point.

Mr Plante acknowledges Mrs Orwell's qualities, her generosity with her time and her money, and what he calls her 'disinterested devotion' to her friends: but it is the many unpleasantnesses, or 'difficulties', of her behaviour that are assiduously reported. He took her to Italy to stay in his house, though her friends warned him against it ('When I said I was going to Italy with Sonia Orwell, he said: "You're out of your fucking mind"'): she didn't like it there and the bits he was particularly proud of she particularly hated. She was often drunk; she didn't like anyone she didn't know (and a large number of people she did know): 'The writer mentioned friends of hers. Sonia said: "They're swine."' One or two people, her protégés, she respected, but mostly she was contemptuous of other people's endeavours and even more contemptuous of their reputations: '*Freddy Ayer. He doesn't think* . . . My God. I know Freddy Ayer. I know he doesn't think.' Having wanted to write and, in her own eyes, failed, she was particularly hard on writers, especially those who hoped for success: a writer was congratulated in her presence on a book he had recently published: 'Sonia said: "I won't read it. I'm sure it's awful."' It seems likely, however, that she found her own behaviour more repellent than Mr Plante did. 'Sonia was difficult, but she was difficult for a reason. She wanted, demanded so much from herself and from others, and it made her rage that she and others couldn't ever match what was done to what was aspired to.' It's an admiring remark but the rage wasn't always admirable. When she was ill, a friend came to stay with her: 'In the late morning, she'd bring a tray up to her, and would either find Sonia in a darkened room, her head lifted a little from the pillow, saying angrily, "You fucking well woke me up just when I'd fallen asleep," or, in a bright room, sitting up in bed, saying, as she stubbed out her cigarette in an ashtray: "*Enfin*. I thought breakfast would never come."'

Mrs Orwell disapproved of Jean Rhys for making a meal of her miseries, but she didn't invariably do better herself. On the other hand, she at least had some idea of what she was up to:

> 'Yesterday a young woman stopped me in the street to ask me the time. I shouted at her: "Do you think I can give the time to everyone who stops me in the street?" Afterwards, I wondered why I had been so rude to her. Why? Why am I so filled with anger?'
>
> I said nothing.
>
> She said: 'I've fucked up my life. I'm angry because I've fucked up my life.'

David Plante doesn't tell us a lot about Jean Rhys that Jean Rhys hasn't. His portrait of Mrs Orwell is persuasive: but there is little reason for people who never knew her – who have never even heard of her – to know now how much and with what cause she loathed herself. Novelists have more tactful ways of saying what they think about their friends.

The year Sonia Orwell stayed with David Plante in Italy he decided to spend a few days with Germaine Greer before returning to England. The first thing he saw when he arrived at the house with Ms Greer was a baby sitting at a table under a fig tree playing with finger paints. 'That's not the way to use fucking finger paints,' Ms Greer shouted at the child, who 'stared up at her with a look of shocked awe that there was a wrong and a right way to use finger paints.' Mr Plante went into the house while 'Germaine taught the baby the use of finger paints'. Inside the child's mother was reading a magazine. 'Where the fuck are you while your baby is making a fucking mess out of the fucking finger paints I paid fucking good money for?' Ms Greer shouted from the garden. Germaine Greer knows a lot more than the right way to use fucking finger paints: as Mr Plante describes her, there isn't a single fucking thing she doesn't know how to do. The next morning he finds her preparing the drawings for a dovecot she wants to build:

I said: 'It looks as if you're designing a whole palazzo.'
'I'm simply doing it the way it should be done,' she said.

They visit a local coppersmith: Ms Greer and the coppersmith speak to each other in the local dialect.

Outside I asked: 'But how do you know the dialect?'
'Don't you,' she asked. 'You live here. Shouldn't you know the dialect?'

They go to a garage where the mechanics stare at her: 'they have never known a woman who could swing her hips from side to side and clasp her hands to her breasts and pucker her mouth and know as much as they did about shock absorbers.' Wherever Ms Greer and Mr Plante go together, in Tulsa or in Tuscany, it's the same story: she is in complete fucking command: he is flummoxed. The only expertise they seem to share is an ability to take care of their own sexual requirements:

At dinner with six others, Germaine said to me across the dinner table: 'I haven't had sex in weeks, not since I got here.' 'Neither have I,' I said. She said: 'Well, I've been happy enough in my little white room taking care of it all by myself.' 'I'm pretty content in that way, too,' I said.

Clearly Mr Plante is dazzled by her: dazzled by the sight of her breasts shining in the candlelight as she sits in a bath with burning candles all along the edge, dazzled by the sight of her pubic hair peeping out through the gaping buttons of her skirt, by her 'bodily presence', by her looks (until he noticed her 'stubby' feet, he had thought she 'was beautiful beyond any fault'); dazzled by her sex life, her stories of fucks in the sea with used-car salesmen and the descriptions of her 'long, violently fluttering orgasms'; dazzled by her 'knowledge of the whole world and what was happening or not happening in it'; dazzled by her understanding of 'what it is to be a woman' (what is it?): 'Her intelligence was to me the intelligence of a woman, because she had, as a woman, thought out her role in the world; the complexity of the role required intelligence to see it, and she had seen it, I thought, thoroughly'; dazzled, above all, by the splendour of her public persona. The chapter ends with a description of the wondrous Ms Greer giving a lecture at the Unitarian Church in Tulsa:

> Powerful lights illuminated the stage so TV cameras could film the lecture; in the intense light, Germaine appeared to have a burning silver sheen about her. As she talked, she moved her arms in loose soft gestures, and I found myself being drawn in, not to a public argument in support of abortion as she defined it, but a private revelation about love . . . I thought: She's talking about herself. And yet she wasn't talking about herself. She was talking about the outside world, and in her large awareness of it, she knew it as I did not; it was as if she had a secret knowledge of it, and to learn that secret from her would make me a different person. I wanted to be a different person. I had never heard Germaine give a public lecture; I had never seen her so personal. I thought: I love her.

What is surprising is not that Germaine Greer finds him a creep but that after everything he says about her he finds her difficult. If that adjective can encompass both the helpless Jean Rhys and the very able Germaine Greer, what hope is there for the rest of us?

John Kerrigan

A Horn-Player Greets His Fate

Horn by Barry Tuckwell
(Macdonald, 1983)

At the climax of Browning's strangest poem, a horn-player greets his fate undaunted by Death or Middle English Philology. Weary of questing and pestered by visions, Childe Roland reaches the Dark Tower with the names of fallen comrades ringing in his ears. The hills encircle him like sprawling giants. His death seems certain –

And yet
Dauntless the slug-horn to my lips I set,
And blew. '*Childe Roland to the Dark Tower came.*'

Inspired though this writing is, it courts lexical absurdity. For the 'slug-horn' which Roland sets to his lips is not an oliphant or lur or bucina or shofar or any other kind of archaic instrument but an early form of the word 'slogan' misunderstood by Chatterton and handed down to Browning.

It is, in one sense, a howler. The poet should have done more homework before employing the word. But there's a sense, too, in which Browning the creator saw further than the follower of Chatterton. However quaint the 'slug-horn' may seem in Chatterton's 'Battle of Hastings II', it has a peculiar rightness in Browning's poem. As Barry Tuckwell, its foremost living exponent, reminds us in his splendid new book, the horn began its history in utterance and has never shaken off its origins. The first horns sent signals across dark forests; they called the clan together, like Ralph's conch in *Lord of the Flies*; they sounded a challenge on the battlefield. And this is where young Roland's 'slug-horn' finds its place. As the hero's 'slogan' it is, as it were, the 'mott' – both 'fanfare' and 'saying' – through which he declares himself, in which his poem ends, and from which ('*See Edgar's song in "LEAR"*' is Browning's crucial note) his quest circuitously starts.

For centuries the horn remained essentially a megaphone, blowing its melodic speech further than the voice could carry. But in the late Middle Ages horn calls reached a pitch of expressive complexity which carried them to the threshold of pure musical development. That threshold was crossed, it seems, in 17th-century France. We hear of *cors de chasse* in operas by Rossi and Cavalli, and in Lully's incidental music to Molière's comedy *La Princesse d'Elide*. Lully's music has survived, and it's possible to see from his 'Air des Valets' – helpfully reprinted in Tuckwell's *Horn* – how accomplished but narrowly venatory the early French hornists were. In England this sort of playing caught on late, but once established it became an important part of aristocratic life and rather slow to change. While the French and German traditions advanced, horn-playing here remained, for the most part, tied to the field, the forest and the noble house. The employment of horn-players became an aristocratic status symbol. As late as 1772, the distinguished naturalist Sir Joseph Banks fell out, preposterously, with Captain Cook because Cook would not let him take an entourage which included two french-horn players to the South Seas on board the good ship *Resolution*. (Banks and his musicians went to Iceland instead.) Exotic and a little wild, horns were thought particularly appropriate in the hands of hunting blackamoors. Lord Barrymore employed four negroes in his band. And the best brass-player of his generation, a black called Cato, began his career as Sir Robert Walpole's footman before being passed, like a favourite horse or dog, first to the Earl of Chesterfield and then to the Prince of Wales and his son, the future George III. The Louis Armstrong of Augustan England ended his days, apparently, as royal gamekeeper at Cliffden and Richmond Park.

On the Continent, meanwhile, things were changing fast. In Baroque Bohemia, as Tuckwell lucidly relates, the horn took a 'great leap forward' from the chase to the chamber group. In the early 1680s, a certain Franz Anton, Count von Sporck found himself so pleased by the *cors de chasse* at Louis XIV's court that he took some horns home to Lissa, together with a pair of valets trained to play them. From this small start, a Bohemian school of horn-playing burgeoned. As Sporck rose in the world, he advanced the cause of music in Bohemia, importing an opera company from Vienna and building up a horn ensemble of legendary powers. Bohemian players became so skilful that they travelled to France, not to learn, but to play. German makers were known all over Europe for their skill and inventiveness. Indeed, it seems likely that the first crooked horns – instruments capable of playing in diverse keys – were made in Imperial Vienna.

Yet the German *Waldhorn* remained, like the *cor de chasse*, a limited instrument. Tonally superb, it was about as melodically flexible as a hosepipe. And this is where the Dresden player A. J. Hampel – the pioneer of 'stopping' – made his mark. When Browning's Childe Roland blew his 'slug-horn' in defiance, he doubtless raised his fictive instrument high into the air. Played like that, or slung around the shoulder in a hoop – as horns invariably were until the 1740s and 50s – even the best instrument can only produce open notes in a harmonic series, clustered in the higher range but widely spaced in the bass. The sparing distribution of low notes on the *Waldhorn* limited its musical value, since it meant that flowing passages could only be played – as in Bach's First Brandenburg – at a stratospheric height. What Hampel showed was that, by pushing a hand into the bell, the horn could be provisionally shortened to produce secondary harmonic series alongside the natural one. With an alternation of 'stopped' and open notes, the horn could thus become chromatic. Of course, the sound was not homogeneous, and in the hands of an amateur the 'stopped' notes might sound execrable. (Dr Burney, the father of Fanny and a formidable music critic, compared them to the shriek of 'a person ridden by the night mare, who tries to cry out but cannot'.) In the hands of a virtuoso, however, the 'stopped' notes apparently sounded veiled and mysterious, with an elfin beauty. And the whole point of stopping was, as Barry Tuckwell points out, to make the horn available for virtuoso performance. With some help from the hand, the *Waldhorn* became fully expressive over three octaves, and its rich middle register was opened up for solo playing. The day of the horn virtuosi – Thaddäus Steinmüller, who played for Haydn at Esterhazy, the cheesemonger Leutgeb, Mozart's friend, and Tuckwell's hero, the great Giovanni Punto – had arrived.

This story has been told before, but never, I think, so judiciously. Tuckwell takes most of his facts from two precursors in the field, Reginald Morley-Pegge and Horace Fitzpatrick. But Morley-Pegge's *The French Horn* (1960) and Fitzpatrick's account of *The Austro-Bohemian Tradition* (1971) are as partial as those titles suggest. While one praises French elegance and the svelte hand horns made in 18th-century Paris, the other concentrates on the fuller-blooded playing which developed in Germany on instruments of a larger bore. Tuckwell takes a middle course, responding to the merits of both schools.

Perhaps his admiration for Giovanni Punto helped him here. For as a player, Punto synthesised at the end of the 18th century what was best in two traditions which still remain distinct. Brought up in Bohemia, under the name of Štich, Punto travelled widely as a soloist, and, finding himself impressed by Parisian horns, switched, at the height of his career, to an instrument made in Paris by Raoux. In this act of cross-fertilisation, he anticipated Dennis Brain – perhaps the greatest player of our century – who in mid-career abandoned the narrow-bore Raoux horn on which he had been trained to take up a German instrument.

The historical part of Barry Tuckwell's book is weakest on the hundred and fifty years between Punto and Dennis Brain, perhaps because the author's heart lies with the late 18th and 20th-century music he has done so much to advance in the concert hall. Whatever the reason for this comparative slightness, it's a pity, since it was during those years that the horn developed most rapidly. It was then that the *Waldhorn* picked up the valves which made it chromatic without 'stopping', then that it gathered much of its solo repertoire, and then that it became, in Schumann's phrase, 'the soul of the orchestra'. The total transformation which the instrument underwent can be seen by comparing Berlioz's *Treatise on Instrumentation* with Richard Strauss's revision of it. In 1843, Berlioz writes warmly but warily about an instrument which, for him, is charming but limited and a little unpredictable: Strauss, by contrast, writes prose poetry. The son of a horn-player, and only too familiar, one would have thought, with the technical demands of this difficult instrument, Strauss chooses to rhapsodise about the 'protean' coil of brass which 'calls ringingly Siegfried's exuberant vitality into the virgin forest', which vents 'the last, hoarse cry of the dying Cossack prince' in Liszt's *Mazeppa*, and 'sings in muted sounds of the miracles of the Tarnhelm'.

The Wagnerian emphasis is just, and so is Strauss's stress on utterance, because the horn developed in the 19th century through its atavistic association with the human voice. Here again, Punto is iconic: more than a '*célèbre corniste*', he was a fine, fluent singer. The great Romantic horn writers were vocal composers too: Wagner, Strauss himself, and Mahler, who all his life drew inspiration from the songs which spill out of *Des Knaben Wunderhorn*. In some respects, Modernism has not changed this. One thinks of the recitative in the last movement of Hindemith's concerto, where the horn wordlessly renders a poem by the composer, or the voice and horn lines interwoven and echoing each other, just this and the other side of language, in

Britten's *Serenade for Tenor Solo, Horn and Strings*. Childe Roland, articulating his 'slug-horn', would have understood.

Whether he would have coped with Hindemith or Britten is another matter. Louis MacNeice was clearly worried by even the limited demands that Browning makes of Roland's musicianship, and in the opening sequence of his radio play *The Dark Tower* he shows the hero taking lessons on the horn before setting out on his quest. 'Mark this,' MacNeice's Sergeant-Trumpeter remorselessly insists: 'Always hold the note at the end.' In future, presumptive heroes will be able to consult Tuckwell's *Horn* over such things as legato, tonguing and tone, and they will still find breath control stressed. Equally important, given their goal, they will find some excellent advice on the way to conquer nerves 'on the night'. Like the other books in Yehudi Menuhin's series of 'Music Guides', *Horn* is excellent on all the points of practice that it touches.

Which is not to say that the book is flawless. It has its share of blunders, and the prose is, as they say, workmanlike. A bibliography would have been helpful – especially for those young players at whom the book is aimed. It seems a shame, too, that so many of Mr Tuckwell's admirably chosen musical examples should lie dead on the page. These days, when even magazines seem to come with cassettes sellotaped to their covers, it's odd that books like the 'Menuhin Music Guides' should be sold without audio aids. At the very least, there should be a discography in *Horn*, with an ample selection from Tuckwell's own recordings. What could be better, after reading this book, than to listen to Tuckwell himself – the latest in that long line of heroes which leads back, beyond Brain and Leutgeb and Cato, to Robin Hood, Siegfried and Childe Roland.

Craig Raine

The Prophetic Book

I will give you the world,
the world we are given:
the turban in a tangerine,
a snooker table, say,
with six suspensory bandages,
the lemon squeezer
in the men's urinal.

You will need to know
the names of stone:
Taynton, Clipsham, Anstrude, Besace,
Headington, Wheatley, Perou,
and then Savonnières Courteraie
which is quarried at Meuse.
Sweet shades of chamois leather.

The passionate kiss
of sellotape, a sofa
with its four cedillas,
the ripple of a running-track,
pincushion harbours, starfish
strong as a tongue
will pleasure you.

Will pleasure you as much
as the sight of a steamroller
seen as a scarab beetle,
or the beach as a ballroom
dancing with steps,
or a bather testing the sea
like a ballerina.

I will bring you the beauty of facts:
Southdown, Dalesbred, Dartmoor,

Derbyshire Gritstone, Bluefaced Leicester,
Herdwick, Hill Radnor, Devon Longwool,
Beulah Speckled-Face, Oxford Down,
Welsh Mountain, North Country Cheviot,
do not exhaust the names of our sheep.

There is so much to celebrate:
the fine rain making midges
on a pool, the appalled moon,
and the crescent moon at morning
which fades like fat
in a frying-pan, the frail
unfocused greens of spring.

You will see the pelting rain
of string in Kentish hopfields
when the weather is clear,
enjoy the sound of squeaky shoes
when doves are beating overhead,
find out flamingoes
with polio legs, elephants

with laddered trunks.
I give you the cracked light
in a goose's quill, like frozen vodka,
a hunter's mane plaited
into peonies, swallows
in their evening dress
performing like Fred Astaire.

There are tiddlywinks
of light in the summer woods.
Play with them. The ironing-board
has permanent lumbago. Pity it.
Pity the man on his motorbike
stamping his foot
and roaring with temper.

Fly in aeroplanes and see
the speedboat like a shooting star
as if someone had struck a match,
the car-park's pharmacy of ampules,
the reef knot on a motorway,

the marquetry of fields,
a golf-course appliquéd with bunkers.

I will give you what is here:
a thousand kinds of bread,
each with a shape and name,
happiness and its haemorrhage,
the homesick hardware store
which can only say home,
Goethe and the gift of death.

Maze of entrails. Solid heart.
Drinker of urine. Channel swimmer
with tiny goggles of flesh.
Penis threaded like a grub
or folded for a clitoris.
Anus plugged with liquorice.
Endive and coral bronchial tree.

Overlapping skull plates.
Mollusc and master yogi,
standing on your head
with ankles crossed,
your horses are waiting
by the fringe of the weir,
cleft like a broad bean with black.

Your train is leaving the station
like a labrador scratching at fleas.
The ticket collector
stands in confetti.
I give you this prophetic book,
this sampler of life
which will take you a lifetime to read.

Three

London Review
OF BOOKS
VOLUME 5 NUMBER 15 18 AUGUST TO 31 AUGUST 1983 60P

Michael Stewart

The Miners' Strike

The present miners' strike compels an appalled fascination of a kind quite different from that exercised by other industrial disputes. It grips like a thriller. It is partly the question – identified by E. M. Forster as a simple but fundamental aspect of the novel – of what happens next. Will other unions be drawn in? Will we be into power cuts by Christmas? What will Mrs Thatcher do then? It is partly – to take another of Forster's categories – the actors: the interplay of the cheeky chappie from Yorkshire and the lumbering pensioner from Florida. But there are other ingredients not normally present in industrial disputes. There is the daily violence – brought into every home by television – on the picket-lines, where hordes of tough young miners and uniformed policemen sway and grapple in physical combat like medieval armies. There is the uneasiness about the accountability of the police. There are the guerrilla raids at night, presumably by striking miners, which leave a trail of damage and destruction. There are the dignity and guts of isolated working miners, and the cowardice of those who telephone their homes to threaten their children. There is the tragic irony that under their feet, as they stand in picket-lines or sit unwillingly at home, the livelihood of many miners is gradually disappearing, as inexorable geological forces, no longer kept at bay by human skill and ingenuity, buckle roadways, crush machinery, obliterate coalfaces and flood whole pits. There is the sombre feeling that in the mining communities a very British characteristic, a comradeship and sense of humour in the face of adversity, a willingness to suffer hardship and deprivation in a good cause, is being exploited and squandered for obscure and questionable ends. And underneath it all, there is something else: dim memories of 1926; the feeling that in Britain perhaps there was never a peace treaty in the class war, just a truce; that the country, split more than ever into two nations by the recession, is evolving in ways that nobody can predict; the first tremors of an earthquake that might merely dislodge a few tiles from the roof –

but could also shake the present painstakingly constructed British political edifice to pieces.

The economics of the dispute are relatively straightforward. The 1974 'Plan for Coal' – endorsed by the Labour Government though drawn up under its Conservative predecessor – was a deal according to which the Government and the Coal Board would invest heavily in new and efficient productive capacity, so ensuring a flourishing industry far into the future, in return for which the union would agree to the phasing-out of the long tail of uneconomic pits. Broadly speaking, the first part of the deal has been honoured; the second part has not. The industry still has a high-cost tail: according to last year's Monopolies and Mergers Commission report, 15 per cent of coal output involves colliery operating losses of £330 million. The closure of this loss-making capacity would significantly improve the industry's productivity and financial position. In spite of this, Mr Scargill argues that no pit should be closed until its reserves of coal are exhausted, no matter how expensive it is to extract the coal from it, and that there should be no job losses in the industry.

While the argument in this extreme form is patently absurd, it is impossible to understand the attitude of some of those involved – such as Neil Kinnock – without appreciating that a weaker version of the argument does have a certain intuitive appeal. The case for going on subsidising uneconomic pits rests on two propositions. First, production of North Sea oil will peak next year or very soon after, and within a decade will be in rapid decline. Britain's reliance on coal will thus increase sharply: therefore, we should not now be closing capacity and running down the mining labour force. Closely examined, this proposition is unsustainable. Declining oil production carries no implication that there should be rising coal production: there is no more reason why a country should aim to be self-sufficient in the production of energy than in the production of steel, cars or tiddlywinks. A country should concentrate on producing the goods and services in which it has a comparative advantage, selling these abroad in exchange for the products in which it has a comparative disadvantage. By the end of the century, Britain ought to be exporting knowledge-intensive goods and services in exchange for cheap coal from Australia and South Africa, and such domestically produced coal as can compete with these imports – and in principle there could be a lot – will come, not from the uneconomic pits which the Coal Board is rightly determined to close, but from the new pits – the Selbys and Belvoirs – that it is anxious to develop.

The second proposition on which the case for subsidising uneconomic pits rests is that there is no alternative employment in many of the mining areas: better that the men produce coal uneconomically than that they produce nothing at all and live on the dole. In all but the very short run, such an attitude is a recipe for industrial ossification and decay. The community as a whole, which benefits from economic growth and progress, has a responsibility to help those on whom the costs of economic progress fall most heavily: miners made redundant at uneconomic pits must be given every assistance in travelling to, or being relocated at, viable pits, or in being retrained for new jobs, or being aided financially in setting up their own small businesses. But they cannot be employed indefinitely in producing a product for which there is no market. And if that means that some of the remoter mining villages cease to be viable communities, that is a cost of progress which, however sad, has to be accepted.

Thus the central concession that the miners' strike is designed to extract from the Coal Board and the Government – that there should be no pit closures except on grounds of exhaustion – makes no economic sense, even when a wider perspective is adopted than the simple accounting one of eliminating the industry's losses. The strike is not about economics: it is about politics. And although the politics are murkier than the economics, a number of features stand out fairly clearly.

Mrs Thatcher, it would seem, hates and fears trade unions. Perhaps this is because they – and the working-class interests they represent – had no place in the scheme of things at her father's grocery shop in Grantham. Perhaps it is mainly an intellectual conviction, derived from her right-wing advisers, who have taught her that market forces are the only true progenitor of economic progress, and that in Britain particularly much the biggest impediment to the operation of market forces is the monopoly power of the trade unions. For whatever reason, she came into office determined to weaken the power of trade unions as far as possible, both by legislation and by appointing tough like-minded businessmen to the chairmanship of the nationalised industries whose restrictive practices and excessive wage demands had – as she saw it – been sabotaging the economy for thirty years or more. Thus it was that the hard-headed Scottish-American business tycoon Ian MacGregor was appointed to sort out British Steel, and sort it out he did: after a doomed 13-week strike, the men accepted new manning procedures which in plants such as Port Talbot raised productivity overnight by far more than had been achieved in a decade of futile negotiation. Following that, Mrs Thatcher seems to have decided – overriding the doubts of close associates – that MacGregor was ready for the big one: the miners. If the miners could be defeated (and they had won a victory over her in February 1981, forcing the Cabinet to retreat over pit closures), then the back of the union movement would be broken.

The present strike was sparked off by the announcement early in March that Cortonwood – a colliery to which miners had recently been transferred from elsewhere, with a promise that the pit had several years life ahead of it – was now destined for closure within a few months. There is a theory that this provocation was deliberately engineered by MacGregor – no doubt with the connivance of the Prime Minister – in order to get the miners out on strike at the most unfavourable time of year for them. Had a strike not begun until the autumn, after coal stocks had been depleted by the overtime ban which started late last year in protest against the Coal Board's 'derisory' 5.2 per cent pay offer, the miners would have been in a much stronger position. A more plausible explanation, perhaps, is simply that this is America's, and MacGregor's, way of doing business: if the pit isn't paying, close it. Whatever the precise explanation, the basic point was clear: the union's attempts to thwart the streamlining of the industry by resisting the closure of uneconomic pits were going to be defeated.

It is at this point that the key figure in the entire drama appears on centre stage. It is difficult to believe that, in the absence of Arthur Scargill, the present strike would have followed anything like the course it has – or even, perhaps, that there would have been a strike at all. He is the most charismatic trade-union leader to appear in Britain for a generation. He is young, he is tough and he is tireless. He is wily, he is articulate. He is a mob orator of genius. And he is completely unscrupulous.

He is, in fact, in the mould of demagogues and would-be dictators down the ages, from those who threatened the Athenian city-state to those who have wrought havoc in our own century. There is the same dedication to the cause, the same disregard for the truth, the same mesmerising oratory, the same repetition of emotive phrases ('American butcher', 'police violence'), the same identification of scapegoats (in Scargill's case the media), the same adulation by mobs of muscular young men looking for a leader and a punch-up, and the same tacit approval of the violence they indulge in.

For what is the cause in which Mr Scargill so fervently believes?

What makes Arthur run? It is very hard to believe that it is the welfare of the miners and their families. It strains credulity that a man of Scargill's intelligence is leading his members down the present road in the firm belief that at the end of the day they are going to be better off. He has a different objective from the one he claims; he is playing a different game from the one he appears to be. It is difficult to resist the conclusion, whatever the instinctive reluctance to draw it of those whose earliest political memories include the disgraceful McCarthy period in America, that the name of Mr Scargill's game is revolution. Mr Scargill does not like the present dispositions of British society, and sees no prospect of securing the election of a Parliament that will significantly change them. Therefore, change must come by some extra-Parliamentary route. The answer, proposed by Marx and adopted by Lenin, lies in the hands of the organised working class. It is the miners' historic role to be in the vanguard of this great movement, and it is the role – nay, the *destiny* – of Arthur Scargill to be at the head of the vanguard, at the very tip of the spearhead of revolution.

It may not be exactly that, but it is surely something very like it. How else explain, for example, the one great loophole in Scargill's defences, which has justified more than a quarter of the miners in their decision to go on working, and which may yet lead to intractable legal difficulties: the absence of a national ballot? The obvious answer is that Scargill had lost on the two previous occasions when he balloted the full membership of the union, and wasn't going to risk losing again. But the point about a democracy is that you are supposed to abide by majority decision: that is the way the system works. Mr Scargill rejected a national ballot, not because it might lead to a setback for him personally (though that, of course, is how the media would present it), but because it might lead to the wrong decision. The mass of ordinary members, influenced and misled in ways they do not understand by the insidious bias of the capitalist media, simply cannot be relied on to make the right choice. Therefore it must be made by the activists, who take the trouble to attend the meetings and debate 'the issues'. This is exactly the argument that the left wing of the Labour Party has been using to resist selection or reselection of Parliamentary candidates by the full constituency membership, as opposed to the party activists alone. The difference between the Labour Party and the NUM is that Mr Kinnock, who is a democrat, is opposed to decision-making by activists alone, while Mr Scargill, who is not a democrat, has not only embraced it in theory but has succeeded in putting it into practice.

The conclusion must be, then, that Mr Scargill has organised a strike which has no basis in the democratic procedures of his union, which is probably opposed by a majority of its membership, which is employing mass picketing of a kind that is now illegal, and which involves violence and intimidation on a scale quite alien to British traditions, in an attempt to force a democratically elected government to abandon some of its policies. Mr Scargill may – ludicrously – be condemned as a collaborationist by leading members of the Revolutionary Communist Party, such as Frank Richards and Mike Freeman, but their vague rhetoric about uniting the working class and 'taking control' does not carry the menace that Mr Scargill does.[1] If the Government surrenders to the miners, agreeing to subsidise uneconomic pits indefinitely and to prevent any job losses in the industry, it will be a conclusive demonstration to other unions of the political effectiveness of industrial action. Mr Scargill will encourage union activists to raise their sights. Other government policies which Mr Scargill does not like will come into the line of fire: the level of public expenditure, the tax structure, defence policy. If the Government does not suitably change these policies, Mr Scargill and his friends will bring the country to a halt. Parliamentary democracy will have become a sham. To anyone who believes in such democracy, therefore, the moral is quite clear: Mr Scargill must be defeated, and be seen to be defeated.

But one cannot leave the matter there. Whatever one may think of Mr Scargill's motives or tactics, it would be foolish to ignore the extent of the discontent and disaffection with the present state of affairs in Britain that he is articulating, or to underestimate the support he is drawing from many white-collar workers, pensioners, unemployed and others, who feel that he at least is taking on Mrs Thatcher in a way that nobody else is. Two statistics reveal a lot about Mrs Thatcher's Britain. One is the unemployment rate, which has more than doubled since she took office, to a rate of over 13 per cent for the labour force as a whole, and around 25 per cent for those in the 16–25 age group. Although unemployment seems more likely to go on rising than to fall, the Government is not proposing to do anything about it: despite ritualistic ministerial statements of concern, it creates the impression of not caring much one way or the other. The other statistic, published in the latest issue of *Economic Trends*, relates to the distribution of income: during Mrs Thatcher's first three years in office (there are no later data) the after-tax income of the top 1 per cent of the population rose by 75 per cent, that of the bottom 50 per cent of the population by only 41 per cent – barely half as much. The fact must be faced that whatever the deficiencies of the Eastern European countries which a Scargillite Britain might come to resemble they do not produce figures like these. There may be a lot of disguised unemployment, but young people who leave school do not find themselves immediately, and for as far ahead as they can see, on the dole. There may be special shops and swanky country retreats for the Party bosses, but there is nothing resembling the glaring inequalities to be found in Mrs Thatcher's Britain or Mr Reagan's America. The comfortably-off in these Western countries may reasonably offer daily thanks that they do not live east of the Elbe: for those at the bottom of the pile the right preference is not nearly so obvious.

However, it is not just Mrs Thatcher's economic policies which help to explain, though not excuse, Mr Scargill's willingness to seek an extra-Parliamentary route to power. Mr Scargill is wrong to reject democracy. But if democracy is to claim the continuing allegiance of its citizens, it must be honoured in the spirit as well as in the letter. A government should be fine-tuned to the legitimacy of its actions, particularly in contemporary Britain, whose antiquated electoral system can give one of the three main party groupings 26 per cent of the vote but only 3½ per cent of the Parliamentary seats. A government cannot realistically behave as though it has a mandate to put into effect every proposal in its election manifesto – particularly a government like the present one, which obtained the votes of only 31 per cent of the electorate. There is no evidence that Mrs Thatcher respects or even understands these precepts. She has used her huge Parliamentary majority to ram through legislation, such as that on rate-capping and the abolition of the GLC and other metropolitan councils, which is at best of questionable legitimacy and at worst the consequence of personal pique. She has made arbitrary decisions, such as the decision to ban unions at GCHQ, without even bothering to consult those of her ministers most directly concerned. It is not surprising that Lord Hailsham's ominous phrase 'elective dictatorship' is being so frequently used.

Scargill must certainly be fought and defeated. Ironically, this calls for those who believe in democracy, the rule of law, and the traditional British practice of settling disputes by peaceful negotiation and compromise, to support the Government in the stand it is taking. But that stand cannot be permanently successful as long as the attempt to flout democracy by the Left can be seen as a response to a willingness to flout democracy on the right. Mr Scargill must be defeated, but so, in a sense, must Mrs Thatcher.

Letters

SIR: No one, surely, can be surprised at the fact that Arthur Scargill reviles the media. Most of them are unashamedly right-wing. Most of them simply assume that he is bent on 'the destruction of the British way of life' and say so in clichés of this kind. But in a paper like the *London Review of Books* it is, to say the least, disappointing to see a long line of such clichés wheeled out under cover of rational reflection (Vol. 6, No 16).

In the first place, it is sad, if scarcely surprising, to see a professional economist taking as wooden a view of what is 'economic' as did the courts in the face of the case against the GLC's decision to reduce London's fares. Australian and South African coal is indeed cheaper than most of our own. 'Comparative advantage' would indeed seem to suggest that we should switch to it. The Japanese did so ten years ago. But if the Japanese had always interpreted comparative advantage as rigidly as Michael Stewart does, 'they would,' as Stephen Marglin has recently said in the *New York Review of Books*, 'still be exporting silk cloth and parasols rather than automobiles, cameras, television sets and semiconductors.' Terms of trade are not easy to predict. One's future advantages and disadvantages are a complicated gamble. 'By the end of the century,' says Stewart, 'Britain ought to be exporting knowledge-intensive goods and services in exchange for cheap coal.' Well yes, it *ought* to be. But one could be forgiven for thinking that the present government, in pricing one such service, higher education, out of the international market, takes a different view. And there is no good reason at all why I should be writing this letter on a cheap and by the standard of 1984 technically very simple word-processor which is imported from the USA, except that there is no British equivalent. It is not inconceivable that by the end of the century we could be importing even more in value, in these goods and services as in others, than we are now. The economics of the present dispute between the NCB and the NUM are not so 'relatively straightforward' as Stewart says they are.

Nevertheless, one might allow the NCB the fact that it's difficult to see future costs and benefits, and concede that on a more immediately narrow economic calculation, some pits should now be closed. Nor is there any doubt, as Stewart grants, that 'the community as a whole has a responsibility to help those on whom the costs of [what Stewart and MacGregor and the *Daily Mail* believe to be] economic progress fall most heavily.' I am not sure what 'the community as a whole' is. I certainly know of no economic or political agency of that name. Stewart must mean the Government, which, as he says at the end of his piece, commands the assent of but 31 per cent of the enfranchised 'community'. And this Government as he also points out – let alone the 31 per cent who voted it in – has a somewhat attenuated sense of social responsibility. More surprisingly, it has a somewhat attenuated sense of economic responsibility too. For if it were to shake itself free of its atavistic dogmas, it would see that the Japanese Government anticipated the diseconomies of domestic coal production, planned its demise, and with the extremely firm financial control that characterises its still very successful capitalism, made sure that most of the members of what economists would call the high-quality work-force were retrained for new firms within reach of their homes. The oddest feature of the British Government's economic policy is the assumption that 'the market' and not it must govern. Even the present Administration in America has got itself out of its recent difficulties with a series of classically Keynesian moves.

But of course, and as Stewart in effect concedes, Thatcher cares less about the economy than she does about the distribution of power within it. When the Social Democrats appear if only by default to agree with her, when the Labour Party havers, and when even the General Secretary of the TUC justifies his recent decision to retire by saying that there is no large issue facing his movement, is Scargill self-evidently mistaken to believe that someone has to do something? Obviously, he cares most about his industry and about his power within it. He would not be worth his job if he didn't. Naturally, he sees that against the NCB, the Government, the media, even the Labour Party and parts of the TUC itself, he has to be clever and on occasion unscrupulous. He would not survive a day in politics if he didn't. Certainly, he is selective in his recourses to 'democracy'. But even Stewart agrees at the end of his piece that what he calls at the beginning – against all the more plausible accounts of how it has come to be – 'the present painstakingly constructed British political edifice' is being dismantled, with breathtaking ease, by the Prime Minister herself.

'Democracy', one is embarrassed to have to point out, is not so straightforward. The law against 'secondary picketing' is not so clearly more acceptable than the law against crossing state lines for the purposes of inciting a riot which was hastily passed by a frightened Congress in 1967. The present interpretation and enforcement of existing laws about disturbing the peace and obstructing the highway and so on is not so clearly more reasonable than the interpretation and enforcement of comparable laws in Alabama and Mississippi in 1965.

And it is by no means agreed that every contentious decision taken by an elected body in the name of its electors should be balloted. If it were, one is again embarrassed to have to say, most of the liberal legislation that people like Michael Stewart and me and no doubt you yourself approve of and enjoy would never have been enacted. Enlightened élitism in the supposed interests of others is not the prerogative of the élite.

If, however, it is advocated by anyone else, it is, so Stewart would have us believe ('how else', he asks, 'explain' it?), clear evidence of Leninist intent. He certainly provides no other. But it is not, of course, evidence of anything of the kind. If it were, we would have good reason to fear the Social Democrats' reason for leaving Labour. Scargill doubtless does believe that things could be arranged better for 'the working class', or however one now describes those whom the economy and its corollaries disadvantage. Who can doubt him? Certainly not Stewart, who agrees that in this respect things are better in Eastern Europe. And if Scargill does believe this, he has some grounds also to believe, as I said before, that there is not much hope to be put in the Labour Party or even much of the TUC. Perhaps he does envisage a revolution, if by that is meant the capture of the state by force of arms in the name of some class or other. But if he is as 'wily' as Stewart says he is, indeed if he is even half-way sane, he almost certainly does not. To impute that belief to him is merely an insult and a smear.

What Scargill doubtless *does* believe, not least because it is a fact, appreciated by all except the most categorical of academic economists, is that the enemy is not now private capital but the state. The state is the largest employer, in the hands of a government like ours the most ruthless, and it has behind it, and behind its cloak of legitimacy, a force to impose its will that would have been beyond the wildest fantasy of a Carnegie or a Frick. Scargill, like almost everyone else, therefore sees that no dispute between a union and a nominally public corporation can be anything *but* political. Stewart's imputation of Scargill's political motive, presented as a discovery for us to wonder and shudder at, is what anyone who knows anything about any Western economy in the past two or three decades would regard as a statement of the obvious. And if, as Stewart does rightly and rather less obviously say, the extraordinary fact about Thatcher is that no one is standing up to her, in Parliament, in her own party, in the press (with one or two exceptions – including, on the matter of the Falklands, your paper) or in the judiciary, there is some reason, even if one is not a miner, and even if one accepts the most optimistic view of the supply of affordable energy at the end of the century, to be grateful for the fact that Scargill is. Indeed, one does not have to think too hard, although harder, it is true, than Stewart seems to be able to do, to see Scargill doing more for the general good than most others, with a more obvious obligation in the 'political edifice' to do so, are now doing.

Geoffrey Hawthorn
Cambridge

SIR: Yes – oh dear yes – the miners' strike tells a story and we have had to wait a while for the *London Review of Books* to give us the privilege of reading an interpretation of it in its pages. And when it comes (Vol. 6, No 16) it turns out to be based on a dream world of medieval armies, guerrilla raids, and edifices being shaken to pieces: an apocalyptic vision, with its own mythical demonology, in which ignorant armies of 'muscular' young men clash by night in their bid to take over and Scargillise Britain. Almost every aspect of the article appals. There is Mr Stewart's inability to see that the information and statistics he gives cannot possibly sustain his interpretation of them; there is his portrayal of the miners in the stereotypes used by government ministers, journalists and newsreaders – culminating in his identification of striking miners with Hitler's Brownshirts; there is his insistence that the economic imperative is the only one societies can live by, his unquestioning faith in the benign ends and motives of market forces; and, worst of all, there is his utter estrangement from what is going on in Britain right now.

Mr Stewart's central assumption is that the economic benefits that accrue to 'the community as a whole' must of necessity override any other considerations. Yet he fails to assure us that he has estimated correctly the relative weights of these putative economic benefits against the known human costs that these benefits demand, or indeed that he sets any limit at all to the 'cost of progress'. And because he assumes that there exists a consensus on what progress is he fails to make clear to us the nature of these benefits or how they will arise. In any case, what does he mean when he says that 'the community as a whole . . . benefits from economic growth and progress'? Whose economy is it? It is obvious, even from his own statistics concerning income distribution and unemployment, that there are a large number of people who can have no reasonable interest in seeing more growth if there is not going to be a more equitable distribution of that growth. Be that as it may, Mr Stewart declares it the responsibility of 'the community as a whole' to look after miners made redundant at uneconomic pits, giving them 'every assistance' in travelling to 'viable pits'. Assuredly, Mr Stewart has Norman Tebbit's bicycle in mind here, but if redundant miners are not prepared to travel – and some miners already travel sixty miles or more every day in order to work – they can be 'relocated' or 'retrained for new jobs'. I do not know what jobs he is thinking about – can he possibly mean the 'knowledge-intensive' ones? – but I have a feeling that his dreams of mass retraining, like his helpful suggestion that redundant miners should open their own small businesses, would be greeted with bitter laughter by those miners who live in areas of 25–30 per cent unemployment, whose only industry is mining and who have already learned from Cortonwood the Coal Board's way of 'relocating' people.

Perhaps realising that these token gestures, smacking so much of ministerial hypocrisy, lack all credibility, he rushes on to insist, in a flourish of specious pragmatism, that the miners 'cannot be employed indefinitely in producing a product (i.e. energy) for which there is no market'. Suddenly, it is no longer a question of insufficient resources of coal, of exhausted or uneconomic pits, but of there being no market for this coal. The NCB, in its plans for a 'flourishing industry', wishes to cut production by four million tonnes a year and it is evident from the Government's proposals to build more nuclear reactors by the end of the century that it intends to reduce by as much as possible the 70 per cent of the Electricity Board's generating capacity that is at present coal-fired. Energy demand will stay at least as high into the next century as it is now. The miners' strike is about what kind of energy we want to meet that demand. But all of this is of no interest to Mr Stewart, who, in his daunting pursuit of progress, understands only that parts of the mining industry must go: 'And if that means that some of the remoter mining villages cease to be viable communities that is a cost of progress which, however sad, has to be accepted.' Remote from whom? Sad for whom? Accepted by whom? From Mr Stewart's academic standpoint a community is like a pit or a production idea – it is either 'viable' or it isn't – but what to him is the 'streamlining' of the industry is, to many communities, the end of a way of life. If miners' livelihoods are destroyed through their supposed refusal to hold back 'inexorable geological forces' it is a 'tragic irony': but if these same livelihoods are wrecked through market forces it is merely 'sad' and 'has to be accepted'. I have every confidence that Mr Stewart will find some way of accepting the loss of other people's jobs and the laying waste of their communities. There is something nobly stoic in the way he finds apologies for MacGregor's methods of closing pits in general and

Cortonwood in particular. Mr Stewart, who works by the same short-term profit-and-loss accounts as the Coal Board itself, suggests that Cortonwood was 'uneconomic': in fact, its losses were attributable to the development of new drivages used to open up remaining reserves. The announcement of the pit's closure was made just when the NCB was coming near to seeing returns on this investment. So what do we mean when we say that something is 'uneconomic'? Is it economic to maintain an army on the Falklands? Or to send huge numbers of police to contain the miners' strike, or to sustain a Political Economy Department at a university?

Mr Stewart acknowledges the theory that the closure of Cortonwood was a provocation deliberately engineered by Thatcher and MacGregor but suggests that a 'more plausible explanation' is that this is, 'simply', MacGregor's 'way of doing business: if the pit isn't paying, close it.' As we have seen, this is also Mr Stewart's economic rationale. But what is it an explanation of? It is supposed to be an explanation of the way MacGregor does business. Question: How does MacGregor do business? Answer: The way he does it. Surely this dispute is about the way public industries *should* be doing business. What becomes of that great 'traditional British practice of settling disputes by peaceful negotiation and compromise' when the chairman of the industry is a North American whose way of doing business is quite alien to this tradition and who has made a mockery of free industrial relations? Mr Stewart himself bears witness to MacGregor's business methods: 'MacGregor was appointed to sort out British Steel, and sort it out he did: after a doomed 13-week strike, the men accepted new manning procedures which . . . raised productivity overnight by far more than had been achieved in a decade of futile negotiation.' Mr Stewart is in such ecstasies of admiration for MacGregor's palpable success in promoting economic growth that he doesn't see that he has just dismissed as 'futile' that traditional British practice of 'peaceful negotiation' which he pretends to advocate. Nor does he understand that it is, in fact, MacGregor who is 'playing a different game from the one he appears to be'. It is he who, whilst waving the flag of economic 'realism', works intimately with the present government to create a subject class whose influence on market forces, already negligible, will be naught. It is not that Mr Scargill has a firm belief that 'at the end of the day' he is going to be better off: it is rather that he knows he has nothing to lose. Faced with this kind of management, with a government that is prepared to follow through its dogmatism by docking £15 every week off the social security payments made to miners' families, and with daily caricatures in the media of those human values that have seen them through the past six months, it is little wonder that some miners have acted in ways quite remote from their usual patterns of behaviour.

Furthermore, it is quite erroneous to say, as Mr Stewart does, that only the NCB has honoured the 'Plan for Coal'. Much of the bitterness within the NUM is a consequence of the Coal Board's refusal to consult the union on how the promised investment was utilised. As for the NUM's resistance to the closure of pits, Mr Stewart should be informed that since 1979 alone, over fifty collieries have been closed – about a quarter of the total. Evidently, this is not enough for Mr Stewart, who will be satisfied with nothing less than the defeat of the miners. But if the miners are to be defeated, who is going to defeat Mrs Thatcher? And in what sense? Mr Stewart sees a left-wing revolutionary reaction to rightist tendencies towards an 'elective dictatorship' and adjures us to support the Right by virtue of the fact that it, at least, has a base in parliamentary democracy and is hence more susceptible to amelioration. He is too involved in his hatred of Scargill, the 'mob orator', the 'demagogue', the 'would-be dictator', to understand his own statistics. With an electoral system that gives 'one of the three main party groups 26 per cent of the vote but only 3½ per cent of the Parliamentary seats', and can give a government with only 31 per cent of the electorate a huge majority, Mr Scargill 'and his friends' cannot make a sham of parliamentary democracy: it already is one.

Paul Milican
London SW4

SIR: If Michael Stewart's article on the miners' strike had appeared in one of Rupert Murdoch's classier papers, or in the *Daily Telegraph*, it would have occasioned no surprise and stirred, I imagine, hardly a ripple. But I was shocked by its appearance in your pages, and by the prominence you gave it. It can certainly be taken as an example of the way in which a dispute of this kind drives even supposedly 'enlightened' sections of the intelligentsia into the camp of reaction. But that in itself is nothing new. Mr Stewart's article falls squarely into the mould of those middle-class cries of anger and fear at working-class or popular militancy which have been repeatedly heard ever since the French Revolution first seriously alarmed the possessing classes.

Many of the classic ingredients are there: the claim that the strike, or its leader(s), is aimed at revolution; that 'democracy' is under threat (I wonder that Mr Stewart did not also talk about Civilisation and Society-As-We-Know-It); that the workers are being exploited and misled by 'demagogues'; that the striking miners constitute a 'mob' or 'mobs'. Anyone who cares to take a look at Matthew Arnold's *Culture and Anarchy* – to take just one instance – will find there much the same heated talk about 'roughs' and 'mobs', and much the same demands for governmental firmness and the defeat of the 'rioters'. All inspired by a Hyde Park demonstration in favour of parliamentary reform which led to the trampling down of some of the railings. *Plus ça change* . . . Added to this is a contemporary echo of the old 19th-century liberal economic version of rationality: if economic 'progress' requires that 'some of the remoter' (remote from where?) 'mining villages cease to be viable' – well, that is 'sad' but, finally, just too bad. The same note was struck by Malthus and his supposedly 'scientific' followers a century and a half ago (and Arnold, to his credit, attacked it). Somehow it is always the working class who are expected to pay the heaviest price for this apparent 'rationality'. Opposition to it is 'patently absurd'. We should be importing cheap coal from South Africa – never mind that it's a racist slave economy – while letting our own coal industry's scale be dictated by the 'market'.

Coupled with this inhuman, and ultimately blinkered, 'economic sense', we find an equal indifference to the hardships endured by striking miners and their families. Mr Stewart finds space to laud 'the dignity and guts of isolated working miners', and to add his ha'p'orth to the condemnations of 'the daily violence . . . on the picket lines' and the 'mobs . . . looking for a punch-up'. But what explanation does he have to offer of the fact that for more than six months more than three-quarters of Britain's miners and their families have been prepared to live in the direst poverty, prepared to forgo every minimal luxury, prepared to depend upon what the active solidarity and support of the Labour movement can provide?

On the one hand, he suggests that a majority of miners 'probably oppose' the strike – a statement for which he offers no evidence at all, and for which, so far as I know, there *is* no evidence. Indeed, there is plenty of evidence that the reverse is true. Miners have had every encouragement, from the Coal Board, from the Government, from the press and media, to break the strike and return to work. Week after week, a crumbling of the strike has been predicted. It has not happened. I suppose that Mr Stewart would attribute that to 'intimidation'. Just as the only explanation he can offer for the solidity of the strike is that the miners have been misled by the 'demagogue' and 'would-be dictator', Arthur Scargill. It almost passes belief that this kind of nonsense can appear in a serious intellectual journal. It rests on attributing near-demonic powers of persuasion and manipulation to Mr Scargill, and virtually nil intelligence, integrity or independence to the miners themselves.

This is such an insulting view of the miners and their families that it is hardly worth discussing. But once again it fits a traditional pattern, identified long ago by William Cobbett: the agitator theory. This is the view that 'behind' every protest or revolt lies a tiny bunch of agitators, troublemakers etc, who, somewhat paradoxically, succeed in manipulating gullible ordinary people into taking extreme actions to which they are 'probably opposed'. It was a silly theory in Cobbett's day, as he pointed out, and it still is. It doesn't even fit the facts of the miners' strike, which was certainly not engineered or initiated by Arthur Scargill, but began with an unofficial, spontaneous stoppage in Yorkshire in response to the sudden threat to close Cortonwood colliery. The 'completely unscrupulous' Mr Scargill, whose 'game is revolution', according to Mr Stewart – although once again he offers no evidence for either of these assertions – is not so stupid as to have chosen to launch a national coal strike at the end of a winter, just when the demand for coal is falling. For a supposed revolutionary, that would be amazingly incompetent.

It is revealing to find an academic accepting so uncritically the media's crude personalisation of the dispute, with his demand that 'Scargill' be 'fought and defeated'. Anyone with any experience of this dispute knows that it is the miners, and the miners' union, who are in conflict with the NCB, the Government and their supporters like Mr Stewart. Mr Scargill leads the miners, but if they were not ready and willing to follow him, he would be utterly powerless. Those, like Mr Stewart, who use the military terminology of 'surrender' and 'defeat' should know that they are opposing, not an individual 'demagogue' and 'would-be dictator', but a large body of working people who, for more than six months, have commanded active support from an even wider range of people who reject both the supposed economic rationality and the unsubstantiated smears of commentators like Mr Stewart.

Anthony Arblaster
Sheffield

SIR: Michael Stewart calls it 'ironic' that 'those who believe in democracy, the rule of law, and the traditional British practice of settling disputes by peaceful negotiation and compromise' should be supporting the Government in the miners' strike. I would have thought a better description would be 'incredible'. Does Mr Stewart seriously

believe that if the Government 'won' the current dispute – to the ecstatic applause of Fleet Street – any further opposition to its policies would be effective, or that people would dare even to initiate it? It is to be hoped that if Mrs Thatcher does secure the 'victory' Mr Stewart is so anxious to see, he will raise no complaint over the assaults on 'traditional British practice' which the Government will launch as the process of creating Thatcher's utopia begins in earnest. Mr Stewart will be amongst those who will have given it its real mandate.
Alan Weston
Crosby

SIR: Whatever may be the other merits of Michael Stewart's diatribe against Arthur Scargill and the NUM (*LRB*, Vol. 6, No 16), he does not further his argument by casting Scargill 'in the mould of demagogues and would-be dictators down the ages, from those who threatened the Athenian city-state to those who have wrought havoc in our own century'. Our word 'demagogue' does have a Greek etymology, being derived from *demagogos*. But that word meant literally 'leader of the mass of the people', and such leaders were as structurally necessary to the direct democracy of ancient Athens as elected representatives are to our own 'Western' democracies. It was hostile critics of Athenian democracy like Plato who gave to *demagogos* its pejorative sense of *mis*leader of the people, and it was men of that ilk rather than the so-called 'demagogues' who not only threatened but (in the words of J. S. Mill) 'on the first show of an opportunity were ready to compass the subversion of the democracy'.
Paul Cartledge
Clare College, Cambridge

SIR: If I had ever had any doubts about the depth of the passions stirred up by the miners' strike, the thoroughly intemperate tone of the replies to my article would have dispelled them (*LRB*, Vol. 6, Nos 17 and 18). I have picked my way as best I can between Mr Hawthorn's patches of intellectual incoherence, Mr Milican's laborious sarcasms and Mr Arblaster's squeals of outrage that the *LRB* should have published my piece in the first place, and tried to focus on the main points they seem to be making. These fall under two headings – economic and political.

My basic economic argument was – and remains – that it is nonsense to demand that no pit should be closed except on grounds of exhaustion or safety, regardless of how much it costs to produce coal from that pit. Yet this is what Mr Scargill has been demanding all along, and is still describing as 'non-negotiable'. The implication of this doctrine is that even if coal can be imported for around £30 a tonne (from Poland, since Mr Arblaster does not like my reference to South Africa), we should nevertheless be made to consume British coal which may, in the uneconomic pits, be costing £50 or £100 a tonne to produce. This process obviously involves heavy subsidies. Mr Scargill, and his intellectual supporters like Messrs Milican and Arblaster, seem to imagine that these subsidies come from heaven, or perhaps are paid for exclusively by the rich. On the contrary: for *any* given macroeconomic fiscal stance (whether it be Mrs Thatcher's present one, or some other much more sensible one) these subsidies must mean either higher taxes or lower public expenditure, and either of these, particularly the latter, is likely to hit those in the bottom 20 or 30 per cent of the income distribution quite hard. Do your respondents understand this point? If so, do they attach no weight to it at all? Do they still think that no pit should be closed except on grounds of exhaustion, regardless of how big these adverse effects on taxes or public expenditure may be?

This brings me to what is clearly one of the most contentious things I said in my article. Since it is central to the debate, and since I stick by every syllable of it, perhaps I may repeat it in full: 'The community as a whole, which benefits from economic growth and progress, has a responsibility to help those on whom the costs of economic progress fall most heavily: miners made redundant at uneconomic pits must be given every assistance in travelling to, or being relocated at, viable pits, or in being re-trained for new jobs, or being aided financially in setting up their own small businesses. But they cannot be employed indefinitely in producing a product for which there is no market. And if that means that some of the remoter mining villages cease to be viable communities, that is a cost of progress which, however sad, has to be accepted.'

Mr Hawthorn has particular difficulty in grasping the concept of 'the community as a whole': 'I certainly know of no economic or political agency of that name. Stewart must mean the Government . . . ' No, I do not mean the Government. When I talk about economic growth and progress benefiting the community as a whole, I mean that the vast majority of the British people are better off than they were fifty or a hundred years ago, or than the vast majority of the Ethiopian or Bangladeshi people are today. By 'better off' I mean that real gross domestic product per capita is higher – and before that definition elicits a stream of protest let me say that I am familiar with the literature on measuring economic welfare, and that my proposition would still hold if one took much more basic indicators such as life expectancy or infant mortality. Mr Milican has some problems with the concept of the community as a whole being better off, too. 'It is obvious,' he says, 'even from his own statistics concerning income distribution and unemployment, that there are a large number of people who can have no reasonable interest in seeing more growth if there is not going to be a more equitable distribution of that growth.' Some odd logic here: if there is not going to be a more equitable *distribution* of income and employment (which is presumably what he means), then the only way for the poor to become better off *is* to have more growth.

The essential point, however, is this: of its very nature, the economic growth that increases average living standards means the displacement of old industries, old products and old skills. Those who suffer from this process ought to be assisted by society (or in this context, if Mr Hawthorn likes, the Government) to adjust to these changes. I don't know why Mr Milican should sneer at the idea of relocating or retraining miners, or financially assisting some of them to set up small businesses: the establishment of small businesses has been responsible for much of the phenomenal growth of employment in the United States over the past twenty years. It may be only a small part of the answer in Britain, though that is not self-evident: but why dismiss it out of hand? If the state does not assist miners in these various ways (and you would never know from your respondents' letters that so far there have been no compulsory redundancies in the industry), then either it has to pay them to produce increasingly uneconomic coal, or it has to sack them and leave them to their fate. In my view, both alternatives are unacceptable.

Finally – on the economic side – let me make it quite clear that while I regard Scargill's case as economic nonsense, I am far from believing that pits should necessarily be closed as soon as they become unprofitable. Of course there are social costs and benefits to be taken account of (and they were taken account of by the Labour Government in the 1960s to which I was an adviser). I welcome the kind of proposal made by David Metcalf and Gavyn Davies: that the pace of pit closures and job losses over the next decade should be determined by these wider social criteria as well as by narrow financial considerations. If Mr Scargill was prepared to negotiate on this basis, a reasonable solution to the dispute might be possible. But as long as he is not, it is not.

I turn now to the political aspects of the matter. My argument, in a nutshell, was that Mr Scargill has organised a strike which has no basis in the democratic procedures of his union, which uses illegal mass picketing and involves violence and intimidation in an effort to change government policy, if possible to bring down the Government itself, and perhaps any future government that Mr Scargill disapproves of; that this strategy is unacceptable in a democracy and must be defeated; that it – and the support it is getting – are nevertheless understandable by reference, not only to Mrs Thatcher's appallingly unfair economic policies, but also to her indifference to the spirit of democracy, and the highly questionable legitimacy of some of her actions.

Your respondents react to this argument in various ways (though all of them largely ignore my categorical condemnation of Mrs Thatcher's policies and procedures). Mr Arblaster challenges my rather cautious statement that the strike was probably opposed by a majority of the union's membership, calling it 'a statement for which he offers no evidence at all, and for which, so far as I know, there *is* no evidence.' Really? If Mr Arblaster is to pronounce on these matters, he should master a few facts. Does he not know that in the 11 areas which *did* ballot last March, 18,002 men voted for a strike, and 40,554 against? That seems to me rather powerful evidence in support of my view. While Mr Arblaster denies that a majority of miners were opposed to strike action, Mr Hawthorn implicitly concedes the point, but makes clear that he is untroubled by it: 'it is by no means agreed that every contentious decision taken by an elected body in the name of its electors should be balloted. If it were . . . most of the liberal legislation that people like Michael Stewart and me and no doubt you yourself approve of and enjoy would never have been enacted.' Presumably Mr Hawthorn is thinking of, for example, the death penalty, which Parliament (belatedly) abolished, and has refused to reintroduce, although there is clear evidence that a majority of the population is in favour of it. This example does, of course, raise some interesting questions about the nature and working of democratic systems, but if Mr Hawthorn considers it justifies the NUM executive in ignoring the union's own rulebook, which states that a strike can only be called if sanctioned by a majority vote in a national ballot, he should say so explicitly, so that the absurdity of the analogy is plain for all to see.

The fact that there is good reason to suppose that a majority of miners were against the strike from the start makes particularly distasteful the conduct of Mr Scargill and his executive, who have been responsible for the six months of hardship in the mining communities – which, incidentally, it does not require Mr Arblaster to explain to us. But it is not the central point. Whether sanctioned by a majority of its members or not, this seems to me in large part a political strike. What is a political strike? It is not easy to provide a precise definition, though I would hope to do better than Mr Hawthorn, who offers us the profound tautology that 'no dispute between a union and a nominally public corporation can be anything *but* political.'

Let me suggest two scenarios. First, if the NUM, after a national ballot, went on strike in support of a 10 per cent wage claim, with the NCB refusing to raise its final offer of 5 per cent, and the Government making it clear that it would not increase the industry's external financing limit whatever the outcome of the strike, I would not call that a political strike. It would be for the Coal Board – like any private employer – to decide whether to concede the wage demand, put up prices and reduce its labour force in response to any subsequent fall in sales; or to sit the strike out in the hope that it would crumble; or to negotiate. The second scenario is at the other extreme: suppose the power workers – who could bring the country to a halt within minutes if they wanted to – announced that they would go on strike in 24 hours' time unless by then Mrs Thatcher had gone to Buckingham Palace and tendered her resignation. Not much doubt about the political nature of that strike. Somewhere between these two extremes there is a murky area one can argue about. My contention is that the present strike is much closer to the second scenario than the first. The NUM is seeking to extract from the Government a large, increasing and open-ended subsidy – in other words, to force the Government to change one of its major policies, or yield place to a government with other policies. To this end, it is using or condoning illegal picketing, intimidation and violence in an effort to get other groups of workers – including, crucially, the power workers – to stop work or at least restrict output, thus producing a general level of economic and social hardship that no government could tolerate. Mrs Thatcher indeed bears a large measure of responsibility for this state of affairs: but that does not legitimise the conduct of Mr Scargill and his executive. Mr Scargill must, as I said in my article, be defeated. 'If the miners are to be defeated,' inquires Mr Milican, 'who is going to defeat Mrs Thatcher?' What a disgraceful question. To his credit – given some of the people whose support he must rely on – Mr Kinnock provided the right answer to it some time ago: she must be defeated at the ballot box, not on the streets.

The only one of your respondents to whom I would concede a point is Mr Cartledge, who objects to my comparison of Mr Scargill with the demagogues 'who threatened the Athenian city-state'. I particularly had in mind Cleon, described in the *Cambridge Ancient History* as 'insensitive, unscrupulous, plausible, vain, resolute and violent'. But I would agree, on reflection, that Mr Cartledge is probably right in saying that leaders like Cleon were structurally necessary to the democracy of ancient Athens. I would certainly not wish, in the context of contemporary Britain, to say the same about Mr Scargill.

Michael Stewart
University College London

SIR: Both Arthur Scargill and Margaret Thatcher seem to me to be demagogues, but Scargill is better at it than Thatcher is. In his rather hysterical response to Michael Stewart's article, Anthony Arblaster (*LRB*, Vol. 6, No 18) assumes that Scargill would need 'near-demonic powers of persuasion and manipulation' to fit Stewart's stereotype. Surely those capacities, working off large-scale feelings of insecurity and economic hardship, are exactly what the finest demagogues have; the history of this century offers many salutary examples, though not in Britain. But why, sadly, should we be exempt?

Andrew Robinson
London N1

SIR: How much does a pit have to cost the country before your correspondents will agree to its closure? The Treforgan colliery in South Wales lost £6.5m in 1981–82, which works out at £13,000 per employee. As Christopher Huhne put it, writing in the *Guardian* of 3 May: 'It would have been cheaper for the taxpayer to pay each Treforgan employee more than double the then male average wage NOT to mine coal.' Where do your correspondents think the money comes from? Defence? The universities? No, it will come from those without the muscle of the service chiefs or the dons or the NUM. I refer to the pensioners, the unemployed and the sick. Funny how they don't rate a mention in this debate: it's as though finite resources are a consequence of Mrs Thatcher. Some people seem to think that pit closures are also a result of a specifically Tory philosophy. Again I quote Mr Huhne: 'the Tories have closed fewer pits in five years than the Labour Government managed to do in the single year of 1968.' Mr Arblaster (*LRB*, Vol. 6, No 18) says there is plenty of evidence that most miners support the strike. Why, then, has there been no ballot?

There are many sticks with which Mrs Thatcher's government could be beaten. Her treatment of the mineworkers is not one of them. She knows that, and she knows that the majority of the country knows it. Mr Huhne's *Guardian* article asked: 'Is Mrs Thatcher in reality the miners' best friend?' We don't know whether she is any more, but it's

quite obvious who is *her* best friend and who is doing the most to ensure her re-election.
R. J. Horesh
York

SIR: Paul Milican (*LRB*, Vol. 6, No 18) fails to inform us of some salient facts in the debate over the miners' strike, which is not surprising because they make his arguments look, in places, pretty silly. He tells us that since 1979 alone over fifty collieries have been closed. Why not inform us at the same time that Mr Callaghan's government closed 300 pits? To read Mr Milican's letter, one would think that pit closures began in 1979, not a decade and a half before. It is true that the NCB has not kept exactly to its pledges in the 'Plan for Coal'. It has bettered them by investing £650 million more in the coal industry than had been agreed under the plan. Of somewhat lesser import, Mr MacGregor is not a North American, as Mr Milican puts it: he was born in, and lived for a considerable number of years in, Scotland.
Paul Fairey
Bristol

1. *The Miners' Next Step* by Frank Richards (Junius, 1984). *Taking Control: A Handbook for Trade-Unionists* by Mike Freeman (Junius, 1984).

Angela Carter

Noovs' Hoovs in the Trough

The Official Foodie Handbook by Ann Barr and Paul Levy
(Ebury, 1984)
An Omelette and a Glass of Wine by Elizabeth David
(Hale, 1984)
Chez Panisse Menu Cookbook by Alice Waters, foreword by Jane Grigson
(Chatto, 1984)

'Be modern – worship food,' exhorts the cover of *The Official Foodie Handbook*. One of the ironies resulting from the North/South dichotomy of our planet is the appearance of this odd little book, a *vademecum* to a widespread and unashamed cult of conspicuous gluttony in the advanced industrialised countries, at just the time when Ethiopia is struck by a widely publicised famine, and the rest of Africa is suffering a less widely publicised one. Not Africa alone, of course, is chronically hungry all the time and acutely hungry some of the time: at a conservative estimate, eight hundred million people in the world live in constant fear of starvation. Under the circumstances, it might indeed make good 20th-century sense to worship food, but punters of 'foodism' (as Ann Barr and Paul Levy jokily dub this phenomenon) are evidently not about to drop to their knees because they are starving.

'Foodies', according to Barr and Levy, are 'children of the consumer boom' who consider 'food to be an art, on a level with painting or drama'. It is the 'art' bit that takes their oral fetishism out of the moral scenario in which there is an implicit reprimand to greed in the constantly televised spectacle of the gaunt peasants who have trudged miles across drought-devastated terrain to score their scant half-crust. ('That bread alone was worth the journey,' they probably remark, just as Elizabeth David says of a trip to an out-of-the-way eatery in France.) Art has a morality of its own, and the aesthetics of cooking and eating aspire, in 'foodism', towards the heights of food-for-food's sake. Therefore the Third World can go suck its fist.

The Official Foodie Handbook is in the same format as, and it comes from the same firm that brought out, *The Official Sloane Ranger Handbook*. That is to say, it is 'a *Harpers & Queen* Publication', which means it springs from the loins of the magazine that most consistently monitors the lifestyle of new British affluence. These 'official handbooks' are interesting as a genre. The idea has been taken up with enthusiasm by *Harpers & Queen*, but the original appears to be *The Official Preppy Handbook*, published in the USA in the early days of the first Reagan Presidency. This slim volume was a lighthearted check-list of the attributes of the North American upper middle class, so lighthearted it gave the impression it did not have a heart at all. The entire tone was most carefully judged: a mixture of contempt for and condescension towards the objects of its scrutiny, a tone which contrived to reassure the socially aspiring that emulation of their betters was a game that might legitimately be played hard just *because* it could not be taken seriously, so that snobbery involved no moral compromise.

The book was an ill-disguised celebration of the snobbery it affected to mock and, under its thinly ironic surface, was nothing more nor less than an etiquette manual for a class newly emergent under Reaganomics. It instructed the *nouveaux riches* in the habits and manners of the *vieux riches* so that they could pass undetected amongst them. It sold like hot cakes.

The British version duly appeared on the stands a year or so later, tailored to the only slightly different demands of a youth newly gilded by Thatcherism. *The Official Foodie Handbook* mentions two fresh additions to the genre in the USA: *The Yuppie Handbook* ('the state-of-the-art manual for Young Urban Professionals') and *The Official Young Aspiring Professionals Fast-Track Handbook*. There seems to be no precise equivalent for the Young Aspiring Professional in Thatcher's Britain: the Tory Trade Unionist (or TUTU) might fill the bill in some ways, but not in others. The Yuppie is, presumably, driven by an ambition he or she now has the confidence to reveal nakedly, an ambition to go *one better* than the *vieux riches*. In Britain, it is never possible to go one better than the *vieux riches*, who always own everything anyway. *Harpers & Queen*, the self-appointed arbiter of these matters this side of the herring-pond, identifies the strivers peremptorily as Noovos, or Noovs. There is something a touch Yellowplush Papers about all this, but there you go. It would seem that

The Official Foodie Handbook is an attempt to exploit the nearest British equivalent to the Yuppie market, for, according to the arbiters, food is a cornerstone of this hysterical new snobbery.

Very special economic circumstances, reminiscent of those of the decline of the Roman Empire and also of the heyday of Edwardian England as described by Jack London in *People of the Abyss*, establish gluttony as the mark of a class on the rise. *The Official Foodie Handbook* notes: 'It takes several things to support a Foodie culture: high-class shops, fast transport bringing fresh produce from the land, enlightened well-paid eater-outers who will support the whole expensive edifice, lower-paid workers to make the food. Suddenly they are all present.'

Piggery triumphant has invaded even the pages of the *Guardian*, hitherto synonymous with non-conformist sobriety. Instead of its previous modest column of recipes and restaurant reviews, the paper now boasts an entire page devoted to food and wine once a week: more space than it gives to movies, as much as it customarily gives to books. Piggery has spawned a glossy bimonthly, *A la Carte*, a gastronomic *Penthouse* devoted to glamour photography, the subject of which is not the female body imaged as if it were good enough to eat, but food photographed according to the conventions of the pin-up. (Barr and Levy, ever quick with a quip, dub this kind of thing 'gastro-porn'.) The colour plates are of awesome voluptuousness. Oh, that coconut kirsch roulade in the first issue! If, as Lévi-Strauss once opined, 'to eat is to fuck,' then that coconut kirsch roulade is just asking for it. Even if the *true* foodie knows there is something not quite . . . about a coconut kirsch roulade as a concept. It is just a bit . . . just a bit *Streatham*. Its vowels are subtly wrong. It is probably related to a Black Forest gâteau.

A la Carte is an over-eager social climber and is bound to give the game away. 'Do you know the difference between a good Brie and a bad one? One made in a factory or on a farm? If *you* don't, your guests might.' Then you will be universally shunned and nobody will attend your dinner parties ever again. This mincing and finicking obsession with food opens up whole new areas of potential social shame. No wonder the British find it irresistible. Indeed, in Britain an enlightened interest in food has always been the mark of the kind of person who uses turns of phrase such as 'an enlightened interest in food'. If a certain kind of upper-class British cookery represents the staff's revenge upon its masters, an enthusiasm for the table, the grape and the stove itself is a characteristic of the deviant sub-section of the

British bourgeoisie that has always gone in for the arts with the diligent enthusiasm of (as they would put it) 'the amateur in the true sense of the word'. This class is more than adequately represented by Mrs Elizabeth David.

In *An Omelette and a Glass of Wine*, a collection of her journalism dating back to the Fifties, there is an article describing the serendipitous nature of provisioning in London just after the war. Mrs David remembers how 'one of my sisters turned up from Vienna with a hare which she claimed had been caught by hand outside the State Opera House.' A whole world is contained within that sentence, which could be the first line of a certain kind of novel and sums up an entire way of life. It is no surprise to discover that Mrs David admires the novels of Sybille Bedford, nor that she was a friend of Norman Douglas. It *is* a little surprising that she has never turned her acclaimed prose style to fiction, but has always restricted herself to culinary matters, if in the widest sense, taking aboard aspects of history, geography and literature. Her books, like her journalism, are larded with quotations, from recherché antique cookery books to Virginia Woolf, Montaigne, Walter Scott. Her approach is not in the least like the gastronomic dandyism of the 'food-for-food's sake' crowd; she is holistic about it. She is obviously a truly civilised person and, for her, knowing how to eat and to prepare good food is not an end in itself, but as much a part of civilisation as is the sensuous appreciation of poetry, art or music. In the value system of the person who is 'civilised' in this way, the word carries the same connotation as 'moral' does in the value system of Dr F. R. Leavis.

Mrs David's journalism consists of discursive meditations upon food and foreign parts, but, in the course of *An Omelette and a Glass of Wine*, one learns a discreet but enticing amount about her private life, enough to appreciate that her deftness with the pans is not a sign of domesticity but of worldliness. She is obviously the kind of woman before whom waiters grovel when she arrives alone at a restaurant. One imagines her to be one of those tall, cool, elegant blondes who make foreigners come over all funny, and it is plain that she is the kind of Englishwoman who, like the heroines of Nancy Mitford, only fully come to life Abroad. Her recipes are meticulous, authentic and reliable, and have formed the basic repertoire, not only of a thousand British late-20th-century dinner parties, but also of a goodly number of restaurants up and down these islands. She has been the conduit whereby French provincial cooking and French country cooking, of a kind which in France is being replaced by pizzas and hamburgers, may be raptly savoured in rural England.

The eponymous 'Chez Panisse' of the *Chez Panisse Menu Cookbook* is directly inspired by Mrs David, who now spans the globe. The cook-proprietor of 'Chez Panisse', Alice Waters, says in her introduction: 'I bought Elizabeth David's *French Country Cooking* and I cooked everything in it, from beginning to end. I admired her aesthetics of food and wanted a restaurant that had the same feeling as the pictures on the covers of her books.' It seems an unusual desire, to create a restaurant that looks like a book-jacket, and most of the cooks from whom Mrs David originally acquired her recipes would think it even more unusual to learn to cook from a book instead of from Mum. But all this must spring naturally from the kind of second-order experience that lies behind the cult of food. Alice Waters is a girl from New Jersey who earned her culinary stripes by resolutely cooking her way through a compendium of French recipes assembled by an Englishwoman, using ingredients from Northern California and serving them up to the me-generation in a restaurant named after an old movie. The result is a Franco-Californian cuisine of almost ludicrous refinement, in which the simplest item is turned into an object of mystification. A ripe melon, for example, is sought for as if it were a piece of the True Cross. Ms Waters applauds herself on serving one. 'Anyone could have chosen a perfect melon, but unfortunately most people don't take the time or make an effort to choose carefully and understand what that potentially sublime fruit should be.' She talks as if selecting a melon were an existential choice of a kind to leave Jean-Paul Sartre stumped.

Behind Ms Waters' wincingly exquisite cuisine lies some post-hippy Platonism to do with the real and the phoney. 'Depersonalised, assembly-line fast food may be "convenient" and "time-saving" but it deprives the senses and denies true nourishment,' she opines. Like anorexia nervosa, the neurotic condition in which young girls voluntarily starve themselves to death, the concept of 'true nourishment' can exist only in a society where hunger happens to other people. Ms Waters has clearly lost her marbles through too great a concern with grub, so much so that occasionally 'Alice Waters' sounds like a pseudonym for S. J. Perelman. 'I do think best while holding a tomato or a leg of lamb,' she confides. For a person of my generation, there is also the teasing question: could she be the Alice, and 'Chez Panisse' the *real* Alice's Restaurant, of the song by Arlo Guthrie? And if this is so, where did it all go wrong?

Frank Kermode

Canons

Holy Scripture: Canon, Authority, Criticism
by James Barr
(Oxford, 1983)
Structuralist Interpretations of Biblical Myth
by Edmund Leach and D. Alan Aycock
(Cambridge, 1983)

For reasons that are not immediately obvious, the question of canons is at present much discussed by literary critics. Their canons are of course so called only by loose analogy with the Biblical canons, so it may be of more than strictly clerical interest that there is a major row going on among the professionals who deal with the real thing. This powerfully written book by James Barr is for the most part a polemic against a new wave of Biblical criticism called by its proponents 'canonical criticism', and to get the hang of Barr's book one needs some idea of what he is attacking.

Canonical criticism is not a one-man operation, but its most distinguished theorist, and Barr's main target, is Brevard S. Childs, a professor at Yale. Barr is Regius Professor of Hebrew at Oxford and a scholar of immense distinction, so this is not a battle of pygmies. The arguments of Childs are most conveniently set forth in his *Introduction to the Old Testament as Scripture* (1979). Briefly, he wants to reinstate in a modern form the concept of canon which, first weakened by the Reformation, has collapsed during the past two centuries, when a predominantly historical style of criticism has directed attention away from the wholeness of the Bible to the study of individual books and segments.

It was plain even in the earliest days of the new German Biblical criticism that the historical critics would dismantle the canon. The Bible was dissolved into its constituent *biblia*. The bringing together of these discrete books into an exclusive group deemed in principle to be uniformly inspired now seemed little more than a historical curiosity. The element of fortuity in the process, and the obsolete mental attitudes it commemorated, were perhaps not without some interest: but the canon as such could no longer be the prime object of study. Childs doesn't want to medievalise our view of the canon, or undo the vast achievements of what he calls 'traditio-historical' criticism: what he wants is to reduce the tension between that tradition and the one he seeks to revivify. He wants to look with a modern eye at the whole Bible as a literary and theological unit 'with fixed parameters', while recognising that the canon was the product of a series of decisions which need to be considered historically.

The climax of this process of decision was the final fixing of the Jewish canon at the end of the first century of the present era. It was about that time that Judaism became a religion of the Book. After the destruction of the Temple in AD 70 there could be no Temple cult, and in any case there were already many more Jews in the Diaspora than in Palestine. The Book, constructed out of elements which had their own disparate histories, became the preservative of national and religious identity, and would remain normative for Jews throughout history.

Childs sounds moderate; he thinks the canonical critics and the historians can live together, only requiring the other party to yield some ground: to admit that the canon isn't simply a wrapping that has to be removed before one can get at the historical goodies inside. The canon remains a unit, endowed with perpetual applicability. Before it existed there could be rewriting and updating; afterwards modernisation had to take the form of commentary, and the sense of the Scripture would be determined by subsequent applications.

Obviously, then, the canon must not be disintegrated. However, this kind of criticism stresses the inseparability of understanding and application, and so it is committed to a hermeneutic position very unlikely to appeal to the 'traditio-historians' Childs would prefer to conciliate.

James Barr is one of them. He takes a wholly different view of what it is to read a book, and especially a book that purports to be history – to speak of events that happened and persons who existed. He thinks it only sensible to hold that individual books are more important than the collections in which they may be found; and he also thinks that what the books are about is even more important than the books themselves. It is not the canon that confers authority on its members, but the events and persons they report. Barr says very forcibly that to behave as if this were not so is dishonest. Childs is his main target, but he deals some terrible blows to less respectable authors of similar persuasion.

Barr notes that the people represented in the Bible managed very well without a canon. It never occurred to Paul, dictating his letters to an amanuensis, that they would later form part of one. When Childs argues for a connection between the identity of a Church and its possession of a canon, Barr replies that the connection is illusory. What harm would be done to the Roman Catholic Church, he asks, if it had to get along without the Book of Wisdom, which is part of its canon? And what harm would come to the Protestant Churches if they had to declare that same book canonical?

In its purest or most extreme form the canonical argument is that 66 books are inspired, and that nothing else is. But this is a position entirely lacking in Scriptural support: moreover it is offensive in its implication that there is no truth outside those books. And who would want to say that Jude deserves canonical privileges denied to the *Confessions* of St Augustine? Well, Augustine, very likely. But it can be made to seem very odd that a choice made seventeen hundred or more years ago, on the basis of arguments of which we don't know the details and probably wouldn't accept in any case, should demand perpetual endorsement.

As to the Old Testament canon, Barr questions whether it is proper to speak of such a thing. The textbooks (with some support from the Talmud) say that the Jewish canon was established at Jamnia about the end of the first century of the present era: but according to Barr, whatever may have happened at that Council had nothing to do with canon. And the so-called Alexandrian canon of the Greek Old Testament isn't a canon at all – just the Torah plus some other books. And even if it were proper to speak of a Jewish canon, it was much less important than it appears 'to those who have seen the notion of canon through the glass of the Calvinistic Reformation'.

All this amounts to saying that even if there is a canon we should be far better off without it. Holding that opinion, it is obvious that Barr rejects any idea of making historical and canonical criticism work together: for the historical critic, the canon is mostly an impediment.

The more general implications of this disagreement may be expressed thus. For Childs, it is the meaning constituted by the canon – the *final* meaning – that is the interesting one. For Barr, only the *original* meaning matters, and it has to be got at by cumulative historical research. The difference, therefore, is in the end a consequence of incompatible hermeneutic predispositions. Barr's is a 'recognitive' hermeneutics along the lines, say, of E. D. Hirsch. Childs prefers the other sort, now by most people associated with the name of H.-G. Gadamer, which denies the separation between understanding and application, between 'meaning' and 'significance'. Thus it appears to Barr that Childs, in neglecting the original sense and context, destroys the meaning, whereas to Childs it must seem that Barr is the victim of a myth which has supported historical criticism throughout its relatively brief history, and which claims that we can have immediate access to objects and texts remote from us in time, that we have no difficulty in liberating ourselves from the constraints of our own historical situation.

Barr admits that his method was discovered only lately, but maintains that it is nevertheless God-given, an 'ultimate datum of faith'. The books of the Bible are valuable because they provide access, however difficult, to real events and persons: to the truth of history. He has little but contempt for his opponents, trained, he says, in hermeneutics, especially in bastard versions of Bultmann's hermeneutics, and having, as he sees it, no interest whatever in the truth. 'The final criterion for theology cannot be relevance; it can only be truth.' The historian's predecessors may be seen to have been conditioned, more than they can themselves have known, by the prejudices of their times: but he himself need not be. Argument to the contrary is simply wrong. The point isn't argued; the rival view is simply treated as self-evidently absurd and repellent in itself and in its consequences, one of which is the practice of treating the Bible as a 'separate cognitive zone'. That it was so treated for centuries is dismissed as an error one should no longer endorse.

Barr remarks justly that some of the rote rejections of history by lesser canonical critics would have disgusted their supposed godfather Bultmann, who was a historian as well as a hermeneutic philosopher. Yet Bultmann shows how hard it is, in the end, to keep history and hermeneutics apart. He believed that 'the interpretation of Biblical writings is subject to exactly the same conditions of understanding as any other literature.' But he also believed that all understanding requires fore-understanding: that is, it depends on something presupposed. In the case of the Bible, that fore-understanding must, for him, be theological. Bultmann's solution was to say that 'historical exegesis rests on an existential confrontation with history and therefore coincides with theological exegesis,' but one imagines that this formula would not attract Barr. It does, however, express rather well the problems of historians who are also believers. In the past, some have even left religious for secular institutions in order to avoid seeming contradictions between their professions of faith and their research. For a prior commitment to the New Testament as the donnée of faith is, on the face of it, in conflict with a posterior commitment to break it up into separate historical documents. Barr solves his dilemma by claiming that there is a religious vocation to pure linguistic and historical criticism.

Writing about these conflicts, Gadamer remarks that the historian is always seeking in the text 'what the text is not, of itself, seeking to provide . . . he will always go back behind the [texts] and the meaning they express to enquire into the reality of which they are the involuntary expression.' The critic, on the other hand, is concerned with the text for the sake of its own beauty and truth. Their practices are now in conflict, after a long period in which criticism allowed itself to be regarded as 'an ancillary discipline to history'. It is Gadamer's opinion that the historical method, as advocated now by Barr, violates the intention of the text; his opponents think that Gadamer's hermeneutics violates the intention of the author.

Whatever one thinks of that, it is interesting to reflect, with Gadamer, that neither the historian nor his opponent behaves as if he were perfectly conscious of the myth underlying his operations. The historian refers his events and persons to a context of total history; the canonical critic establishes his total text and context with fixed parameters. In Gadamer's terms, then, both sides undertake a task of application: so the historian is, presumably without wishing to, performing in relation to 'the great text' – the history of the world itself – what the canonical critic attempts in relation to the world of his 'separate cognitive zone'. Again one can hardly suppose that this argument would appeal to Barr.

The new canonical criticism might conceivably, in some very qualified way, revive older modes of attention to the canon. If you treat the canon as a self-sufficient world, with many mysterious, occult correspondences within it, you are in touch with ancient techniques that may be modernised, possibly with some help from secular literary criticism. In that field, books which may, by analogy, be called canonical, are given special sorts of attention. The whole idea of literary canons, undogmatic though it must be, is at present under attack by those who regard it as arbitrary or authoritarian, and wish to end the distinction between 'inside' and 'outside' books. This attitude is, ultimately, founded on the same sort of fore-understanding as Barr's: when the Bible is reduced to *biblia*, the *biblia* retain no privilege and are accorded the same kind of attention as any other book. Yet *Paradise Lost* and *Ulysses* continue to get attention of a different degree and quality than that made available to *The Purple Island* and *Sorrell and Son*; and analytic techniques are usually designed with special reference to the 'inside' books. There is, of course, an act of faith involved in the decision to continue thus. Its consequences are that we do not treat certain books as mere historical records but as possessing each its own kind of integrity, and also as belonging to a larger whole. Their virtues may be entirely independent of any historical reference they might have. Nobody reads *Ulysses* to find out what happened on 16 June 1904. My conclusion is therefore that if we take seriously the rule that scripture must be read under exactly the same conditions of understanding as other books, Childs complies with the rule more closely than Barr: which is surprising.

The Barr-Childs dispute is not one in which one might expect Edmund Leach to be very interested, but if by chance he were, one assumes that for all his religious scepticism he would be on the side of Childs and not of Barr, though he would probably prefer Barr's prose style. He has his own challenging, even boisterous way of talking, and will not say things by halves. In the present book he continues the structuralist analysis of Biblical myth which has interested him over the past fifteen years. He contributes five essays, and there are two more, using similar methods, by D. Alan Aycock; with one of these Leach expresses forcible though good-natured disagreement in his Introduction.

This Introduction states his general position. His approach to Biblical narrative is synchronic, and he has no time for the historical critics who for the last century and a half or more have been trying to 'unscramble the omelette'. Before they came on the scene it was always assumed that the Biblical stories had mysteries encoded in their texts; the prehistorical interpreters pointed out the patterned structures underlying the narrative transformations, just as *he* does. But nowadays 'truth' is 'equated with "historical truth" . . . If only we could know what really happened in history we should understand the truth, including religious truth.' This seems as absurd to Leach as the contrary view does to Barr; and what we have here is another attempt, quite different from that of the canonical critics, to throw off the yoke of the historical method and get back to occult patterns immanent in the text.

The quest now is for myth, defined as 'a sacred tale about past events which is used to justify social action in the present'; it is true for those who believe it, which is all that matters. It is as important to Leach as it is to

Childs that the makers of the canon saw all their disparate materials as hanging together, and it is the hanging together that matters, not whether there were real people called Moses and David, who may or may not have done this or that.

Of course the patterns and fulfilments of the old interpreters were different from Leach's; the resemblance lies only in that they are concealed, and require to be detected by elaborate methods of investigation. The structuralist technique elucidates relationships previously unsuspected by showing how invariant motives reappear in structural permutations. Biblical texts prove susceptible to techniques developed by anthropologists for the interpretation of myths in any society; they offer sacred tales, unconnected with history and having meanings quite other than their manifest senses.

An instance of the practical difference between this approach and that of the historians is this. The Old Testament has many contradictions and inconsistencies: these are explained by historical scholarship as the result of the Bible having been assembled as an edited compendium of distinct documents of different provenance, so that overlapping or contradictory versions were brought together. This is, in Leach's words, the omelette they seek to unscramble. To the anthropologist, however, these phenomena are not simply to be explained away, for they are highly significant.

Mythologies are clusters of stories which seem to make sense in themselves but often contradict one another. Considered as parts of a corpus, they have a different import, which is to be sought precisely at the junctions between them. Those joins and conflicting versions have real religious significance; they indicate liminality as a temple does, and give a subliminal sense of betwixt-and-betweenness that seems an essential part of communal religious feeling. It is as if the parapraxes of the canonical texts gave us access to their deepest meaning. It may be worth adding that some Jewish Old Testament scholars, working with more literary presuppositions, have also been studying these bad joins and contradictions, and they, too, defy the historian's wish to explain them away.

Leach's thesis is illustrated in some fascinating exercises. One chapter is entitled 'Why did Moses have a sister?', and the answer to the riddle, achieved after a prolonged but masterly journey through a labyrinth of evidence, is 'because mytho-logic requires that his mother be no older than himself.' The trail has led from Abraham as a double of Pharaoh to Michelangelo's Pieta in St Peter's. Why are there in Mark and Matthew not one but two magical feedings, of 5000 and 4000?

Because the feedings are eucharistic and tied to epiphanies: since these Gospels have two relevant epiphanies there must, at the cost of whatever narrative awkwardness, be two feedings also. The feeding stories work like parables (St Augustine knew that, by the way), but indeed all the Biblical narratives work like parables. Believing that to be so, Leach does some work on the parables themselves, and produces some novel results. The Sower parable has had thousands of pages of explanation devoted to it, but I doubt if any one else has said it was part of a *rite de passage* and a figure of the Resurrection made manifest in the Eucharist. Of course all these results depend on the assumption that time in the Gospels is mythical time, in which no event happens before or after any other event.

I can no more give a fair idea of the ingenuity, or incidentally of the fun, of these essays than I can of the brio with which they are composed. They will undoubtedly meet with resistance: Leach will enjoy that. That there are, in disciplines remote from his own, indications that the grip of conventional historical scholarship on Biblical studies is being loosened doesn't at all mean that he would approve of these other approaches, or, despite his lively proselytising in lectures to theologians, that the others will approve of *him*. And finally one should not underestimate the power of the historians' resistance: Barr's strong-minded book is a sufficient reminder of that.

Jon Elster

Socialism

The Politics of Socialism: An Essay in Political Theory
by John Dunn
(Cambridge, 1984)

Optimism and wishful thinking have been features of socialist thought from its inception. In Marx, for instance, two main premises appear to be that whatever is desirable is possible, and that whatever is desirable and possible is inevitable. John Dunn's short book is much concerned with the disastrous consequences of this utopian strand in socialism. He argues that socialists, if they want to be taken seriously, must show that the society they propose is economically viable, and that the process of getting there is politically feasible. He also comes close to saying, without ever actually doing so, that neither demonstration will succeed. The cumulative impact of the difficulties that he urges socialists to confront is such that one wonders why he doesn't simply tell them to pack it in.

Plain talk, however, is not in Dunn's repertoire. His circumlocutory style is as exasperating as ever. When discussing Macaulay's prophecy that adult suffrage would destroy society through the use of its capital stock for current consumption, he remarks that 'the present Conservative government in Britain might well be thought to have gone further in this direction than any of its Labour predecessors.' Well, yes, but has it? Having noted that John Rawls's *Theory of Justice* captures very well the cultural revulsion from capitalism, he adds that 'this is not to say that his theory necessarily gives a very compelling account of how we should in fact conceive social justice.' No doubt, but does it? (And if not, why not?) What substitutes for plain talk is trite pomposity. There is a whole paragraph that consists of the single sentence: 'Human beings simply are what they are.' And surely readers who are intelligent enough to follow Dunn at his most convoluted do not need to be told that 'in politics what is likely to happen is more important than what just conceivably might happen.'

The ground covered is familiar. The economic and political developments of the last century give reasons for doubting most of the classical socialist propositions. After Bernstein it has increasingly been accepted that in advanced capitalist societies, characterised by a high degree of industrial development and a democratic political system, a revolutionary strategy for socialism is implausible, undesirable and superfluous. It is implausible, because capitalism simply isn't so irrational that it can be counted on to create increasing poverty in the midst of plenty. It is undesirable, both for the intrinsic reason that oné cannot ask one generation to sacrifice itself for the sake of its children or grandchildren and for the extrinsic reason that the end tends to become infested by the means. And the reformists have argued that revolution was superfluous because one could achieve the economic goals of socialism by a gradual process.

Recent developments provide grounds for being sceptical about these goals themselves. It has become clear that classical socialism massively underestimated the importance of economic incentives. The incentive structure of Soviet-type economies is an obstacle to efficiency, both in the individual unit of production and in the system of national planning. The idea that classes will disappear when the means of production are nationalised has not been confirmed, to say the least. One can always try to counter these objections by referring to the low initial level of development in the socialist countries and to the hostility of the capitalist environment, but it becomes increasingly difficult to produce this argument with any degree of confidence.

On the one hand, then, there are 'the increasingly evident political and economic hazards of socialism'. On the other hand, there are 'the proven cultural deformations of capitalism'. The central idea of *The Politics of Socialism* seems to be that while the pull from socialism has lost much of its force, the push from capitalism has not. Dunn argues that 'the conjunction of huge aggregations of inherited personal wealth with the ugly and alarming conditions in which millions still have to live is far more important as a cultural affront than it is as an economic injury.' Capitalism may deliver the goods, but it does so in a way that undermines the self-esteem and capacity for self-realisation of most people. The inherent ugliness of capitalism ensures that there is a perpetual impetus towards socialism, but contemplation of actually existing socialism perpetually tends to stop it in its course. 'The modern democratic capitalist state,' Dunn says in the last paragraph of the book, 'is the natural political expression of a form of society irritably but rationally aware of its own internal contradictions, but also irritably but rationally unconvinced of the possibility of transforming itself into a less contradictory form.'

In the broad spectrum of forms of socialism, there are two main proposals for creating a society in which 'culture rules economics.' One postulates a transformation of man, who will become 'noble, virtuous, disciplined, generous, dedicated, indefatigable, selfless, rational, patient, gentle, resolute, courageous, friendly, independent, co-operative, adaptable, discerning, cheerful', as Dunn puts it in one of his more extravagant strawman constructions. The other takes for given man's mean and envious nature, but tries to harness his activities into culturally beneficial channels. Rawls's *Theory of Justice* is indeed the best statement of this social-democratic attitude. It suffers, however, from the internal tension of any system of political philosophy that assumes people to be guided by very different motivations from those underlying the theory itself. This 'cultural contradiction of capitalism', in Daniel Bell's phrase, will inevitably lead to movements in the direction of (some less extravagant version of) the first proposal, with disillusionment and a return to social democracy setting in after a while. Capitalist societies are prone to cultural cycles of disenchantment.

This, I take it, is Dunn's main argument. Flaws of exposition apart, *The Politics of Socialism* surely has a good deal of merit, but it seems to me quite seriously incomplete. To explain why it needs to be supplemented by other considerations, I must first comment on two general, related flaws of the book. First, it does not identify and name the socialists who are taken to task for holding the various, often absurd views which it discusses. Dunn never argues against actual assertions made by specific writers within the socialist tradition. Instead he constructs his own composite pictures of strawmen, to whom he then imputes various degrees of ineptitude, stupidity and dishonesty. I am not saying that actual representatives of these different views could not be found, but surely it is an important rule of intellectual debate to single out the best proponents of the theory one is discussing.

The second, more important flaw is that Dunn does not have a clear and consistent notion of socialism. His explicit definition is that 'socialism is an analytical term indicating aversion to the private ownership of capital,' but he also writes that 'the main thrust away from capitalism comes from the anarchic character of capitalist production' – which is not at all the same thing. The first statement suggests that the argument is about exploitation and justice, the second that it is mainly about (economy-wide) efficiency. Moreover, Dunn also argues that productivity (i.e. efficiency at the level of the firm) and the quality of work experience are part of the socialist aspiration. These are four different values, which for their implementation point in quite different directions. Socialists are not committed to the belief that it is just as possible to realise all of them simultaneously as it would be to realise each of them taken separately. Nor are they committed to the view that socialism must retain everything which is good in capitalism. It is pure caricature when Dunn asserts that socialists must show 'socialist policies to be a necessary remedy for, or at least a beneficial alleviation of, some of the major existing demerits' of society as it is 'and to threaten none of its existing merits'. This statement mirrors the very utopianism he is criticising, by the implicit denial of trade-offs between values. Surely the goal of any serious form of socialism is to create a society which *on balance* is a marked improvement on capitalism, not one which is better in many respects and worse in none.

If the anarchy of the market is the main culprit of capitalist production, we are led towards Soviet-type economies as the remedy. There are, however, good reasons for thinking that this would be worse than the disease. If private ownership of the means of production is the most objectionable feature, we may but need not seek the same remedy. An alternative would be a system of worker-owned and worker-managed firms selling and buying in the market. It is an astonishing lacuna of the book that it mentions neither the extensive theoretical literature on market socialism, nor (except in passing) the Yugoslav experience. Nor does it refer to similar developments in capitalist countries, in the form of individual experiments (Mondragon) or in the form of legislated industrial democracy.

The book fails, then, because it has no real focus. It contains the reflections of a very intelligent person who has read too many stupid arguments about socialism, and who wants to tell us about his frustration. This is not what we need in our present circumstances, or in any other circumstances. The difficulties of inventing and implementing socialism are substantial, but world-weariness is not the right response to them.

Denton Fox

Admirable Urquhart

Sir Thomas Urquhart: The Jewel
edited by R. D. S. Jack and R. J. Lyall
(Scottish Academic Press, 1984)

Sir Thomas Urquhart, who is known today, if at all, as the 17th-century translator of part of Rabelais, must have been a most peculiar man. At a guess, he may have had to a preternatural degree that quality of mind, not unknown among modern scholars, that causes a man to believe that whatever he thinks, says or does is infallibly true and right, and that whatever he observes in the world is true and right only insofar as it coincides with what is already in his mind. It would be wrong and unkind to call him a liar, as he has been called: he simply stated his own truths. Since he also seems to have been almost completely devoid of common sense, and to have been given to violence, he was hardly likely to have had a smooth life. The wonder, indeed, is that his troubles were not more immediately fatal; what saved him, I suppose, is that no one took him seriously.

The little we know about Urquhart's early life comes mostly from his own pen, and is therefore not likely to be true. But there is one incident, vouched for in the records, that seems somehow emblematic. In 1636, after his father had succeeded in wasting most of the family estates (around Cromarty, in the north of Scotland), and presumably because of this, Sir Thomas and his younger brother imprisoned their father in an upper room for five days. When the father gained his freedom he instituted legal proceedings, but nothing much came of them, and eventually all were reconciled. What is interesting is the question of Sir Thomas's motives. Did he think his action would win back the estates or increase his patrimony? Did he propose to keep his father prisoner permanently? Did he suppose the neighbouring gentry would come out in favour of rebellious sons? But it was still a valiant act.

It is reasonably certain that some time before this incident he had been at university in Aberdeen, and had gone on an extended Grand Tour. After 1636, as a Royalist and an Episcopalian, he engaged in some minor warfare with his neighbours, and then took refuge in England, where (according to his own testimony) he was knighted by Charles I in 1641. In 1645 he brought out the *Trissotetras*, a work which apparently 'expresses trigonometrical formulae logarithmically'. Urquhart's biographer, Willcock, says that 'no one is known to have read it or to have been able to read it,' and that it 'dropped at once into the depths of oblivion'. This last statement, at least, is not quite true: Samuel Colvil, in 1681, said of another peculiar book that it

> comes from Brains which have a Bee,
> Like *Urquhart's Trigonometrie*.

After that he returned to Scotland, and finally joined the Royalist army that was crushed by Cromwell at Worcester in 1651, in the last battle before Charles II fled abroad. Urquhart, with many others, was taken to London as a prisoner, where, apparently, he determined to recover his freedom and his estates by using his pen. His first effort was a genealogy in which he names and describes his ancestors, going back to Adam. They were a notable line, and distinguished in their marriages: Pamprosodos Urquhart, for instance, married 'that daughter of Pharaoh Amenophis which found Moses', while Cainotomos Urquhart married the daughter of Bacchus. The prefatory letter is written in the persona of one 'G.P.', who explains that he had acquired the genealogy by chance, and that he thought it his duty to publish it: he expresses devout hopes that 'the greatest State in the world stain not their glory by being the Atropos to cut the thred of that which Saturne's sithe hath not been able to mow in the progress of all former ages, especially in the person of . . . ' A modern reader might think this Urquhart's clever trick to prove that he was not guilty by reason of insanity, but such a pedigree was perhaps somewhat less startling then. Hector Boece's history of Scotland, which was, in Scotland, still highly regarded in the 17th century, begins by relating how a Greek, Gathelus, went to Egypt and married Scota, the sister of the pharaoh who was drowned in the Red Sea. Urquhart certainly expected others to believe his genealogy, and I think that, at least in some sense, he came to believe it himself.

Cromwell's reaction, unfortunately, is not known, but Urquhart found it necessary to try again with the *Jewel*, or, to give it its full title, which in some sense describes it accurately (I transliterate the hybrid term in Greek type, which is meant to signify 'from dung, gold'): 'EKSKUBALAURON: OR, The Discovery of A most exquisite Jewel, more precious then Diamonds inchased in Gold, the like whereof was never seen in any age; found in the kennel [gutter] of *Worcester*-streets, the day after the Fight, and six before the Autumnal Aequinox, *anno* 1651. Serving in this place, To frontal a Vindication of the honour of SCOTLAND, from that Infamy, whereinto the Rigid *Presbyterian party* of that Nation, out of their Covetousness and ambition, most dissembledly hath involved it'. Here again Urquhart uses a persona, as a useful mouthpiece for praising himself. This persona, who styles himself 'Christianus Presbyteromastix', relates how, after the battle at Worcester, Urquhart's lodgings were plundered, and over 3200 sheets of his writings, in three portmanteaux, were taken. (Before jumping to the conclusion that the plunderers must have been illiterate, one should remember that there is not likely to be the slightest bit of truth in this story: it speaks well for the morality of modern scholars that so many of them should have speculated why Urquhart took all his manuscripts to war with him.) The fragment that, by chance, survived, and ultimately reached Mr Presbyteromastix, is the 'Jewel' proper, a prospectus for Urquhart's universal language.

In their excellent introduction, the editors justly point out that in the 17th century there was considerable interest in the possibility of a universal language, and that Urquhart was responding to this vogue. But parts of his prospectus must have seemed absurd even then. It is divided into 134 articles, including such items as these:

> 93. Three and twentiethly, every word in this language signifieth as well backward as forward; and how ever you invert the letters, still shall you fall upon significant words, whereby a wonderful facility is obtained in making of anagrams.
>
> 101. One and thirtiethly, in the denomination of the fixed stars it affordeth the most significant way imaginary; for by the single word alone which represents the star, you shall know the magnitude together with the longitude and latitude, both in degrees and minutes, of the star that is expressed by it.

Presbyteromastix says that he has consulted Urquhart, who has assured him that he can recover the language if he is given his freedom, and who has shown his 'modestie in requiring no more', as a recompense for so great a public service, than that 'the same inheritance which for these several hundreds of yeers, through a great many progenitors, hath by his ancestors without the interruption of any other been possest, be now fully devolved on him'. Presbyteromastix adds that still greater benefits may follow in the future from an inventor 'whose brains have already issued offsprings every whit as considerable with parturiencie for greater births if a malevolent time disobstetricate not their enixibility'.

The prospectus, in this edition, fills only 19 pages; the remaining 130 are given over to the 'vindication' of Scotland from 'tergiversation [faithlessness?], covetousness or hypocrisie, the three foule blots wherewith his [Urquhart's] country is stained', interlarded with praises of Urquhart, requests that he be rewarded properly, attacks on the Scots Presbyterian ministers, and other matter. Most of the vindication consists of descriptions of notable 17th-century Scots savants and soldiers; in particular, almost forty pages are given to a highly romanticised biography of the Admirable Crichton. Crichton's universal learning and his superlative swordsmanship are the qualities most stressed, but he is also the best man in the world at all other activities: in short, another Urquhart.

Willcock described Urquhart's style as 'a combination of that used by Ancient Pistol with that of Sir Thomas Browne', which is witty, but grossly unfair to Browne. One might better say Pistol and Holofernes, but unfortunately there is too little Pistol. In Bacon's phrase, Urquhart studied words and not matter, and while he undoubtedly had a way with words, it is mostly a very long-winded way. Even one of his longer sentences – and there are many of them – would be too long to quote here, but I will quote one of the very few bits of eroticism, if that is the word for it, in the *Jewel* (Urquhart shows a gross enough vein elsewhere), the description of Crichton's consummation of his love.

> Thus for a while their eloquence was mute and all they spoke was but with the eye and hand, yet so persuasively, by vertue of the intermutual unlimitedness of their visotactil sensation, that each part and portion of the persons of either was obvious to the sight and touch of the persons of both. The visuriency of either, by ushering the tacturiency of both, made the attrectation of both consequent to the inspection of either. Here was it that passion was active and action passive, they both being overcome by other and each the conquerour. To speak of her hirquitalliency at the elevation of the pole of his microcosme or of his luxuriousness to erect a gnomon on her horizontal dyal, will perhaps be held by some to be expressions full of obscoeness . . .

Urquhart has the odd felicity. In describing one of Crichton's duels, he remarks: 'as if there had been remoras and secret charms in the variety of his motion, the fierceness of his foe was in a trice transqualified into the numness of a pageant.' The reference to the remora, the small dread sucking-fish that can stop dead a ship under full sail, seems a happy bit of learning. And I like the spirited way in which he defends his friend Duncan Liddel, who should, by all rightful nepotism, have had the chair of mathematics at Aberdeen, but was debarred from it because he had got a wench with child. Urquhart points out that Socrates, whom he conceives to have been a bigamist, was still allowed to practise philosophy, even though neither of his wives, 'whether Xantippe or Myrto, was either so handsome or good as Master Liddel's concubine'. But in the main, the *Jewel*, if not quite unreadable, is unlikely to be read except under duress.

The introduction to this edition contains the most accurate available account of Urquhart, and also an acute analysis of the *Jewel*, which the editors, as their duty requires, take with some seriousness. They dismiss, I think quite rightly, the suggestions that the proposal for a universal language was a spoof, or satirical, or the work of a disingenuous charlatan (I am less sure than they are that it is not the work of a 'deluded crank'). It is disconcerting that he borrows from Rabelais for serious purposes – the resemblance of Urquhart's genealogy to Pantagruel's has been pointed out, as have the parallels between Crichton's and Pantagruel's intellectual triumphs – but Urquhart's vision was too single to permit irony, nor, perhaps, did he have any sense of humour. At a guess, Urquhart thought that he had the idea for a universal language in his head, and that this was really just as good as having written it all down. The editors seem also right in suggesting that the work is essentially a panegyric, in the hyperbolic mode, praising Urquhart for his nobility, learning, martial prowess, and political and religious views. Whether it was a carefully contrived work seems more questionable, though, since hyperbolic self-praise seems to have been an automatic reflex with him: one imagines that he conversed only in a shout, and always about himself, and in the same ways. What is incredible, but still must be true, is that Urquhart really hoped that this work, in which he shows himself as a would-be aristocrat (a list of his 152 ancestors is included), a fop (to judge from his prose, and indeed contemporary engravings confirm this), a duellist, and a holder of views on politics and religion which would have seemed at best highly questionable to the government of the time, would so enrapture Cromwell that he would reverse the forfeiture of Urquhart's property and even (surely almost an impossibility) restore to Urquhart the estates which his father and he himself had let slip away.

But undeterred, Urquhart next year brought out another book about his universal language, in which, however, he says very little more about his language, but much about his vast deserts, the injustices he has suffered, and the rapacity of his creditors, whose importunities have prevented him from emitting 'to publick view above five hundred several Treatises on inventions, never hitherto thought upon by any', to the great benefit of society. In the same year, 1653, his translation of the first two books of Rabelais was published, but that was to be the last benefit that he would confer. In 1654 or 1655 he went abroad, perhaps exiled, and apparently settled in Middleburg in Zeeland (this is a discovery of the editors). There is evidence that he died in 1660, but it is pleasant to note that he had a spirit which time and ill fortune could not humble. In 1658, when he must have been in his late forties, he sent a long and ornately abusive letter to his cousin, challenging him to a duel at a place Urquhart would later name, 'quhich shall not be aboue ane hunderethe & fourtie leagues distant from Scotland'. If the cousin would neither make amends or accept the challenge, Urquhart proposed to disperse copies of his letter 'over all whole the kingdome off Scotland with ane incitment to Scullions, hogge rubbers [sheep-stealers], kenell rakers [gutter-scavengers] & all others off the meanist sorte of rascallitie, to spit in yor face, kicke yow in the breach to tred on yor mushtashes . . . ' (I have slightly emended the Luttrell Society print of this letter). Nothing much came of this, either.

The annotations in this edition, while concise, are numerous and valuable. Almost all of Urquhart's frequent Classical quotations have been tracked down, which must have been no mean task, considering Urquhart's habits of misquotation and misattribution. And most of the innumerable more or less obscure Scots soldiers and savants that Urquhart mentions have been located, so that this edition will be very useful for anyone dealing with 17th-century Scotsmen. The only one I can see whom the editors missed (in the way that one will miss names on a map that are written in too large letters) is one of the few that most people will know. Urquhart's reference, 'nor is Master Ogilvy to be forgot, whose translation of Virgil and of the fables of Aesop in very excellent English verses . . . ', is annotated: 'Ironically, no 17th-century vernacular poet of this name is now recorded.' But this is of course John Ogilby, the dancing-master turned voluminous poet, whom Pope repeatedly gives us licence to call 'great' ('Here swells the shelf with Ogilby the great' and 'thy great fore-father, Ogilby' in the *Dunciad*; Ogilby also ornaments *MacFlecknoe*).

This edition is intended for all classes of readers, which seems fair enough, since the work is not likely to be re-edited (though there is some evidence that the edition is intended partly for beginning students, which worries me a little: if anyone thinks he can flog such students through this work, I wish him luck). While reviewers for the *TLS* used to point to the explanations of fairly obvious Classical allusions in American editions for students as a symptom of, and indeed a major cause of, the Decline of the West, I rather like this practice: it makes me feel superior, and I keep hoping that if I am told Livy's dates enough times I will remember them. But the editors, so expert and indefatigable in dealing with hard problems, are occasionally nonchalant in dealing with these simple matters. For instance, it is true enough, I suppose, to say that Alcibiades (an ancestor of Urquhart's, incidentally) was a 'statesman' and 'a brilliant disciple of Socrates' (though this is a bit like describing T. S. Eliot as a banker from Missouri), but what is relevant is (page 63) that he was renowned for his beauty, or (page 106) that he was supposed to have had all the gifts of nature.

The glosses at the foot of the text are very necessary and helpful, but a few of them seem slightly misleading. In some cases this may arise from a sense of humour, as when 'gallop galliard' is explained as a 'brisk dance for two horses' (the *OED* unfortunately offers a more likely explanation). When Urquhart, arguing that the English should treat the Scots more gently, says that they should apply 'lenitives rather than cauters', he is not really asking them to send 'gentle laxative medicines'. Urquhart quotes Bacon, who in making the same general argument, says of the Scots, 'for the goods of the mind and body they are *alteri nos*'; it is perhaps overly patriotic of the editors to make a silent emendation by glossing *alteri nos* (the plural of *alter ego*) as 'above us'. When a prince, attempting to kill himself, is prevented by his gentlemen, who hinder 'the desperate project of that autochthony', 'autochthony' is glossed as 'son of the soil', which makes poor sense: the *OED* is doubtless right in suggesting this is a mistake for 'autoctony', 'suicide'. Since some words of no great difficulty are glossed, such as (*pace* Molly Bloom) 'metempsychosis', 'fervencie' and 'buckler' (incidentally, I think 'gratifying', on page 144, means 'gratifying', not 'requiring'), it is surprising that there are some really difficult words left unglossed. But these are all very minor blemishes in an excellent edition.

Blake Morrison

Xerox

They come each evening like virgins to a well:
the girls queuing for the xerox-machine,
braceleted and earmarked, shapely as pitchers
in their stretch Levis or wraparound shirts,
sylphs from the typing-pool bearing the forms
of their masters, the chilly boardroom gods.

But this one, this nervous one, is different.
She doesn't gossip with the others and pleads,
when it's her turn, *no, you go first*.
Not until they've gone, their anklets chinking
down the corridor, does she lift the hatch
and dip her trembling hand into the well.

A lightshow begins under the trapdoor:
it flashes and roars, flashes and plashes,
each page the flare of a sabotaged refinery
or the fission of an August storm.
Minutes pass, they slide into the wastebin,
but something is committed for all time.

Sweetface, twoface, little sulky one,
you were never so alone again:
they took a week or more to find you
but they found you, your cheeks lit palely
not from the photocopier's shuttle
but in the lightning of a Nikon swarm.

And what has this to do with it? How you sat
one night by a heifers' drinking-trough
near Yelverton, afraid and down-at-heel
in a mud-churned, midge-drizzling negative,
then saw the country rising from its shadow
under the sudden candour of a moon.

David Lodge

A Martian Goes to College

(with apologies to Craig Raine)

Caxtons are bred in batteries. If
you take one from its perch, a girl

Must stun it with her fist
before you bring it home.

Learning is when you watch a conjurer
with fifty minutes' patter and no tricks.

Students are dissidents: knowing
their rooms are bugged, they

Take care never to talk
Except against the blare of music.

Questioned in groups, they hold their tongues,
or answer grudgingly, exchanging sly

Signals with their eyes
under the nose of the interrogator.

Epilepsy is rife, and the treatment cruel:
sufferers, crowded in dark and airless cells,

Are goaded with intolerable noise
and flashing lights, till the fit has passed.

Each summer there's a competition
to see who can cover most paper with scribble.

The sport is hugely popular; hundreds
jostle for admission to the gyms,

And must be coaxed out when
their time is up. A few, though,

Seem unable to play, and sit staring
out of windows, eating their implements.

Fiona Pitt-Kethley

Sex Objects

I learned from a friend's porno mag that men
can buy the better class of plastic doll
(posh ones are hard and unyielding, not the
pneumatic sort that fly from windows when
they're pricked), in slow instalments, torso first.

Well-qualified in wanking, Mark saves up
his pennies till they grow to pounds and then
invests in Ingrid, just the body, for
his carnal press-ups – a bit too flesh-pink
for human, and she sports a ridgy seam
where back meets front. Mark humanises her –
steals her a black lace bra that doesn't fit
(he's not that used to seeing naked tits),
and puts a cover of a *Cosmo* girl
up on the pillow where his doll's neck ends.

Six months on, tired of screwing her pink trunk,
he spends his pocket-money on a head
(a bald one comes by post), mouth a red O.
He buys his girl a man-made fibre wig,
and, graduating to fellation, talks
about her to his friends.

He gets the arms for Christmas and soon gives
his doll a voice – a steamy tape: he's good
at it by now, he thinks, and she should tell
him so. The tape's a great success at first,
until he starts to get the timing wrong,
and Ingrid, moaning, says, 'It's wonderful'
after he's gone.

Mark's not a legs-man, so these limbs come last:
a duty – something to hook round his back.

He's shocked when they arrive – one black, one white.
The firm's in liquidation and could just
supply him with the halves of two whole pairs.
(The black's from 'Sonia', another doll.)

That limb cures his Pygmalionitis quite.
He starts to look for human girls to fuck,
but finds they usually need persuasion first,
their fannies aren't so neatly set in front
and, unlike Ingrid, they can criticise.

Four

London Review
OF BOOKS
VOLUME 6 NUMBER 12 5 JULY TO 18 JULY 1984 70P
DAVID MARQUAND: INTERDEPENDENCE

Christopher Ricks

Dark Tom

Beyond the Pale: Sir Oswald Mosley 1933–1980
by Nicholas Mosley
(Secker, 1983)
Rules of the Game: Sir Oswald and Lady Cynthia Mosley 1896–1933
by Nicholas Mosley
(Fontana, 1983)

'The human craving to believe in *something* is pathetic, when not tragic; and always, at the same time, comic.' The life of Sir Oswald Mosley was pathetic, tragic and comic, and his son's humane deliberated biography is itself a notable contribution to 'The Literature of Fascism' which T. S. Eliot was judging with that sentence in 1928. In 1928 Oswald Mosley was still an up-and-coming Labour MP. It was the year after Eliot had made manifest that the something which satisfied his own craving to believe was Christianity. Mosley as Fascist soon came to crave this craving in others; he could always tap it, but he could never satisfy it for long, since the drugging or hypnoidal power would necessarily wear off and then the faithfully addicted would need a new fix of their *idées fixes*. What Mosley gives (to apply Eliot's fearful evocation of history, in the immediate aftermath of the great mowing-down in 1914–1918) he gives with such supple confusions that the giving famishes the craving. To famish a craving is to incite a cycle of short-lived satisfaction and life-long insatiability.

Fortunately for English public life and for his salvation, Eliot believed, saw indeed, that Fascism and Christianity were irreconcilable. Writing a letter about the Blackshirts in the *Church Times* in 1934, he of course observed every propriety, and – while quoting four immitigable statements by Mussolini – affected only to be asking about Fascist compatibility with Christianity. 'I am not answering this question, but putting it.' But to put it so was to permit of only one responsible answer. 'The point is not whether a large number of people, with or without the inspiration and example of Sir Oswald Mosley and Lord Rothermere, are both zealous Fascists and devout Christians.' But in 1934 the 'inspiration and example' of Mosley would have been words drily to call up rot dry and wet. The caddish effrontery of Mosley's private life (Eliot made the relevance of this explicit though not for publication) had culminated in 1933 in the death of his long-suffering wife and in the ensconcing of a short-suffering Mosley with his other helpmeet Diana Guinness *née* Mitford. Mosley's biographer Robert Skidelsky avers that 'Mosley always tried to maintain the old English distinction between private life and public life.' But Mosley came up against that other, even more powerful, old English tradition or law which has recently snuffed out Parkinson's individual talent, the tradition of countenancing no such distinction. It was fortunate, though not merely lucky, for English anti-Fascism that Mosley was a bounder. He was a veteran liar both in public and in private life, a master of the untrue categorical denial: why should one think it a mere confusion of categories to infer a deep untrustworthiness seeping both ways? There are those who will never be able to bring themselves, even under the threat of Reagan, to want Edward Kennedy as President.

Mosley did appreciate the existence, though not the nature, of the human craving to believe *something*. What he really offered to meet, though, was different: the human craving to believe *in someone*. (Not the satisfaction which looks smaller but is larger – believing someone.) His son will always be, as every son is but momentously more so, the victim-beneficiary of being his father's son. Nicholas Mosley wanted when young to believe in his father; he moved on to wanting to believe his father; he moved on again to wanting to believe that his father –well, many things, but mostly that his father was not a monster and that his survival into an old age which had much love and happiness in it was in the end less unjust than just. Nicholas Mosley's own survival is remarkable, not least as being so much more than survival. Without priggishness, with undull decency, he makes it clear how and how much he has learnt, and the deepest personal sadness in the book (personal as against the pity of war and of peace) is the inescapable admission that his father learnt nothing.

We reviewers ought to acknowledge that we are not likely to be doing justice to this book, because Sir Oswald will not have it so – Sir Oswald, still peremptory, oppressive, charming, and brutal, is determined to claim more than his share of Limehouse and limelight. The book itself is alive with counterpointings, comic and touching; the account of the author's courage, his winning the Military Cross fighting in a war in which he did not then believe and which his father fought against, is un-ingratiating, piteous and finely paced. The same is true of the visits to, and correspondence with, Mosley in prison during the war, with all the sad and weird affinities to the son's boarding-school. But Sir Oswald's power to impel and repel – compounded as it is by the recent Government decision to release much of the hitherto secret material about Mosley and British Fascism – will necessarily and not unreasonably loom larger in discussion of the book than it does in the book's own art. One of Mosley's books was called *The Alternative*; Nicholas Mosley's is constituted as *An Alternative*. In sum: you might think from the extensive praising reviews of this book that you needn't actually read it, because it would seem to be the kind of book that reviews can sufficiently gut and précis and anthologise for you, but you would be wrong, since much of what gives the book its patient power – its balance and sustenance of alternate tones and of alternating currents – will not be figuring in reviews.

A tribute to Nicholas Mosley needs to acknowledge not only the difficulty but the impossibility of his enterprise. Both are endemic in the simplest, most recurring, matter of all: how to refer to the man. *Rules of the Game* spoke of him well-nigh throughout by the name by which his friends knew him: Tom. Chapter One was called 'Tom'; its first words were 'My father Oswald Mosley', whereupon the naming by relationship and by the name Oswald Mosley fell away. It had a disconcerting effect, this use throughout of Tom. It made the reader feel as if he too were a friend of Mosley's, of Tom's indeed; it made all the personal and intimate parts of the record feel illuminatingly continuous with the daily life that Mosley actually led, while all the public parts felt darkly discontinuous and even peripheral. Since the person who was doing and saying all these public things, even while spoken of as Tom, wasn't Tom to all those people out there, it somehow can't really have been Tom who was that person. Then again the name Tom was disconcerting because Mosley didn't seem to be one of nature's Toms. One may speak of the demonology of Mosley without implying that there was not indeed a great deal, hideously much, that was demonic about him: that said, it can be admitted that 'Sir Oswald' was and is a powerful contributor to the demonology. It is not only that Oswald is an insufferable name (*Who was Oswald Fish?* asks the initialled onomast A. N. Wilson), awash with the sub-Shakespearean sinister and histrionic, and darkly seconded by Mosley's middle name

('Sir Oswald Ernald Mosley'). For Tom is such a relief of a contrast to Oswald. It would have been difficult, however well-justified, to animate the demonology of Sir Tom Mosley: why, he sounds like a thoroughly homespun trade-union leader or vice-chancellor. There is a post-war anecdote about the father of Nicholas Mosley's girlfriend, exclaiming: 'But I would rather shake hands with Oscar Wilde than with Oswald Mosley!' Mosley was not amused but bemused: 'Does her father think I'm a bugger?' 'No, Dad, it's not that he thinks you're a bugger.' But one of the good things about the anecdote must be its onomastic antics: for Oscar was always a difficult name which Wilde made impossible, and the same goes for Mosley's Oswald.

This second volume, *Beyond the Pale*, eschews Tom almost entirely. (The name occurs once in a quotation, is decoded, and then escapes into the neighbouring text before being promptly apprehended and liquidated.) Instead it mostly says 'my father' even when family or familiar matters are not in question; sometimes it says Mosley; sometimes, wary and ceremonious and on edge, it dilates to 'Oswald Mosley'. There is nothing dishonest or disingenuous about these decisions and variations: what there is, though, is unignorable testimony to the unsatisfactoriness of all the ways of referring to the most important and (*pace* John Vincent, who has been wonderfully at it again) the most interesting person pondered in the book. There is no one way that is neutral, or natural, or complete, of referring to Sir Oswald Mosley in this book, nor could there be. And if the difficulties of tact and the problems of principle arise with so immediate, so small and so omnipresent a matter as how to refer to the man, what then must the full complexities and delicacies be? To find for any father, and then for such a father, words at once true and kind, or not untrue and not unkind: this is to seek to combine Larkin's domestic truth-telling with Lowell's visionary acumen about those soldiers (Napoleon's, Mosley's) who have 'Grand opera fixed like morphine in their veins'. To a follower, Mosley was the Leader (agreeable how much the English language falls short of the thrill of *Führer*): to his son, he is mostly 'my father'. The son himself, in a small-scale way which brings home what the large scale is, presents a difficulty to his reviewer. Must I keep saying Nicholas Mosley? To say Mosley would be confusing; to say Mr Mosley would sound circumspect, and not the usual practice in these pages, and moreover our author is really Lord Ravensdale (or Nicholas Mosley the author, but not 'Mr Mosley').

'British Union stands for peace' – and for no nonsense from those who question the claim, or who believe that peace with Hitler is impossible. Mosley came, or came on, as a man of peace. But then, in the opening words of a song from Bob Dylan's new album *Infidels*:

Look out your window, baby. There's a scene you'd like to catch.
The band is playing 'Dixie'. A man got his hand outstretched.
Could be the Führer, could be the local priest.
You know sometimes Satan comes as a man of peace.

The Führer or the local priest? Does the Church collide with or collude with Fascism? But as Skidelsky acknowledges, Mosley's 'peace campaign' was notable for 'its absolute refusal to criticise any German actions'. Mosley's ability to deceive himself was even more remarkable than his ability to deceive others, and it looks as if he, or some part of him, did genuinely and self-deceivingly believe that he was mustering, in Nicholas Mosley's words, 'a fascist movement dedicated to peace' and 'an army that would march to prevent future wars'. He even managed to persuade himself that had it not been for this (needless) war, Hitler would never have murdered the Jews. His refusal to contemplate how early Hitler was insane is scarcely sane.

Even when Mosley came to repudiate Hitler, he managed to make it sound as if he were only scorning and deprecating him. 'My father never, it seemed, much liked Hitler: in old age he used to refer to him as a "terrible little man".' Those three words are cited again later in the book. Their reduction of opprobrium to social condescension, especially in that 'little', is evidence of Mosley's insensibility and worldly fortification. It is characteristic of him that he should warp to his own brutal polemic purposes the bone-deep fatigue of Macbeth at what mankind had come to seem; Macbeth's corrupted vision of man, 'that struts and frets his hour upon the stage', becomes in 1946 Mosley's derision of corrupt (other) men: 'What a chance for every mediocrity and dunce on the fringe of politics; for every little "Tadpole" and "Taper" to strut his little hour!'

'I withdraw not a word I have ever uttered, nor ever will.' He never repented or recanted, so there are no words of contrition to assess stringently, but even when he came to dissociate himself he yet cultivated guilt by dissociation. In 1933 he said that 'Hitler has made his greatest mistake in his attitude to the Jews': but this did not stop him from taking a leaf out of Hitler's black book. 'His greatest mistake': this rang a cracked bell for me. Less than twenty pages later, we bump into Ezra Pound at Mosley's Black House, along with his pamphlet for the British Union of Fascists, 'What is Money for'. Pound, who eventually came to contrition's lockjaw, spoke too of a mistake – his own, which is at least some advance on Mosley's disembarrassment. Donald Davie has spoken for Pound: 'To take only the most blatant and damaging of the charges, his anti-Semitism, should we not respect him for admitting, however belatedly, "the worst mistake I made was that stupid, suburban prejudice of anti-Semitism"? It appears not. On the contrary one gets the clear impression that for Pound to confess his faults is almost worse than having committed them.' This is tinged with forgiveness as inattention. For Pound's confession is marred by the insufficient gravity of the word 'mistake' (it is Davie who speaks here of *faults*), and it is vitiated by the prejudicial vehemence of 'suburban' ('terrible little man'). In the very moment which we are urged to respect for its rising above prejudice, Pound sinks back into it: 'that stupid, suburban prejudice of anti-Semitism'. The word 'suburban' can be so counted upon to do its prejudicial work as not even to be visible, it seems, as prejudice. That the remark is inaccurate (one might wish that it was only or mainly suburbs which had housed anti-semitism) is important, but less important than the incorrigible habit of mind which found it useful.

Anti-semitism, which is more than a mistake, is unmistakably the nub of the Mosley question. A man is not his sister-in-law's keeper, though Unity Mitford stood in need of one, but her demented forthrightness is always a dark undercurrent in the Leader's followers: 'Today he' – Hitler – 'was so kind and so divine I suddenly thought I would not only like to *kill* all who say and do things against him, but also *torture* them. It is wonderful to think that someone like him can ever have been thought of.' On the next page of this book there follow her words: 'I want everyone to know that I am a Jew hater.'

To the end Mosley claimed that he was not against Jews as such, only against their dragging England into a war that was not Britain's business ('Mind Britain's Business,' and 'Britain Fights for Britain Only'). Jews could be forgiven for not deducing this from Mosley's cry that 'stronger than even the stink of oil is the stink of the Jew,' or from the congratulatory telegram from Streicher about 'the forces of Jewish corruption'. All of this was riven with contradiction and worse: Mosley so little succeeded in disciplining and controlling rabid anti-semitism in his henchmen, his followers and his publications as to make it impossible to believe that he could have controlled an empowered Fascism even if he had wanted to. Among his turbulent wishes was this one, to ride and reap this whirlwind.

'A revolutionary idea,' wrote Eliot in 1929, 'is one which requires a reorganisation of the mind; fascism or communism is now the natural idea for the thoughtless person.' A political movement as thoughtless and even mindless as Fascism needed scapegoats, needed to find its energy in negation, not in the positive positing of anything. As early as 1929, and à propos of Italian Fascism, Eliot had thrown in a syntactically comic throwing-up of the hands: 'The really interesting thing about fascism is its syndicalism, its organisation of workers, and its financial policy, if it has any.' Odd to say that the really interesting thing includes a policy which may not even exist. But in the 1930s, as again in the 1980s, no one except a historian or philosopher of Fascism could mount even a five-minute lecturette on Fascist syndicalism and the workers: that was not the hiding place of its power. Mosley's Fascism was not only null, it was dedicated – devoted, in the old double sense of pledged and doomed – to nullity. When Nicholas Mosley says that 'there was nothing in the philosophy of fascism necessarily to do with racialism or the desire for conquest which were the drives which pushed Hitler to destruction and eventually to self-destruction,' he does, honest as he is, have immediately to add: 'On the other hand some archetypal drives (even excesses?) seem to be necessary if groups are to be welded dynamically into a single force.' Or dynamitically. For his words could be interrupted: 'there was nothing in the philosophy of fascism' – exactly. There was nothing in it, and there was *nothing* in it. The human craving to believe in *nothing* is pathetic, when not tragic; and always, at the same time, comic.

'One of the points of these books – biography or autobiography – has been the attempt to create an attitude by which the darkness in people (there is always darkness) might be made to seem not so much evil as somewhat ridiculous.' The difficulties of the enterprise can be seen in the slight wobble of 'might be made to seem': might be seen to be?

Mosley made promises lightly; he also promised light. But it was darkness, black-shirted, which was alluring. In a superb poem about the tragic compromises with tyranny which democracy may be moved to make, 'Eisenhower's Visit to Franco, 1959', James Wright flashlit the dark disingenuousness of Fascism:

Franco stands in a shining circle of police.
His arms open in welcome.
He promises all dark things
Will be hunted down.

The Fascist leader proceeds with a travesty of ordered enlightened equability; he promises all dark things will be hunted down. No, he really promises what was fleetingly intimated, a discreet amputation of that, an apocalyptic line-ending. He promises all dark things. There was nothing in the philosophy of Fascism.

The anti-Fascist is not immune to the convenience of the scapegoat. It cannot exactly be said that this book inculpates William Joyce since William Joyce, sick in the head and foul in the mouth, is sheerly culpable: but the book is sometimes tempted to suppose that Joyce's direct guilt for Fascism's anti-semitism somehow lessens Mosley's devious guilt. The book wrestles with the fallen angel, and in the end it wins. An unforgettable page describes Mosley rebuking an inordinate subordinate:

> There was an incident from the early days of Union Movement just after the war that stuck in my memory. My father had summoned to him one of his lieutenants who had disobeyed orders that members should not become involved in the breaking-up of opponents' meetings: my father reprimanded the man in a room next door to where Rosemary and Diana and I were having dinner. My father shouted at him for a time; the man was saying, 'Yes sir, sorry sir'; then my father said quietly, 'Well don't do it again.' And as he showed the man out into the passage some sort of wink seemed to pass between the man and my father – some touch on the arm perhaps – a recognition of comradeship or complicity beyond the demands of discipline. And it was as if we all knew that the man of course would do whatever he had done again; my father knew this; the man knew that my father knew this – it was as if the reprimand was just some ritual by which my father might effectively not quite let his left hand know what his right hand was doing. And it must have been something like this, I supposed, that had happened in the Thirties – both with my father, and with other national socialist leaders.

No one can write seriously and at length about anti-semitism without giving offence, and Nicholas Mosley will be held to have palliated or extenuated his father's evil. One might go further: not only must it needs be that offences will come, but woe to that man by whom the offence cometh. It is unimaginable that anyone could ever judge these matters exactly right, alive fully to justice and to mercy. There are, of course, offences and offensivenesses; the smart thing to do in the New Right of Cambridge lately was to quote (oh of course to quote, not to take the rap for coining) the remark that the real charge against Hitler was that he had made an intelligent anti-semitism impossible.

Nicholas Mosley's honourable words sometimes carry an intimation that is not quite what he meant to say but which is a wrung admission. He himself draws our attention to the 'perhaps tellingly ambiguous phrasing' of the *Jewish World* when it urged Mosley to repudiate

William Joyce and said of Mosley: 'either his or Mr Joyce's scurrilous claptrap is the authentic revelation.' So when Nicholas Mosley writes that 'during 1933 Oswald Mosley went out of his way to try to disassociate himself from Hitler's anti-semitism,' we might want to think about certain implications of 'went out of his way'; and when, three pages from the very end, he says of Mosley, 'He did come more to accept the horror of things that had been done under the Nazis,' we might notice the perhaps tellingly ambiguous phrasing that gathers around 'accept' there. The first page of the first chapter says of Mosley's fore-marchers, the British Fascisti, that they were 'not particularly anti-semitic'. Those words rang another warning bell. A greater writer than Nicholas Mosley – one whose poems fortified him during the war, and moved him to imitation, and one who was loathed by the British Fascists ('It is time that Mr Eliot was told that mankind has plenty of use for courage and sense of direction, none at all for defeatism and disease') – once delivered himself of, and up with, such words. Eliot in 1944 replied to a review by Lionel Trilling of his selection of Kipling's verse. Trilling had said: 'Mr Eliot, it is true, would not descend to the snippy, *persecuted* anti-Semitism of ironic good manners which, in "The Waster", leads Kipling to write "etc" when the rhyme requires "Jew".' Within his letter of reply, Eliot remarked: 'I would observe that in one stanza, at least, the rhyme required is not to *do* but to *done*: and the obvious rhyme for *done* is not *Jew* but *Hun*. Kipling made several opportunities for expressing his dislike of Germans; I am not aware that he cherished any particularly anti-Semitic feelings.' With a felicitous infusion of Eliot's dryness of manner, Trilling turned upon that phrase: 'As anti-Semitism goes these days, I suppose Kipling is not – to use Mr Eliot's phrase – particularly anti-Semitic.'

It is all a minefield, and being innocent, or not particularly guilty, will not save anyone from being blown up. Even the demolition people sow their own bombs; it was thought reasonable for a philosopher in *Scrutiny* in the very month of September 1939 to say as mere say-so that 'the German people are *as a people* politically young; their political philosophy is philosophically immature,' and then to proceed: 'Those of us who have not the misfortune to be Germans . . . '

Susannah Clapp

'You are my heart's delight'

A Portrait of Fryn: A Biography of F. Tennyson Jesse
by Joanna Colenbrander
(Deutsch, 1984)

According to Rebecca West, F. Tennyson Jesse was 'ideally beautiful. I have never seen a lovelier girl.' A sketch in Joanna Colenbrander's biography shows a flat, winsome face with wide, rather fishy eyes; her thin limbs are splayed out with flapperish elegance. It may be that her attractions – a fat bundle of love-letters was destroyed when she died, and Mrs Colenbrander finds several witnesses to testify to her 'aura' – had less to do with ideal beauty than with loquaciousness and flair. She published more than thirty books,[1] and was praised for her 'masculine insight into human motives', but her most enduring fictional creations are women who passed themselves off as gorgeous.

She was born in 1888, the second daughter of an amiably evangelical clergyman (Tennyson's nephew) and a mother who retired to her sofa at 25. He had asthma and she had migraine – and they very soon ceased to have sex. Home life was irregular and inequitable. Her elder sister was first dumped with and later adopted by prosperous maternal relations who pampered her. 'Fryn' (a self-made contraction of 'Wynifried' which seems to have been quite typical of her chatter) spent parts of her childhood with both parents in exotic and hopeless clerical postings abroad, and parts in what are described here as 'dingy lodgings', alone with her mother who didn't much like her. In *The Alabaster Cup* she gives a vehement third-person account of her early years – full of religious anxiety and aesthetic epiphanies – and a poisonous picture of her mother. Edith Jesse, who quickly decided against her husband and his 'interferences', liked women and dallied with a succession of them. This is made to seem more innocent – less glandular and less malevolent – in Mrs Colenbrander's account than in

Tennyson Jesse's. Both tell the story of how one fading female companion was banished because her skin was 'like a crocodile's'; the story of how Edith Jesse had earlier gone hand-in-hand with this woman to her husband and asked him to bless their special friendship does not appear in Mrs Colenbrander's book.

Edith Jesse managed to turn even her sanctimoniousness into spite, and surviving such a hateful mother gives Tennyson Jesse a claim to wonderfulness which Joanna Colenbrander is eager to uphold. She was for many years Tennyson Jesse's secretary: she has access to a lot of first-hand information, and records much of it as if she were taking dictation. When she comes to student days at the Newlyn School of Painting she is helped by an effervescent diary in which Tennyson Jesse detailed gypsy beanos, picnics at which girls imitated the noise of water coming out of bottles, and a weird episode when she and a friend dressed up in black and spent a night at a hotel pretending to be interesting widows. All her friends had nicknames – 'Damit', 'Horse', 'Aunt' – and favoured a mewing private language: 'I began a big pastermiece – a dragon, and a lady in a birthday-suit – for which Dod is going to sit.' They dressed up as butterflies and bacchantes, and squeaked about sex over cocoa and boiled eggs; Mrs Colenbrander tells us that when Harold and Laura Knight arrived: 'Their brilliant painting stunned the whole colony.'

After Damit and Horse, there was Tottie Harwood and literary London. Edith Jesse didn't want her daughter back at home after college, so she started to write to keep herself: paragraphs about mannequins for the *Times*, a short story for the *English Review* and a novel, *The Milky Way*, which the *Daily Mail* called 'fresh and blithe', and she thought 'very bad'. She wore a hat 'like a coal-heaver's, with a pink quill', was courted by publishers, and gossiped about: 'I hear that William Heinemann has given you a black pug,' spat Ivy Litvinov at a party. H. M. Harwood, a big, relaxed, bossy doctor-turned-playwright, wrote to her admiringly, and they began to gad together. They went to Madeira and played roulette, and to Paris where she wore 'an opalescent dress with a zigzag hem', and he called her a foolish virgin.

Then they went to Windermere, and she was changed. Joyrides were being offered over the lake in an old-fashioned aeroplane, a 'pusher' machine with the propeller behind the pilot. People went up one at a time, and Tennyson Jesse went first:

> We took off. I peeped round and down and put out my right hand to wave – and it got struck. It didn't really hurt. I pulled the hand back into my lap, and watched fascinated as a pool of blood reached to my knees. My pretty new pleated skirt had formed a basin for it.

Her hand was mangled and her self-esteem badly wounded: 'I thought no one would ever be in love with me again.' During the next year she had six operations: each time the hand failed to heal; each time a bit more of it was chopped off. Eventually she went to New York, where she had an introduction to a surgeon, and the treatment there included morphia injections. At this point Mrs Colenbrander becomes magisterial. Confronted with Tennyson Jesse's taciturnity about her treatment, she deals with the matter as if it were the subject of a High Court action: 'It has been affirmed that . . . [she] became an addict, eventually a registered addict'; 'It was known positively that Dr Armando Child treated her for the addiction . . . He is said to have been a charming man.' Mrs Colenbrander invites pardon rather than understanding: she is vague about the period of time for which the addiction lasted, and quotes only one acquaintance on what seems to have been a much-discussed subject. This is Rebecca West, who suggests that the problem was more than fleeting: 'Her tragedy was that she was put on drugs almost at the start . . . The wonder is that she achieved so much.' Throughout this book there are hysterias and obsessions which bear out her words.

There is also much achievement and activity. Fitted with a new hand in New York, Tennyson Jesse sailed for the West Indies, with the alcoholic nurse who administered her injections; on the voyage she collected two proposals of marriage. She went to Havana, shark-fished, and made friends with a salesman who gave her his models of ladies' underwear. The New York *Evening Sun* found her 'gowned in a debutante frock, twirling a purple streamer hat in her artistically moulded fingers', and talking about adventures. Back in London, she wangled an assignment from the *Daily Mail* to go to the Front. Mrs Colenbrander is duly admiring of her bravery, but seems no more amazed by her success as a war-reporter than she is by her shark-fishing.

She could be efficient as well as bold, organising a household in which her father could shelter from his wife, and in which her stammering sister Stella (an actress who never stuttered on stage) could play the ingenue. Mrs Colenbrander thinks that one of the most striking features of this life was the number of 'distinguished' people who took an interest in Tennyson Jesse. She lists some sirs, some publishers, and, at various points, Conrad, Maugham, Coward and Walpole, but she doesn't tell us enough of what they said about her subject to persuade us that they are peculiarly valuable testaments to her incandescence. She does have a lot to say about the queue of eager aides and secretaries who acted as administrators, amanuenses and buffers. There was May, who fled from a grim family and remained with Tennyson Jesse for the rest of her life, suspecting men and sewing the household initials on bedspreads; Minnie, who had hair like a dandelion and 'scattered melodious notes like a skylark'; there was Letty, who was dear and unselfish; Mrs Colenbrander, who was instantly captivated. And there was 'Tiger', an Irish empathist, who shortly after she joined the household felt the small form of her hostess creep into bed beside her, 'the mothlike hands, that were yet so strong, clutching spasmodically'. This visit seems to have been prompted by anxiety, not desire, but, despite Mrs Colenbrander's warmth, it is difficult not to see in Tennyson Jesse's treatment of these women – encouraging one, ignoring another – some echo of her mother's capriciousness.

In 1918, when she had known him six years, Fryniwyd Jesse married Tottie Harwood. The terms of the marriage were enough to turn anyone's brain. It was to be kept secret, because for years Harwood – whom 'it was said that nobody had ever refused' – had been having an affair with a married woman. Her husband was 'distinguished', her son was Tottie's, and Harwood's reasoning seems to have been that by concealing his marriage he could maintain a hold on his child. His stance was one of sonorous integrity; his wife's of submission. Mrs Colenbrander quotes an exchange which could have come from one of Harwood's less good plays: 'He had said to her: "I have responsibilities which you would be the last person to make me wish to evade," and she had answered: "I know."' His family thought that he was a philanderer and she was an adventuress, a maimed person using her torn hand as a hook. As usual, Rebecca West was able to give the literary view: 'It was cruel and pointless . . . His mistress was protected from scandal by her position in life, and Fryn had enough to contend with already. There had been talk, which I knew to be baseless, about her friendship with dear Alfred Mond. When she and Tottie began going away together, naturally nobody knew what to make of it, and Fryn's reputation must have suffered.'

Tennyson Jesse, who made rather a speciality of going to hotels in strange guises, seems at first to have got a thrill from living as if she were her husband's lover. After three years the charm had worn off. In an account occluded by a garbled time sequence, and delivered in tones of great mystery and complication, Mrs Colenbrander pinpoints a crisis on their wedding anniversary. They met on Harwood's yacht: there had been some discussion of his plans (public school and money) for his son's future, and he had given her a pair of jade ear-rings. Then he told her to run along, because he was expecting 'guests'. She knew who he meant: she ran along, and fell ill. She may have had a miscarriage; she was treated, with a flurry of eyeshades and injections, for migraine; she certainly suffered some sort of nervous collapse. The immediate effect was that Harwood took his marriage out of the closet and his wife on holiday. The long-term consequence was more bitter. Year after year for the rest of her life she lashed him and herself with the certainty that he had once let her down and the possibility that he didn't now love her best. From hospital beds and holidays, from her own bedside, she wrote him letters: the occasion of these is often obscure, but their theme is always of injury and their tone invariably see-saws between lament and elegy. In 1931: 'it remains that it was I who have been sacrificed . . . Oh my heart, I'm so excited at the thought of seeing you.' Three years later: 'Dearest – It isn't that I don't love you, but I felt your hatred of me was setting me back.' Twenty years after this she was still compiling lists of the things he had 'spoilt' for her, and telling him: 'I love you so terribly it hurts me to look at you.'

It's difficult to know from these letters what was actually going on. Harwood's responses are in turn affectionate, bewildered and exasperated: '*What* has not been cleared up?', and Mrs Colenbrander does not go outside their exchanges to establish a chain of events and delinquencies. Harwood was probably arrogant and definitely a male-chauvinist pig – in response to a complaint that his wife couldn't cook, he explained that he wanted her 'as a pet' – and in attempting to smother all news of his marriage he didn't display much sign of the big brain with which Mrs Colenbrander credits him. Tennyson Jesse's pain and resentment were increased by several miscarriages and by well-wishers who were eager to supply her with details of the other ménage and its offspring. But at some point her grievance lost touch with its source and became obsessional: fuelled by drugs or drink, she would periodically turn to anyone who would listen and transfix them with a tale of muddled misery.

For much of the time things were quite jolly. Harwood had leased the Ambassadors Theatre, and there produced a number of his lightly-turned plays – among them, *The Pelican*, written with his wife, which treats the case of a disinherited son. The couple had comfortable houses from which they found it easy to exit. In 1922, while they cruised down the Thames in their yacht, May and Stella Jesse were knee-deep in Harwood weeds, clearing a stream which ran through the grounds of their new house, a 15th-century mill near Chichester. The householders returned in time to admire a new wing and give a well-publicised feast for the construction workers. Several house-parties later, they were off to India and Burma. Here Tennyson Jesse got the idea for *The Lacquer Lady*, a lusciously written novel about palace life in Mandalay, and found the Marquis of Reading and his wife completely 'unspoilt . . . Alice arranged the flowers in my room herself.' In Cairo she put henna on her hair, and 'floated up the Nile looking like a giant tangerine'. Back at the mill, she and her sister lolled in the bath, talking about their mother and their 'wombys' – and Tennyson Jesse started to write about murder.

She produced crisp introductions to *Notable British Trials*, and a study, *Murder and its Motives*, which oddly features 'elimination' as one motive. Her best-known novel, *A Pin to See the Peepshow*, was based on the Thompson and Bywaters case, in which Edith Thompson was hanged with her lover for the murder of her husband. The book was published in 1934; it is an expansive, romantic novel, full of dresses and decor, which tells its story – that of a young woman bewitched by the possibility of glamour and intent on the joys of sexual activity – with ease and dash. There are some sentimental snobberies: it is hard to believe that the trim and capable heroine sprang from a family so uniformly weedy and ill-favoured, and difficult not to feel that the author to some degree supports the view that there is nothing so terrible as suburbia – there is a sprinkling of Jesse attributes on Julia Almond, who is short-sighted and devoted to her dog as well as her appearance. The novel's chief pleasures are provided by furnishings as much as by psychological sharpness: it speaks clearly of a time when the Goldhawk Road was lined with elm trees and cows, when young women draped their rooms in pagoda-figured wallpaper, and when boutiques were stuffed with debs in hats yelling darling. A strong condemned-cell scene led some to suppose that the book was designed to deliver a plea against capital punishment: it hardly seems to favour it, but although Tennyson Jesse, along with others, was disturbed by the sentence in the Thompson–Bywaters case, she elsewhere proclaimed it more humane as well as more thrifty to 'kill more people'.

While Tennyson Jesse was writing about murder she was making regular attempts to kill herself. In 1926, yachting around St Tropez, the Harwoods had seen another house they liked, and in which they lived with extravagance and strain. Tennyson Jesse wrote a chirpy memoir of their life there, which turns on a minute and anthropomorphic examination of their cats and dogs – with a brief excursion into the habits of the fancily named goldfish which cavorted in the fountain. In it, she quotes, apparently condoningly, from an essay written by a visitor who, though seemingly bent on celebrating a deliciously tangled existence, conveys an atmosphere of self-consciousness and wilful intimidation: there are animals and guests and baby-talk everywhere; Harwood runs round naked but for his corduroy shorts, while his wife, terrifically got up, makes grand entrances in cartwheel hats and 'very ordinary, frightfully old' frocks. Mrs Colenbrander also draws on this guestschrift, though she misses out from the middle of her quote a point which makes Tennyson Jesse look both wee and weird: 'She is always on the lookout for daddy-long-legs, they frighten her – though to be entwined from head to foot by a cobra is her heart's delight.'

All this enshrining of her daily life in print suggests some precariousness, and Mrs Colenbrander reluctantly makes it plain that Tennyson Jesse wasn't always a joy to be with. In long spells of wretchedness she attacked her friends and worried at her husband, demanded sudden trips for what she called 'migraine injections', and chirruped strangely about having found the secret of eternal youth. Again and again she took overdoses, leaving hellishly accusatory notes for Harwood: 'You did this to me, by your lack of self-control.' How much of this can be laid at the feet of Harwood – who seems a good instance of the fact that loyal conduct isn't enough – how much was morphia, how much was madness, Mrs Colenbrander leaves open.

There was dippiness as well as damnation in their lives. At one moment Harwood was devoting himself to domestic economies – and discovering that they had 80 pairs of necessary sheets; at the next, he was bathing in Hollywood with Garbo (topless). In the Second World War he set himself to the study of vitamin supplements, while Tennyson Jesse wrote excitingly about the crew of a burning oil-tanker. Together they published a volume of letters addressed to American friends, in which, with a larding of 'my pets', they deliver wartime news. It's surprising that Mrs Colenbrander doesn't make more use of these letters, for they have a lot to say about the Harwoods. He boomed about destruction: 'There were a few righteous men in Sodom, but the Lord . . . didn't allow that to influence him.' Tennyson Jesse was alternately brisk and gossipy, chatting about stray cats, about Old Bailey murder trials, about Noel Streatfeild being accosted by a French tart in Bond Street. She declared herself left-wing, but this seems to have been mostly a way of announcing a caring spirit: few of the 'little ordinary people' she commends for behaving so well in the Blitz would have warmed to her description of East End evacuees as 'savage, verminous and wholly illiterate', or have wept for her as she bewailed the exit of domestic help from London.

1. Virago publish *A Pin to See the Peepshow* (1979), *The Lacquer Lady* (1979), and *Moonraker* (1981). The Hogarth Press publish *The Baffle Book*, edited by F. Tennyson Jesse (1984).

Richard Rorty

Against Belatedness

The Legitimacy of the Modern Age
by Hans Blumenberg, translated by Robert Wallace
(MIT Press, 1983)

Lots of people blame the way things have been going lately on 'false consciousness'. We are, they say, trapped in a conceptual scheme which distorts the way things really are. All our ways of talking, acting and hoping are infected by these concepts. We cannot expect things to get any better until we rid ourselves of them and adopt a new form of intellectual life, one which helps to encourage the emergence of new forms of social life. On this view, we are just not with it if our highest social hopes are, for example, that Somozas and Castros will be replaced by Allendes, that larger numbers of people will lead longer, more leisured lives, and that we shall eventually get solar power and nuclear disarmament. For we are still thinking in a 'liberal' or 'hegemonic' or 'scientistic' or 'technocratic' or 'rationalistic' way. This way of thinking is, we are told, 'bankrupt'. What we *should* be hoping for is that, in our capacity as the vanguard of human thought, we shall be able to break out of the vocabularies which we have inherited from the 19th century, and thus 'unmask' what is being done by people whose highest hopes are still those of John Stuart Mill.

When people who take this line are asked what alternative concepts they would recommend, they usually reply that the question is premature. Self-criticism must come first. We need to deconstruct the metaphysics of presence, or to become aware of the repressive character of the most benevolent-looking of contemporary institutions, or to see the distortions induced by innocuous-seeming linguistic expressions. Time enough to think of some new metaphysics or institutions or language when we have gotten rid of the old. This is a predictable reply, for those who accuse us of 'false consciousness' would risk self-refutation if they replied: 'Right. Here are the new concepts you need.' The danger is that the rest of us might say: 'They sound pretty good – we'll give them a whirl.' Such a reply would falsify the original claim that we had all been imprisoned within old ways of thinking. If intelligible alternative concepts are available for the asking, then the old concepts were not deep and tacit and unquestioned enough to have created 'false consciousness'. Chains that easy to break cannot count as bondage. No 'epistemological rupture' will be required. So people who use such notions cannot tell us what is false about our consciousness by spelling out what undistorted consciousness looks like. They have to gesture in the direction of a place where such consciousness exists or existed.

Marxists usually gesture in the direction of a working class which has not been corrupted by 'consumerism', and hence retains a revolutionary consciousness. Others gesture in the direction of a monastery in Ladakh, or a commune in Oregon. But mostly the gesture is towards the past. Nietzsche, at his worst, gestured towards some narcissistic and inarticulate hunks of Bronze Age beefcake. Carlyle gestured towards some contented peasants working the lands of a kindly medieval abbot. Lots of us occasionally gesture in the direction of the lost world in which our parents or our grandparents told us they grew up. Heidegger, the great master of nostalgia, kept gesturing towards those pre-Socratics whose one-liners left most room for retranslation (or, as he put it, the most open space for Being).

It is to the credit of such post-Heideggerian philosophers as Derrida and Foucault that they avoid this insistence on the belatedness of the modern age. They are trying to work out from under the notion of 'false consciousness' by admitting that 'false' is not the right term, and that 'unmasking' is the wrong rhetoric. They recognise that if we are going to set aside the reality-appearance distinction, typical of what Heidegger called 'the metaphysics of presence', we must be careful not to smuggle it back in, disguised as a distinction between the pristine old and the nasty new. So what we get from Derrida and Foucault, and from other contemporary French writers, is not so much attempts to unmask the realities of the time as warnings to eschew 'totalisation' – to avoid the 'metaphysical' impulse to place everything within one great big 'privileged' ahistorical context. From this point of view, Heidegger's downbeat history of philosophy (with everything getting more impoverished and constrained and etiolated as you go along) is just Hegel stood, yet again, on his head – the inverse of Hegel's upbeat story of everything having gotten richer and freer and more colourful. What we want, on this view, is acknowledgment of discontinuity and openendedness and contingency, rather than either nostalgia or exuberance.

Given this state of intellectual play, about the last thing one would expect to come down the pike is a great sweeping history of the course of European thought, built on the Hegel-Heidegger scale, which has Francis Bacon as one of its heroes, speaks well of the Enlightenment (of all periods), and suggests that the future lies (of all directions) ahead. It has been a long time since anybody with pretensions to historical depth has agreed with Macaulay about Bacon. The Enlightenment has been a favourite target ever since Adorno blamed it for Los Angeles. The belief that things might well get better and better the more technological mastery we acquire has almost vanished, even from the popular press. But Blumenberg's book makes all the things that Heidegger made look bad look good again. He turns Heidegger's story on its head, but does not fall back into the totalising metaphysics which backed up Hegel's story. He gives us good old-fashioned *Geistesgeschichte*, but without the teleology and purported inevitability characteristic of the genre, and condemned by liberals such as Popper and Berlin.

Die Legitimität der Neuzeit was published in 1966, and has been much discussed in Germany, though not much elsewhere. Badly educated English-speaking philosophers like myself (the kind who read long books in German only if they absolutely have to, *non sine ira et studio*) owe a great deal to Robert Wallace. He has translated eight hundred pages of very tough German as lucidly as literalness permits. (We also owe a lot to the MIT Press series 'Studies in Contemporary German Social Thought', which promises more Blumenberg books in the future.) Those of us who agree with Nietzsche and Heidegger that the philosophical tradition is pretty well played out, with Carlyle and Foucault that the arts and the sciences have not been unmixed blessings, and with Marxists that we should not believe what the lying capitalist press tells us about the modern world, but whose highest hopes are still those of Mill, now have a champion. Or, if not exactly a champion, at least somebody whose upbeat history we can cite against those who revel in belatedness, and against those who fear that telling big sweeping *geistesgeschichtlich* stories will reinforce our bad old totalising urges.

The German mode of gearing up to think about something – starting with the Greeks and working down through, for example, Cicero, Galileo and Schelling before saying anything off your own bat – is easily parodied. But it is an explicit and conscientious way of doing something that we all do, usually tacitly and carelessly. We all carry some potted intellectual history around with us, to be spooned out as needed. Those of us who don't do the historical work ourselves are fated to pick up, usually at several removes, somebody else's story (for example, Augustine's, Macaulay's, Marx's, H. G. Wells's, Will Durant's). Such stories determine our sense of what is living and what is dead in the past, and thus of when the crucial steps forward, or the crucial mistakes or ruptures, occurred.

Most intellectuals still think that the most decisive step of all came in the 17th and 18th centuries, when we got out from under prejudice, superstition and the belief in God. Since then we have been becoming freer and freer thanks to the developing natural sciences, the proliferation of new artistic forms, increasingly democratic political institutions, and similar aids to self-confidence, necessary for life in a Godless universe. The alternative, minority view (which has become the majority view among French and German intellectuals in the last few decades) is that the 17th and 18th centuries merely 'secularised' various religious themes. This story dismisses such visions of human progress as Mill's, Marx's, Dewey's and Rawls's as merely anthropomorphised and vulgarised versions of Christian eschatology. This view is nicely summed up by a quote from Karl Löwith, included by Wallace in his very clear and helpful 'Translator's Introduction': 'The modern mind has not made up its mind whether it should be Christian or pagan. It sees with one eye of faith and the other of reason. Hence its vision is necessarily dim in comparison with either Greek or Biblical thinking.' From this point of view, it does not make much difference whether you prefer Socrates to Christ or conversely, as long as you despise the dim moderns. Löwith here follows Nietzsche, who was equally nasty about both Socrates and Christ, but insisted that either was infinitely preferable to us feeble late-comers. Löwith's view chimes with Heidegger's slogan 'We are too late for the gods and too early for Being', and with similar slogans in Ortega, Strauss, Adorno etc. Whatever else these people disagree about, they unite in despising the hopes of contemporary liberals.

Blumenberg gets his book off to an unfortunately slow start with a hundred pages on the notion of 'secularisation', designed to undercut the cliché that liberal belief in progress is just warmed-over Christian hope. This section is filled with arch and allusive replies to critics of the first edition of the book – replies which Wallace does his best to elucidate in footnotes, but which are often pretty confusing. Still, the drift is clear: just because we have recognised the silliness of the claim that Christianity was 'just superstition and priestcraft' we need not run to the other extreme and say that Enlightenment beliefs in Nature and Progress were 'just heretical re-formulations of Christian dogma'. What the Enlightenment gave us was not 'the transposition of authentically Christian convictions into secularised alienation from their origin, but rather . . . the *reoccupation* of answer positions that had become vacant'. That is, people still needed answers to questions like 'What is it all for?' but once they had given up trying to make sense of a relation between themselves and Omnipotence they found some genuinely new answers to give to this question, answers which had nothing to do with Omnipotence.

These answers consisted in variations on the claim that the point of our lives lies in our contribution to an infinite task – the acquisition of Baconian knowledge-as-power, the satisfaction of theoretical curiosity – which lies before the species as a whole. This is not a Christian heresy, any more than Christianity was 'just' Gnosticism plus some new proper names. The Enlightenment did not just rechristen the Incarnate Infinite 'man' instead of 'Christ'. Rather, from Hobbes on 'the infinite serves . . . less to answer one of the great traditional questions than to blunt it, less to give meaning to history than to dispute the claim to be able to give it meaning.' The substitution of an infinitely long time in which progress can occur for a pre-existent infinite which will redeem our finitude is not just a 'transposition'. It is a leap in the dark of the same magnitude as the 'leap' which Kierkegaard said separates the Christian from the Socratic. Here as elsewhere in the book, Blumenberg shows us how easy and misleading it is to pick a description sufficiently abstract to encompass ancient, medieval and modern beliefs, and then to say that they are all 'merely alternative forms' of the same superseded way of thinking. This facile use of abstraction ignores the struggle and the labour which were required to forge these 'alternative forms', and the fact that no one would have gone through such struggles for the sake of a 'transposition'.

In Part Two of the book – 'Theological Absolutism and Human Self-Assertion' – Blumenberg hits his stride, and swings into his story. He thinks that the Middle Ages reached a predestined crisis when the notion of Divine Omnipotence was thought through by Ockham to its bitter end. Ockham urged that there was no reason knowable to man why God actualised this possible world rather than another. This left us no alternative but Baconian pragmatism: the attitude that says: 'Who cares how things look to God? Let us find out how they can be made to work for *us*.' On this view, Ockham cleared the ground for Galileo: 'It was not a matter of indifference which of the possible worlds God had in fact created; but since man could not hope to fathom this decision, it had to be made a matter of indifference. The search for a set of instruments for man that would be usable in any possible world provides the criterion for the elementary exertions of the modern age; the *mathematising* and the *materialising* of nature.'

To view nature as matter in motion was not, on Blumenberg's view, a live option until the medieval dialectic had played itself out – until the hope that nature was created for the sake of man had destroyed itself from within. It is not that 'science' (incarnate earlier in Lucretius and reborn in Galileo) 'discovered' what the world was really like, and thus no longer needed the hypothesis of a divinity. Rather, there was intellectual room for what we now call 'science' only when another, initially more promising, alternative had been worked through.

Baconian pragmatism and what Dyksterhuis called 'the mechanisation of the world-picture' made possible the modern age – the age of what Blumenberg calls 'self-assertion'. His attempt to legitimate the modern age is an attempt to defend all the things which Heidegger despised about the 20th century: its proliferating curiosity, its urge for technical mastery, its refusal to be interested in something larger than itself which contains it and makes it possible, and its consequent orientation toward an unknown future. For Blumenberg, the Romantic attempt to discredit the Enlightenment, and the continuation of this attempt by Nietzsche and Heidegger, confuse a justified criticism of the Enlightenment's attempt at 'self-foundation' with an unjustified criticism of its ideal of self-assertion. The Enlightenment was, indeed, wrong to see itself as the discovery of the true, ahistorical framework of human existence – as the first occasion on which humans had seen themselves as they truly were. But one can agree with Nietzsche's and Heidegger's and Derrida's criticisms of the very idea of such a framework ('the metaphysics of presence') without despising the mode of life which the Enlightenment made possible for us. Blumenberg wants to abandon Husserl's nostalgic Cartesian hope to escape from history into presuppositionless philosophy (a hope still shared by many analytic philosophers). But he insists that the fact that the modern age lacks 'foundations' is to its credit, not a reason for mistrusting it. It is an indication of courage, not of weakness or of self-deception. The legitimacy of our modern consciousness is simply that it is the best way we have so far found to give sense to our lives. This is to say that it beats the only other two ways we know about – the ancient attempt to find philosophical foundations, and the medieval attempt to find theological ones. So Blumenberg can pretty much agree with Heidegger's account of the stages we have traversed since Parmenides, but whereas Heidegger sees these stages as successive fallings-away from primordial greatness, Blumenberg sees them as rational rejections of alternatives that didn't work out. The rejections were rational not by reference to ahistorical criteria, but merely by reference to what he calls 'sufficient rationality' – rationality as pragmatic choice among available tools, without recourse to antecedent standards of preference. This is just enough rationality 'to accomplish the post-medieval self-assertion and to bear the consequences of this emergency self-consolidation'. Blumenberg wants to make a virtue of what the Romantics rightly diagnosed as a necessity for those who think of empirical science as the paradigmatic human activity: viz. the abandonment of a context for human life larger than that provided by the activities of our contemporaries, and the abandonment of some more definite object of hope than the unknown fortunes of our descendants.

The story which is adumbrated in Part Two of *The Legitimacy of the Modern Age* is told again, at greater length and with more attention to the ancient world, in Part Three ('The "Trial" of Theoretical Curiosity'). This is the longest part of the book, and is a series of reminders that the sentence which begins Aristotle's *Metaphysics* ('All men by nature desire to know') has not always had the sense it has for us. It has not always meant that our curiosity about how things work is an essential and laudable part of us. For the ancients, this phrase implied both that knowledge of theoretical truth was necessary for happiness and that 'the truth in its totality was at the disposition of the individual' (as opposed to the race, in the course of a potentially infinite future). Our modern concept of happiness has to do (as Heidegger rightly says) with mastery rather than with contemplation or participation. It is a Baconian conception of happiness which, Blumenberg says, 'reduced the necessary knowledge to the amount fixed by the requirements of domination over natural reality. The recovery of paradise was not supposed to yield a transparent and familiar reality but only a tamed and obedient one.' Blumenberg tells a story of how the assumption that reality was transparent and familiar yields to ancient scepticism about both of the implications which Aristotle had drawn from his maxim. He then shows how the Sceptics' renunciation of knowledge of reality ('for the last time in our tradition down to Nietzsche,' Blumenberg provocatively but dubiously says) is trumped by Tertullian's claim that Christ has made theoretical curiosity obsolete. This claim detaches happiness from the pursuit of knowledge, and puts Christian faith in the vacancy left by the sceptical dissolution of the possibility of a contemplative life. From then on, the burden of proof was on those who (like St Thomas Aquinas) thought that Aristotle was not wholly wrong, and that curiosity might not be simply a vice (the excitation of an unruly member, the inquiring eye as homologue of the pushy penis).

Blumenberg takes very seriously indeed the episcopal condemnation of St Thomas for having cast doubt on divine omnipotence, interpreting it as an indictment for *curiositas*. He sees the medieval period as driven to insist on that omnipotence by the break which it had made with ancient thought. So he thinks it was fated to wind up with Ockham's nominalist and voluntarist rejection of the Aristotelian and Thomistic claim that the human mind naturally grasps the essences of things. But this rejection leaves theoretical curiosity without excuse. Bacon's desertion of the idea of 'the essences of things', and the infinitising of space and time which followed Copernicus, provided a new excuse – one which the ancients had never thought of, and which the medievals would have regarded as blasphemous. Blumenberg traces the further development of this excuse in discussions of (among others) Galileo, Descartes, Voltaire, Hume and Kant. He ends this section of the book with a sympathetic restatement of Feuerbach's claim that 'the future heals the pains of the past's unsatisfied knowledge drive,' and a sympathetic interpretation of Freud's remark that 'the postponement of loving until full knowledge is acquired ends in a substitution of the latter for the former.' Both men are interpreted as recognising that 'ancient efforts to understand the infinite, the absolute, the self-sufficient, the self-enjoying turn out to be necessarily roundabout attempts by man to grasp himself . . . as having a right to self-enjoyment.'

The concluding Part Four of the book is a very beautiful diptych called 'Aspects of the Epochal Threshold: The Cusan and the Nolan'. Blumenberg thinks that what happened between the time of Nicholas of Cusa and Giordano Bruno (of Nola) was a genuinely 'epochal' change, but that 'there are no witnesses to changes of epoch. The epochal turning is an imperceptible frontier, bound to no crucial date or event.' So he offers us the view from Cusa's side of the threshold ('the world as God's self-restriction') and from Bruno's ('the world as God's' indefinitely long and wide 'self-exhaustion'). Here the discussion becomes much more detailed and exegetical than in earlier portions of the book, and I shall not try to summarise it. Suffice it to say that Bruno, like Bacon and Feuerbach, is one of Blumenberg's unfashionable heroes. For Blumenberg, Bruno 'only accepted a challenge that was historically posed. He gave it an answer that went to the root of the formation of the age that had come to an end. What was received as "joyful tidings" and in the toil of centuries had become "Scholasticism", he experienced as trauma.'

In the sketchy plot-summaries I have been giving I have barely been able to hint at the subtlety, richness and originality of Blumenberg's book. There is not a stale sentence in it. Everything has been thought out anew. This makes it a slow book to read, for one constantly has to chew over novel interpretations of familiar texts. (Not to mention having to deal with texts one never knew existed – like Peter Damian's discussion of whether God can restore lost virginity.) Although the scholarship is overwhelming (and, like all scholarship, disputable and likely eventually to be corrected), one never feels that a fact or a text has been dragged in so that the author can show off. On the contrary, there is a moral earnestness about the book which is extremely impressive. Blumenberg clearly feels that the damage done to the liberal intellectuals' self-confidence by Nietzsche's and Heidegger's contempt for the modern needs to be undone. It took considerable courage to try to do this: to be unfashionable enough to insist that, despite all the continuities which scholarship has detected, the traditional divisions between ancient, medieval and modern are just as important as we always thought them, and then to argue that our technological civilisation has nothing to be ashamed of (even though it has a great deal to be wary of).

It should not be thought, however, that Blumenberg wants to revive Enlightenment scientism. He should not be seen as a champion of 'reason' against what is sometimes (misleadingly) called 'Heideggerian irrationalism'. He rightly criticises Heidegger's own 'history of Being' as a revived form of Ockhamite theology, but he is equally adamant against the idea that the modern age is the one 'in which reason, and thus man's natural vocation, finally prevailed'. As he says, 'the idea of reason liberating itself from its medieval servitude made it impossible to understand how such servitude could ever have been inflicted upon the constitutive power of the human spirit . . . Another dangerous implication of this explanation was that it was bound to inject doubt into the self-consciousness of reason's definitive victory and the impossibility of a repetition of its subjection. Thus the picture of its own origins and possibility in history that the epoch of rationality made for itself remained peculiarly irrational.' On Blumenberg's view, the Enlightenment's scientistic attempt to *ground* itself as well as to assert itself – its urge to regard itself as something more than just a further desperate attempt by the species to give itself a point – was bound to produce Heidegger's reactive attempt to get beyond 'grounding' (and, also, one might add, the popular French parlour game of *mettre en abîme*).

It seems to follow from what he says, though Blumenberg does not make this explicit, that the way to stop the pendulum swinging between 'irrationalism' and 'defences of reason' is to let historical self-consciousness take the place of metaphysics. Such historical self-consciousness would not require ahistorical metaphysical or epistemological back-up, but merely a vocabulary which, as he says, has 'a durability that is very great in relation to both our capacity to perceive historical events and the rate of change involved in them'. In other words, if we can tell a story about why we moderns are in better shape than the ancients and the medievals, we've got what he calls 'sufficient rationality' – the same sort of Whiggish rationality as we use when telling stories of scientific progress. We can ignore the question of whether the heuristic vocabulary we use in telling this story – the vocabulary which describes 'the constant matrix of needs' which humans fulfil by telling themselves philosophical and theological and historical stories – is grounded in anything. (As we ignore the question of whether the vocabulary of modern physics, which we use heuristically when writing the history of ancient physics, is more than 'just' *our* vocabulary.) If such a vocabulary makes enough sense of the past to let us avoid unanswerable riddles like 'How did human reason let itself be repressed for so long?' or 'How did we ever get stuck with the "metaphysics of presence" in the first place?' that will be justification enough.

Blumenberg resembles Foucault in his attempt to get intellectual history out from under 'the dilemma of nominalism and realism in interpreting the validity of the concept of an epoch'. He shares Foucault's distrust for 'the logic of continuity' which 'takes as its only alternatives the constancy of what "was there all along", or preformation extending as far back as documentation is possible'. But whereas Foucault settles for striking discontinuities, abjuring 'totalising' stories which cover twenty-five hundred years, Blumenberg thinks that we can keep on writing such stories if we recognise that 'all logic . . . is based on structures of dialogue.' But the dialogue in question is one which only belatedly finds out what it has been about:

If the modern age was not the monologue beginning at point zero, of the absolute subject – as it pictures itself – but rather the system of efforts to answer in a new context questions that were posed to man in the Middle Ages, then this would entail new standards for interpreting what does in fact function as an answer to a question but does not represent itself as such an answer . . . In a cartoon . . . De Gaulle was pictured opening a press conference with the remark, 'Gentlemen! Now will you please give me the questions to my answers!' Something along these lines would serve to describe the procedure that would have to be employed in interpreting the logic of a historical epoch in relation to the one preceding it.

Here Blumenberg seems to be saying that, just as the history of science represents Aristotle as talking about inertia even though he did not believe there was such a thing, so we must read the ancients and the medievals by our own lights. We need not worry about whether those lights pick out 'what was there all the time', nor about whether we can translate our jargon and theirs into a common 'neutral' vocabulary. It is enough that we should find a story which treats our predecessors neither as heroes nor as fools, but simply as fellow inquirers who lacked the advantages of hindsight.

The first edition of Blumenberg's book was published four years after Kuhn's *Structure of Scientific Revolutions* and one year before Foucault's *Les Mots et les Choses*. But the latter book waited only six years to be translated into English. Ever since it has stood side by side with Kuhn's on many bookshelves, profoundly affecting the way we English-speakers think about intellectual history. It is a pity that Blumenberg's book went untranslated for 17 years. If it had been on those same shelves for the past decade our reflections on such topics as 'progress' and 'rationality' would have been greatly enriched. For Blumenberg, as aware of 'incommensurability' as Kuhn and of 'ruptures' as Foucault, helps us see that we have to keep right on being 'Whiggish' in our historiography, and that what matters is the subtlety and self-consciousness of our Whiggery. He thus helps us see that the demand to unmask completely, to make all things new, to start from nowhere, to substitute new true consciousness for old false consciousness, is itself an echo of the Enlightenment. It is precisely that part of the Enlightenment which really *is* 'bankrupt'.

A. J. P. Taylor

Diary

It is some time since I wrote a diary here. It will be seen I have had plenty to write about. I should explain that there are two versions of a period of my life. One is the version of other people, a version which others try to impose upon me. The other is my own version, a version equally genuine and much more unusual.

According to others such as my doctors and the members of my family, I had a mental breakdown, was the victim of fantasies and never moved from the hospital bedroom except to have a bath and did not read even the newspaper. This version can be disregarded. According to my recollection, I had a life of adventure interrupted by periods of relaxation, and never encountered insoluble difficulties. Most of my life seems to have been passed in some part of the North of England and at different periods. My first stretch was in Roman Britain, when I lived in York and was afterwards stationed on the Wall. These experiences were very instructive to me as an historian.

The Romans did not remain long. Nor did I waste much time at the court of King Arthur. The outstanding figure of my attraction was the king, though I did not manage to encounter him often. This was the period when I spent most of my time on the Yorkshire moors. I got lost pretty often, though always rescued by other wanderers. Gradually I moved into a more civilised existence. The centre of my life was now Harrogate, a place I have never visited in my life. I had difficulties here obtaining regular copies of the *Manchester Guardian*, which did not surprise me at all. I also attended a very expensive luncheon party one Sunday in Harrogate given by my daughter Amelia, who is not in the habit of giving expensive luncheon parties.

I gradually resumed a family life. The principal figures in it were my mother and father, both of whom had, I thought, been dead for some time. My father had taken over a medieval monastery – was it Furness Abbey? – which he had transformed into a boarding-house for holidaymakers. My father was as delightful as ever and as efficient. I spent an occasional night with him during the summer. Though friendly, he never displayed much interest in my activities whatever they might be.

I sometimes went shopping with my mother in Manchester, a thing I had done often enough in real life. I found Kendal Milne a great obstacle against getting from one end of Manchester to another. One afternoon I encountered a birthday party given by some shop assistants. I wanted to get through, not to take part in it. My father took me out to his monastery, an event which somewhat puzzled me because in the general puzzle of my existence I was aware that I lived in the 18th century when motor-cars did not exist. It also puzzled me that my hospital rooms were sometimes in London and sometimes in France, probably in Paris, though the nurses were always English. No one ever tried to explain to me where I was or what I was doing. It was a long period of bewilderment which I gradually accepted as one of total incomprehensibility. It then just disappeared along with the figures who populated it, including my father and mother. I was sorry to lose him, otherwise I did not worry.

In the last episode of my medical career some of it became clear to me. I recognised that I was in a hospital, though it was not clear to me where – probably London, though it might be somewhere in France. It was also clear to me that wherever it was it was difficult or impossible to get out of it. In the quiet of lunchtime I would pack a small bag and set off for the way out. Sooner or later a nurse would catch me and ask me where I was going. Patiently I would be led back to my own quarters without any explanation. I must have read something during this long and dreary period. But apart from the *Times* every morning, I can only remember reading *The Good Soldier Schweik* in its most extended edition – something over seven hundred pages. It is still an incomparable war book.

One morning, without any explanation, I was told that I was moving out. There was my wife waiting for me. I had to admit that I had spent all this time in University College Hospital, not in France, but I still found many things hard to explain – what had been wrong with me, what treatment I had received, why it should end. The important thing was to be out. I have firmly resolved never to enter a hospital again. If this means the end of my life I shall not care. Anything is better than to be imprisoned in a hospital.

Life has begun to stir since I was released. I opened an exhibition of the works of David Low, which had been locked up since his death. Some years ago I opened a similar exhibition of Low's works which the University of Canterbury had managed to acquire. Now I launched another set which his daughter had at last revealed. It is the finest collection of radical art in existence. A week or two later I attended a commemoration of Bronterre O'Brien, perhaps the greatest of the Chartist leaders. I must confess that I had forgotten about O'Brien until I looked him up. Once I read again his enthusiasm for the radical cause I recognised his greatness. We made something of a pilgrimage to his tomb in Abney Park cemetery, Stoke Newington. This was wild land for us. I had no idea that Stoke Newington was so near the centre of London, still less that Abney Park cemetery was a collection of some historic merit. However, after some toil, we made the journey. The cemetery was much overgrown. Even O'Brien's table tomb was obscured by vegetation. But a way had been cleared. I was glad to praise the great radical even though his memory is somewhat faded. Stoke Newington has an active group of his admirers, mostly Irish, led by Chris Maguire, an Irish electrician whose acquaintance I was glad to make. Of such men were radicals once made.

That ends my expedition. I cannot walk any distance and easily fall asleep. It is a relief not to go to the theatre or a cinema. I miss chamber concerts more than any other form of public activity. One day, perhaps, I shall manage to attend one. One day life will begin again for me. I cannot say that I miss it very much.

Lawrence Gowing

Human Stuff

Day after day I find an excuse to be in Piccadilly and once there give up any attempt to stay out of the galleries at the Royal Academy.[1] Venetian art of the 16th century is running in one's head like music, complete with its resounding orchestration. One abandons oneself to it. Yet it is not merely indulgence. One is drawn by the magnetism of an idea: the idea of art invented in Venice soon after 1500, at just the moment when this incomparable exhibition begins, an idea that one recognises, without reasoning how, as the modern idea.

In gallery after gallery at Burlington House the melodies of Venetian painting hang in the air. Anything that Giorgione had to do with seems to have been implicitly musical – and he surely had to do with far more than he painted. The pictures at Venice and Dresden, the *Tempest* and the *Venus*, which are most certainly his work, are remembered whenever in the galleries the goddess lies nude and dreaming while turbid storm clouds roll up from the horizon to discharge their passion in the evening sky.

A dream was the natural medium of Venetian imagining. A print entitled *The Dream of Raphael* (apparently because the engraver later worked for him) is the opposite of rational Classicism. Baby monsters out of Bosch, just such monsters as infest Giorgione's *Sunset Landscape* in the National Gallery, crawl from a canal into a catastrophic townscape, there to haunt two slumbering Giorgionesque nudes. The flaming town is a darkened arena for an extraordinary mastery of graphic tone. Imaginings like this are the common context for the musical harmonies of Venetian art.

The visual music is an extension of consciousness which is in both senses as fantastic as the widening frontiers of thought in Tuscany and the Rhineland. It was akin to the exploratory resource of Leonardo, who was in Venice twice in the first years of the century, perhaps showing Giorgione a roundness as impalpable as smoke and teaching Sebastiano how to model an eerily palpable thigh under St Louis's robe. The music was there already. It flowed through the Alpine passes with the Northern travellers. Nightfall in the countryside above Bergamo was the setting in which Cariani's *Lutenist* – like an offspring of the couple in Giorgione's *Tempesta*, brought up to just their suspenseful mood – thoughtfully attended to his melody, while a shepherd with a pipe (sheep were herded to the flute in Venetian painting) walked through a darkening farmyard towards the mountains. The *Pastoral Concert* must have been inspired by Giorgione, even though Titian painted the picture (in the Louvre). In mid-century (and often in this exhibition) the concert reassembles to celebrate erotic delight and fate. In one print the band is conducted by an *écorché* figure and a skeleton, bodies flayed for art. The subject is known as the 'Aviary of Death'.

At the very start, in the Large South Room, which at other exhibitions one is inclined to miss, yet now cannot stay away from, one meets one of the great puzzles among the pictures that Giorgione had to do with, the *Judgment of Solomon*, unseen for a generation in a country house in Dorset. It is found to be a highly intellectual picture, by someone who was seriously interested in the receding depth of a basilica and the justice that was dispensed in it, with a stepped perspective as exact and spacious as in Giorgione's Castelfranco altar-piece. So much in the picture is so personal that it should surely be possible to recognise its painter. The taut, diagonal creases in the judge's cloak, for example, which are so well conceived to agree with the lunging and retiring diagonals of the action: they inaugurate the zigzag folds which catch the light in Venetian painting, not only modelling shape but proposing pictorial directions, prompting the significant gestures of the brush, which *are* Venetian painting. It is clear that Sebastiano del Piombo, lately the favoured candidate for the honour of having painted the *Judgment of Solomon*, which, unfinished and damaged as it is, is still an indubitable masterpiece, is unlikely to be the right one. His organ shutters hanging opposite disqualify him. The mothers, between whom Solomon must judge, are clearly, coolly drawn, one of them in *profil perdu*: they are quite evidently not Sebastiano's monumentally sultry sybils.

What great draughtsmen these painterly colourists were! Perhaps Giorgione drew with such functional clarity precisely because he insisted on launching straight into colour. The series of hues strung out across the *Judgment* now emerges as one of the most serenely resolved colour-scales in art. On the left, the soldier in silver and red is the brother of the soldier in the same square cap who has been severed from but now restored to the so-called 'Adultress' from Glasgow. The women beside him in moss-green and mauve lead to the constable in apricot and silver; the boy behind has a relative, similarly breaking out of the penumbra, in the *Pastoral Concert*. The judge in slate-grey and blue, with his pronounced, diagonal decisiveness, is the pivot of the whole picture, against the mauve pink cloth of honour that hangs with such exact chromatic justice against the depth of space. Then the sequence continues, with its consistent freshness. The bearded sage from among the Vienna *Philosophers*, with his eloquently drawn hands, is softly, gently modelled, like the old man in the Glasgow picture and in the San Rocco Bearing of the Cross – modelled with transparent roundness as only one painter did it; he is in cinnabar and indigo. The true mother's goodness is epitomised (and aligned with Solomon) by a chord of blue white and emerald. The agonised courtier who understands takes up the indigo and apricot. The sequence leads at last to the executioner in whose dusky colour and diagonal thrust the picture is concentrated and concluded.

We are present at the exact moment when the local colour of the 15th century changes into the tonal colour of a new age through a system of finely intelligent and intelligible modulations that allow the eye to exchange the scales of value and hue – a system of tuned affinity and compromise achieved without apparent impurity or loss, analogous to equal temperament in the keyboard to come. Now that the *Judgment* hangs beside the Glasgow picture (in which I persist in seeing Susanna and the young Daniel), both reveal their beauty as never before. It is a sign that we have pictures in their right context. Can we really doubt who these two masterpieces were predominantly due to? Looking at the *Judgment of Solomon*, we can imagine the radiance and clarity of Giorgione's vanished frescoes on the outside of the German Warehouse (now the post-office) at the Rialto. In the Glasgow picture the obsession with light on crumpled drapery is found to be the special property of the flickering brush, which points – and how pointedly – towards the greatest Venetian painting of the century.

Veronese, whom we honour for limpid, daylit iridescence, was equally lucid and gracefully specific as a draughtsman. We can judge his feeling subtlety when he is modelling a head with colour – Procris, for example, mourned by the careless and repentant Cephalus, in a picture (borrowed from Strasbourg) which balances with tragic gravity the buoyant blue and orange of its pendant (from Madrid), the famous *Venus and Adonis*, in which consummated love is lazily triumphant. Venus and Adonis are posted up triumphantly all over London, and for once a poster does something useful, apart from attracting us to an irresistible exhibition. If you wonder why the Prado picture has never looked so good, you can thank the poster for restoring its concentration by silently omitting the equivalent of half a metre along the top, which is an unlucky addition.

Under the leadership of Titian, Venetian painting turned in a direction that what we know of Giorgione barely suggests. Form was generated by colour as it had never been before. Colour marked the quality of things that were luminous of their inward nature – and still are when a painter has the constancy to achieve the steady, sensuous state that can be wrought in the ductile stuff of paint. In the 12-year-old Ranuccio Farnese's tunic, painted by Titian in 1542, crimson breeds a golden lustre which condenses into glistening embroidery and materialises, bulging, in the buttons. 'Finally *splendour* was added, which is something quite different from light.' Painters who read Pliny would eagerly have sought that splendour. Movements of the brush are direct and purposeful, like the impulsive gestures that spread the crumbling incandescence along the zigzag folds of drapery, moulded by the wearer or billowed by the wind and reflecting, in its directional impetus and chromatic magnificence, both the outward glamour and inward emotion of painting. The two culminated together in the pictures that flowed from Titian through the third quarter of the century.

A richness of material and imagining that was intrinsic to oil paint is the dominant theme of the exhibition, and its dominance was due to Titian. Lotto, the most individual talent that Venice bred, was only himself in Bergamo. One can see that the sensational disproportions in his manner, or the amusing fear and ferocity inspired in the Virgin's household cat by the Annunciation, would have been excluded by the convention of grandeur that Titian promoted in Venice. Conversely, young men from Bergamo, like Cariani and Palma, who sought their fortunes in the capital, made more use of the Giorgionesque example than any painter native to the city. Paris Bordone from Treviso must have been schooled in conformity. He made the *Mystic Marriage of St Catherine* into the most courtly and fleshly of sacred conversations, surprisingly set in a landscape almost unaltered from the *Pastoral Concert*. In later life Bordone made a corner in florid realisations of mythology with abundant rosebuds and shot silk, which were the height of poetic luxury. Wherever the spell of Venetian power and wealth was felt, Perseus armed and Venus crowned would have been thought of as Bordone painted them. The sumptuous figurative resource of the Italy and the Antiquity imagined by Shakespeare was not far away.

Across Gallery III the accumulating coolness and warmth of

Veronese and Titian face one another with staggering effect, broken only by a splendidly energetic full-length of a cavalry commander ascribed to a certain Brusasorci, which, if it was really by him, would make him at a stroke one of one's favourite painters. The armour is striped in shining bands, which echo the contours with arresting kinetic effect: as one moves gingerly past, the commander strides too. His family thought that he was painted by Veronese and such a presence was hardly within the reach of lesser men.

At the far end of the gallery Lombard realism takes over, and sustains the comparison with Venice better than anyone could guess. The catalogue describes Brescia (where the striped armour was made) as 'the most avant-garde artistic centre in the Veneto': it is delightful when historians permit one another such liberties, and makes one wonder what the expression can mean. Certainly the cool objectivity of Brescia anticipates a common temper of 17th-century painting, just as the other kind of Brescian picture, the hallucinating visionary grey in which Moretto painted a dramatic Ecce Homo, offers a phantom foretaste of Zurbaran.

It is not at all clear what such unhistorical observations are really about. Painters in the hill-towns of the Terraferma certainly recorded human likeness with a social awareness that was not encouraged by the stately nobility of the capital. Lombard sobriety had by comparison a hard-bitten existential reference that must have been apparent and attractive. Northern travellers stopped at Brescia and there are drawings of Lombard pictures in Dutch sketchbooks. Across the next hundred years there are delightful coincidences: Cariani has a splendid brothel scene (always mistaken for a family portrait) which is like a prototype for Vermeer's *Procuress*, just as Vermeer's *House of Martha* at Edinburgh resembles a Moretto. One begins to doubt whether anything in the image stock is wholly unknown to any participant and presently ex-historians fall to wondering about a collective unconscious. The only undoubted fact is that Lombard painters maintained the empirical method that was one potentiality of the Giorgionesque innovation, and there in Lombardy it remained until a young man with a pathological depression came along to lay hold of it with a fury that set *disegno* at naught. At the end of the century a good judge could see nothing in Caravaggio's St Matthew pictures but 'the thought of Giorgione'. The mysterious avant-gardism and the impression of a Lombard current flowing strongly towards the future are due to the fact that Venice and the Veneto offered to European painting the 17th-century revolution and its 15th-century source, both at once.

In the centre of Gallery III, dominating the unparalleled assembly of Titian's last pictures, hangs the *Flaying of Marsyas*, which has not been exhibited in the West since 1673, when a bishop in Bohemia won it in a raffle. All these months – it is not too much to say – London has been half under the spell of this masterpiece, in which the tragic sense that overtook Titian's *poesie* in his seventies reached its cruel and solemn extreme. At most hours on most days there is a knot of visitors riveted and fairly perplexed in front of it. It is a controversial picture, not only in the way that late canvases by Titian are apt to be. Some of those who know the artist best doubt whether in basing so much of our view, and not of Titian only, on canvases that were left unfinished, we do not miss the coherence and deliberation of his purpose. That doubt can be set at rest: the *Marsyas* is as consistently and in detail as finely wrought as pictures that Titian valued and sold – and the canvas was signed. The serious doubt about the *Marsyas* is felt just because the story is so explicitly told.

In the autumnal woods a satyr is tied head down to a tree, from which his pipes are hanging, to suffer the punishment for challenging Apollo to a musical competition, which he could not by definition win against an antagonist who was none other than the inventor of music. With a rustic assistant (wearing a Phrygian cap) Apollo, identified by golden hair and a wreath of laurels from Parnassus, with almost loving attention is skinning him. A puppy laps up the blood that is shed and a hound is restrained by a child of the woodland people; another satyr comes with a bucket of water, and Midas, the judge, broods sadly on his failure to defend the mortal from the god. Behind, as god-like as anyone, a musician in crimson plays a *lira da braccio* with feeling. The controversy is an old one. Lessing thought Ovid's account disgusting and those who have difficulty with the picture, in which Titian followed Ovid closely, are echoing a painter of the Enlightenment who told Goethe that Raphael himself would have done better to avoid it. At the Academy people still ask, and on the radio well-meaning critics debate, how it is possible that a horribly painful subject should be the occasion of beauty or greatness in art.

As always with painting, we must look at what the picture is about. Certainly it is about the fate of a victim – which is to say, it is about identity and suffering. Ovid tells that Marsyas cried out: 'Why are you stripping me from myself?' It is about the presence in a body. The shaggy haunches are spreadeagled like a Vitruvian figure upside down, as if to demonstrate the satyr's noble proportions. Titian models his body to show how 'his nerves were exposed unprotected, his veins pulsed with no skin to protect them. It was possible to count his throbbing organs and the chambers of the lungs clearly visible within his breast.' Titian rubbed the golden colour into tender opalescence over the modelling of the chest. We notice what our own art has equipped us to see; Francis Bacon, who sometimes compares the exposure of a human subject with a carcass split in half, paints what is inherently vulnerable in a body. Ovid tells that 'the fertile earth grew wet with tears . . . received the falling drops into itself and drank them into its deepest veins.' Marsyas was indeed poured out like water (the account is curiously like the psalmist's prophecy). Not even the dogs that compassed him are missing from the picture. The stricken judge is enough to show that the painter knew grief, as Ovid did: 'the woodland gods, the fauns who haunt the countryside mourned for him; his brother satyrs too, and . . . all who pasture woolly sheep or horned cattle in these mountains.'

It is not easy for us that a picture which is about the punishment of arrogance should also be seriously to do with music. It was on behalf of order and the laws of harmonious proportion, which sound in the music of strings, that Apollo claimed victory over the chaotic and impulsive sound of the pipes. The disproportion was not musical only: Minerva, who invented the pipes, threw them away when she saw in the water that blowing them distended her cheeks. The punishment to which arrogance was submitted was itself a Dionysian rite, a purification that peeled off the ugliness of the outward man. Apollo's ideal, inscribed on his temple (from which Socrates, outwardly a satyr, adopted it), was self-knowledge, and Dante began the *Paradiso* with a prayer to him: 'Enter my breast and infuse me with your spirit, as you did when you tore Marsyas from the covering of his limbs.' Plato said that the strains of the pipes, which he excluded from the Republic, indicated those who were in need of the Gods. With Titian's Marsyas, so far from suffering cruelty, it appears that a need has been fulfilled. His eyes have a rapt and trance-like gleam. He is spellbound, transported by the rite.

One follows the story across the canvas, watching the smouldering colour, fanned or flicked into incandescence, then dwindling and swept broadly into shadow. Then one turns back to the magnetic player of the *lira da braccio*, as if to listen; very likely he is accompanying himself in song. Philipp Fehl, whose study illumines this picture, has connected him with the remaining figure in Ovid's account. He is a musician called Olympus, the pupil of Marsyas who loved him, and the mourner to whom Apollo gave the body. Olympus was converted by Apollo's music to harmony and to the lyre; he wrote a hymn to Apollo; perhaps he is singing it. He remained 'dear to Marsyas even then'. The melody which he contributes to the picture is the reconciliation of opposing principles, and it reconciles us to the theme.

It is quite a moving moment in Piccadilly in which we understand even a little of the mystery. There has been nothing quite equal to it in Gallery III since Mussolini unpardonably shipped the *Birth of Venus* to London in 1929. I saw it as a schoolboy; the sight of it over the heads of the crowd, and the awareness of the mystery, remain almost untouched by familiarity since. Tuscan painting has more in common with the Venetian experience than one would think. Bordone's St Catherine, for example, in her Giorgionesque landscape, advances with just the tripping step of Botticelli's Hour of Spring. Perhaps the painters were both imbued with the same lines of Ovid. But this year one attends to what is unique to Venice, and there is much more of it in this exhibition, more enlightenment, than one can possibly tell. The roomful of pictures by Jacopo Bassano produces the kind of knowledge that only a one-man show by a very good painter ever yields, the all-embracing knowledge of a personal context which adds to the meaning of every separate picture. It is a circumstance of this incomparably personal art of the West with which it remains for criticism and aesthetics fully to deal. Bassano, whom we are taught to respect for his bucolic inelegance and voracious country appetite, turns out to be a refined, discriminating intellect apparently of the opposite kind. Not instead – as well.

Who could have guessed, when the story of the Tintoretto family's *Paradise*, in the Doge's Palace, seemed complete and fairly wearisome, that a glorious *modello* (now at Lugano) was in store, as marvellously virile and wholly autograph as anything that 'the strongest of the Venetians' painted in his Herculean old age? Almost the only great master in Venice who was a natural-born Venetian, there was always within his power a spectral (yet bodily, muscularly corded) transformation-scene, which would contribute still more to the specifically Venetian discovery. Venice made the West aware of its least Platonic intuition: that it is the actual physical material that comes to life in Western art. The material of Western art has nothing to do with impurity: it is the stuff of imaginative embodiment. I should regret the immense success of the show if the genius of Venice were known simply as a notoriously good exhibition. In fact it is a dimension of the human potential which one is completed in, or impoverished without.

1. *The Genius of Venice 1500–1600*, edited by Jane Martineau and Charles Hope (Royal Academy of Arts in association with Weidenfeld, 1983).

Clive James

N.V. Rampant Meets Martin Amis

'This is the big one,' I told myself nervously. 'The Martin Amis interview. This is the one that could make you or break you.' As I neared his front door my heart was in my mouth.

No doubt he would have said it more cleverly. He would have said his heart was palpitating with trepidation like a poodle in heat in a monastery of mastiffs. Oh yes, he had the long words, Martin Amis. And he knew how to use them. He not only had the metaphors, he knew exactly what words like 'metaphor' meant. He knew what 'trepidation' meant. They had told him at Oxford. He had the education. He wasn't going to let you forget it. I asked myself: Why not cut your losses and get out now? But no, I told myself: because you've got something to offer too. Otherwise why would the oh-so-famous Amis be available at all?

'Come in,' said a familiar voice when I knocked with trepidation. (Yes, I knew what the word meant. I was only fooling back there when I pretended I didn't.) 'The door's open. Just push it.' Yeah, *pushing it*, I couldn't help thinking. Maybe that's what you've been doing, Martin, old son. Or Mart, as your friends call you. Your very powerful friends who can make or break a reputation with a flick of the telephone.

On the hallway occasional table was a copy of the collected works of Shakespeare, left oh-so-carelessly lying around so as to impress the less well-read. Well, I had heard of Shakespeare, so no luck there, Martin. But where *was* Martin?

Then I saw him lurking behind the volume of Shakespeare. Martin Amis, the oh-so-lauded so-called giant of his literary generation, was only four inches high.

'Glad you could make it. Glad in more ways than one,' said Martin in his self-consciously deep voice. 'Usually I drop down to the floor on a thread of cotton at about this time and start for the kitchen in the hope of getting a drink by dusk. But I've lost the thread.'

Lost the thread in more ways than one, I thought, Martin, old son. Especially in this new book of yours, *Money*. But I didn't say so. I couldn't risk the notorious scorn, the laser-like contempt of his brilliantly educated mind. And I hated myself because I didn't say so. And I hated him. But not as much as I hated his book. 'Congratulations on a masterpiece,' I said non-committally. 'I laughed continuously for two weeks and finally had to be operated on so that I could eat.' It was a tactful way of saying that I hadn't been as bowled over as he might fondly imagine.

'Thanks,' said the oh-so-blasé so-called genius, taking it as his due. 'Do you think you could give me a lift?'

He stepped into my open hand and I carried him into the study, where I put him down on his desk beside his typewriter. I could see now that I had been wrong about his being four inches high. He was three inches high. To depress the typewriter keys he must have to jump on them individually, and altering the tab-set would need a mountain-climbing expedition. I began to pity him. I could see now why he had chosen literary success.

But I could also see why I had not chosen it. So I was grateful to him. Grateful to Martin Amis, the post-punk Petronius. Yes, Mart. I've heard of Petronius. You didn't get *all* the education. There was some left over for the rest of us, right?

Through the ostentatiously open door of the bathroom I had noticed that the bidet was full of signed first editions of books by Julian Barnes, Ian McEwan and other members of the most powerful literary mafia to hit London since old Dr Ben Johnson ruled the roost. When I carried Martin through into the kitchen for that so-long-delayed welcoming drink, the refrigerator was full of French Impressionist lithographs piled up ostentatiously so that the casual visitor couldn't help seeing them. 'Antonia gave me those,' said the would-be neo-Swift oh-so-self-deprecatingly. 'She said after *Money* I should write a book about Monet or Manet.' He chuckled, pleased with his ostentatious modesty. Pleased with the secret language he shares only with his friends. With his friends and the beautiful Antonia Phillips, who just happens to control the *Times Literary Supplement*.

All of Martin's friends control something but this is the first time he has married one. Perhaps he will marry them all. I began to wonder who would marry me. Suddenly I noticed that Martin Amis was now only two inches high.

'Look,' said Martin. 'I feel I'm sort of disappearing. Do you think we could cut this short?' I was only too glad.

For finally I couldn't see what it was all meant to prove. Yes, he had published a novel every two months for ten years, was talked of in the same breath as balls-aching old Balzac, and had won the hand of one of the leading beauties of the day. But so what? He had never written a profile for the *Sunday Times Magazine*. He had spent too much time locked away reading all those books to know what was really going on in the London he was oh-so-celebrated for allegedly knowing intimately. Had he read any of *my* books, for instance? Had he read *The Sandra Documents*? Had he read *Offered Infants* and *Tonto People*? Would he even bother to hear about my soon-to-be-forthcoming *The Aimed Sock*?

I should never have taken this assignment. He was afraid of me. Afraid of what I represented. Afraid of someone who was better at what he had always been best at – being young. Being unknown. Once *he* had been unknown. That had been what he had been famous for. But now he was not, and it was killing him.

When we shook hands in farewell at his front door, Martin Amis was barely one inch high. There was an empty milk bottle on the doorstep. I started to put him down carefully beside it. Then I changed my mind and put him down carefully inside it. Half-way down the street I looked back. No bigger than a bacillus with delusions of grandeur, he was drumming with microscopic fists as he slid down inside the curved wall where the side of the bottle met its base. His thin voice cried: 'I need you! I need you!'

I had him where I wanted him at last.

Hugo Williams

Aspects of My Case

Leaving School

I was eight when I set out into the world
wearing a grey flannel suit.
I had my own suitcase.
I thought it was going to be fun.
I wasn't listening
when everything was explained to us in the Library,
so the first night I didn't have any sheets.
The headmaster's wife told me
to think of the timetable as a game of 'Battleships'.
She found me walking around upstairs
wearing the wrong shoes.

I liked all the waiting we had to do at school,
but I didn't like the work.
I could only read certain things
which I'd read before, like the Billy Goat Gruff books,
but they didn't have them there.
They had the Beacon Series.
I said 'I don't know,'
then I started saying nothing.
Every day my name was read out
because I'd forgotten to hang something up.

I was so far away from home I used to forget things.
I forgot how to get undressed.
You're supposed to take off your shirt and vest
after you've put on your pyjama bottoms.
When the headmaster's wife came round for Inspection
I was fully dressed again, ready for bed.
She had my toothbrush in her hand

and she wanted to know why it was dry.
I was miles away, with my suitcase, leaving school.

When Will His Stupid Head Remember?

Mr Ray stood behind me in History,
waiting for me to make a slip.
I had to write out the Kings and Queens
of England, in reverse order, with dates. I put,
'William I, 1087–1066'. I could smell the aeroplane glue
on his fingers as he took hold of my ear.
I stood in the corner near the insect case,
remembering my bike. I had the John Bull
Puncture Repair Kit in my pocket: glass paper,
rubber solution, patches, chalk and grater,
spare valves. I was 'riding dead' –
freewheeling downhill with my arms folded
and my eyes shut, looking Mr Ray in the eye.
Every time I looked round he added a minute to my sentence.

Mr Ray held his red Biro Minor like a modelling knife
to write reports. He drew a wooden spoon.
'I found it hard to keep my temper
with this feeble and incompetent creature.
He was always last to find his place
and most of his questions had been answered
five minutes before . . .' I called my father 'sir'
when he opened the envelope and shouted.
I was practising stage-falls from my bike
in the fading spotlight of summer lawns,
remembering the smell of aeroplane glue and inkwells
with a shiver down my spine. The beginning of term
was creeping up on me again. Every time I looked round
Mr Ray was standing there, stockstill.

Three Quarters

I wasn't happy with aspects of my case.
I shut myself in the bathroom,
a three-sided looking glass open like a book.

I couldn't understand my face. My nose stuck out.
I combed my hair down over my eyes
in search of a parting that would change all this.

I opened the mirror slowly, turning my head
from full to three-quarter face.
I wanted to stand three-quarters on to the world,
near the vanishing point.
I sat in front of the sunray lamp
with pennies in my eyes. I dyed my skin

a streaky, yellowish brown with permanganate of potash.
I must have grown up slowly
in that looking glass bathroom,
combing my hair straight down and pretending to wash.
I made myself dizzy raising my arms above my head
in a kind of surrender. No one else could get in.

Early Work

When I came downstairs my hair looked extraordinary –
a turmoil of popular styles and prejudices,
stiff with unreality and fear.
My scalp stung from onsets of a steel flick-comb.
My parting was raw from realignment.
I'd reintroduced the casual look so many times
I'd forgotten what it was. The whole thing
looked like an instrument of self-torture
with a handle and a zip.

I made my entrance and everyone wanted to know
where I was off to looking like that.
My brother did a comb mime with his knife,
tongue hanging out, jacket pushed back like a Ted.
My father made me go upstairs and start again.
I'd been working on my hair for so long
I thought it was natural to have a whirlpool
on your head, or a ship. I couldn't grasp the fact
that my hair was my hair, nothing more.

Waiting to Go On

I turned the pages slowly, listening for the car,
till my father was young again, a soldier,
or throwing back his head
on slicked back Derby Days before the war.
I stared at all that fame and handsomeness
and thought they were the same.
Good looks were everything where I came from.
They made you laugh. They made you have a tan.
They made you speak with conviction.
'Such a nice young man!' my mother used to say.
'So good looking!' I didn't agree with her,
but I searched my face for signs of excellence,
turning up my collar in the long mirror on the stairs
and flourishing a dress sword at myself:
'Hugh Williams, even more handsome in Regency!'
The sound of wheels on the drive
meant I had about one minute
to put everything back where I'd found it
and come downstairs as myself.

Raids on Lunch

Every lunchtime I came under threat
from my father's parting,
a venomous vapour trail
set at right angles to his profile.
I was the enemy,
po-faced and pale
and armed with a sort of quiff.
I had to make him laugh.
'Ett, ett,' he snapped,
shooting down a joke,
when I made the mistake
of pronouncing 'ate'
as if it rhymed with 'late'.
I hated the way his jaw went slack
as he calmly demolished me.
I couldn't resist
saying something tasteless
about the Royal Air Force,
having seen him disguised as a nun
in 'One of Our Aircraft is Missing'.
I should have run for cover.
Hooking a forefinger
over his much-admired nose
was the remains of my father's
camera-consciousness.
It meant he was critical:
the moment of sloth
before the nun takes off her head-dress
and opens fire on the Nazis.

Scratches

My mother scratched the soles of my shoes
to stop me slipping
when I went away to school.

I didn't think a few scratches
with a pair of scissors
was going to be enough.

I was walking on ice,
my arms stretched out.
I didn't know where I was going.

Her scratches soon disappeared
when I started sliding
down those polished corridors.

I slid into class.
I slid across the hall into the changing-room.
I never slipped up.

I learnt how to skate along with an aeroplane
or a car, looking ordinary,
pretending to have fun.

I learnt how long a run I needed
to carry me as far as the gym
in time for Absences.
I turned as I went,
my arms stretched out to catch the door jamb
as I went flying past.